Kung-Fu Masters

Kung-Fu Masters

Jose M. Fraguas

UNIQUE PUBLICATIONS
Burbank, California

Disclaimer

Please note that the author and publisher of this book are NOT RESPON-SIBLE in any manner whatsoever for any injury that may result from practicing the techniques and/or following the instructions given within. Since the physical activities described herein may be too strenuous in nature for some readers to engage in safely, it is essential that a physician be consulted prior to training.

First published in 2002 by Unique Publications.

Copyright © 2002 by CFW Enterprises, Inc.

All rights reserved. No part of this publication may be reproduced or utilized in any form or by any means, electronic or mechanical, including photocopying, recording, or by any information storage and retrieval system, without prior written permission from Unique Publications.

Library of Congress Catalog Number: 2002 155301
ISBN: 0-86568-211-9

Unique Publications
4201 Vanowen Place
Burbank, CA 91505
(800) 332–3330

First edition
05 04 03 02 01 00 99 98 97 1 3 5 7 9 10 8 6 4 2

Printed in the United States of America.

Editor: Todd Hester
Design: Patrick Gross
Cover Design: George Chen

"Our firmest convictions are apt to be the most suspect;
they mark our limitations and our bounds.
Life is a series of collisions with the future;
it is not the sum of what we have been,
but what we yearn to be."

—José Ortega y Gasset (1883–1955)
Spanish philosopher and author

Dedication

To the memory of Wong K. Yuen, who taught me my first kung-fu kuen and helped me to understand Chinese culture as way of life, work and art.

Acknowledgments

I would like to express my gratitude to those who provided valuable assistance in the preparation of this book. Assistance is an inadequate term for all the patience, time and knowledge that my numerous colleagues and friends so generously provided.

Special thanks goes to Todd Hester, the editor of the work. Also of particular assistance were Ed Ikuta (one of the world's greatest martial arts photographers), Greg Rhodes of London, England (a long-time friend, martial artist and photographer), John Steven Soet (director and writer), Dave Cater (editor of *Inside Kung-Fu*, the world's leading Chinese martial arts magazine), France's Thierry Plée (President of *Budo Editions);* Bey Logan (my long-time English friend who now resides in Hong Kong), and finally Curtis F. Wong, the man who has carried martial arts in America on his shoulders for more than 30 years, and who was ever-willing to share his expert knowledge on Chinese kung-fu.

A word of appreciation is also due Joe Hyams, famous screenwriter and true Hollywood icon, for honoring me by writing the foreword to this work. My admiration for Joe started in 1979 when, as a teenager, I read his masterpiece, "Zen in the Martial Arts." He gave me one of my greatest birthday gifts ever in 2001 but won't know until he reads this. My thanks go out to him for his true friendship and unwavering support.

I would further like to give my heartfelt gratitude to all the masters appearing in this book. They not only generously gave me an enormous amount of personal time for the long interviews, but also provided wonderful photographs to illustrate the book. Without their work ethic, sacrifice, and commitment to preserve Chinese culture, this book would not exist.

I would also be remiss if I did not recognize the many writers, philosophers, and martial arts masters whose works I have read but whom I have never met. Through the written word, their lives and spirits have greatly impacted me and given me invaluable insight. These people are treasures and my life is far richer because of them.

Finally, this book would never have been completed without the support of my family.

—Jose M. Fraguas

Contents

XII
Foreword

by Joe Hyams

XVI
About the Author

XVIII
Introduction

1
Jackie Chan

The Uncompromising Dragon

15
William Cheung

The Terror of Wing Chun

31
Robert Chu

A Perfect Balance

57
Vincent Chu

The Quest for Knowledge

69
Adam Hsu

A Modern Kung-fu Scholar

89
Shi Xing Hung

Spreading the Shaolin Roots Around the World

101
Buck Sam Kong

Opening Doors and Minds

113
Brendan Lai

A Labor of Love

131
Jim Lau

The Intelligence of Wing Chun

功夫

151
Eric Lee

The King of Forms

169
Wong Shun Leung

The Logic Behind
Wing Chun

179
James Lew

Breaking the Mold

191
Henry Look

The Virtue of Honor

203
Yang Jwing Ming

The Correct Way of Life

211
Gerald Okamura

Heart of the Dragon

229
Vernon Rieta

The Shaolin Journey

249
Randy Williams

A Wing Chun Crusader

269
Ark Y. Wong

Grandmaster of Shaolin

279
Doc Fai Wong

Deliberate, Steady,
and Solid

301
Y.C. Wong

The Whipping Power
of Hung Gar

317
Li Jian Yu

The Power of the Mind

foreword

by Joe Hyams

Kung-fu was only the name of some esoteric Chinese martial art to me on August 3, 1964, the day I went to the *International Karate Championships* at the Long Beach Municipal Auditorium in California. Martial artists from all over the country had come to Long Beach to compete in the first major karate tournament in the United States. The weekend event, sponsored by Ed Parker, had been sold-out for months; nearly a thousand people were turned away at the door. I was there anticipating great action on the hardwood floor of the auditorium, and to encourage some of my mates from Mr. Parker's kenpo karate studio.

The hundreds of entrants—male, female, young, and old—in the various rings were cheered-on by wild partisan applause. Midway through the final day of competition Mr. Parker introduced Bruce Lee who, he said, was going to give a demonstration of kung-fu.

Few of us in the audience had ever heard of Bruce and were probably unfamiliar with kung-fu. Bruce walked into the center ring wearing a black kung-fu uniform and boots. With him was Taky Kimura, his most advanced student, who looked like the Michelin tire man in a padded suit of body armor, shin guards, and what appeared to be a catcher's mask over his face.

Bruce started his demonstration immediately bringing down the house with the explosive speed and obvious power of his hands, kicks, and variety of techniques. His ability and cockiness—some called it arrogance—were forgiven because of his unquestioned ability.

I left the auditorium that night determined to find Bruce and study with him, but he had returned to his home in Oakland. When he came back to Los Angeles more than a year later to teach in Chinatown I arranged to meet him in a restaurant for *dim sum*. Bruce was shorter and slighter of build than I had imagined. At one point during the meal he picked up a piece of Peking duck with his chopsticks, tossed it in the air, and caught it. I was mightily impressed. I told him that my friend, Oscar winning writer Stirling Silliphant, and I wanted to take private lessons from him and said we were both black belts.

Bruce shrugged and said, "So are most of my students."

"How long do you think it will take us to become reasonably proficient in kung-fu?" I asked.

"A lifetime," he said, and grinned.

"Your lifetime or ours?" I asked.

"Yours," he said.

On that note he agreed to teach Stirling and I twice weekly in the driveway of my home. He arrived for our first lesson in a battered old car. He was wearing a blue jump suit and sneakers. The car's trunk was overflowing with kicking shields, boxing gloves, focus mitts, and wood and plastic *nunchakus*.

During our first few lessons he demonstrated and explained that every block in *wing chun* was an attack that can also be a defense, just as a defending hand can become an attacking hand—even attacking and defending with the same hand at the same time. He called that "the way of the intercepting fist," a translation of the Chinese words *Jeet Kune Do*.

We spent hours drilling on *chi sao*, or sticking hands. He often put on a blindfold and challenged us to hit him. Each time, at a touch from one of us, he either hit, trapped our hands or was out of range before our attack could be completed. I was so frustrated by his ability that one day I asked to examine the blindfold. He smiled and gave it to me. I held it up to the light. There was no way I could see through it.

One morning when Bruce was demonstrating his one-inch punch, a friend of mine, who had studied judo in Japan, came to visit at the same time my wife needed to remove her car from the garage. We went to the pool area where Bruce continued his demonstration. My friend watched, obviously unimpressed and skeptical.

Bruce went to him and said quietly, "I'll show you the punch if you like." My friend, bulkier by far than Bruce, smirked. Bruce handed him a focus pad saying, "Hold this against your chest," Bruce placed his extended finger tips lightly on the pad, collapsed his fingers into a fist, and slammed my friend's chest with an explosive, almost imperceptible shift of his weight. My friend flew back about ten feet into the pool.

On another day Bruce arrived at my home with a teak dummy composed of a trunk, three levels of arms and one leg. He formally introduced us to *mook jong*, who was to be our "new best friend." We mounted mook jong on the side door of the garage. For weeks thereafter Stirling and I practiced hand and foot trapping, punches, and kicks against mook jong.

Bruce taught us some basic skills with the plastic nunchakus. Sadly, neither Stirling nor I gained enough skill to use the real thing without getting creamed.

One morning Bruce announced that he was going to Hong Kong to make a film. "I'm going to test both of you," he said.

The test was simple. First, we broke two boards with kicks, fists, and a heel-palm strike. Next, Bruce placed a brick on two supporting bricks on the ground and had us break it. Then Stirling and I sparred for three two-minute rounds. Finally we demonstrated our skills on the teak dummy. Test completed, Bruce gave us a diploma certifying our level in Jeet Kune Do. As we were saying goodbye, I asked Bruce what he wanted me to do with mook jong.

"Keep it until I get back," Bruce said. "And here's a gift for you. Don't kill yourself with it." He handed me his black wood nunchakus.

"What do you suggest we study while you're away?" I asked.

"Wing chun," he said.

That was the last time I saw Bruce.

Stirling, who had written Bruce into several television shows while we were training with him saw Bruce again, however. He went to India with Bruce and James Coburn to make "The Silent Flute," a film he had written for Bruce. Sadly, the film was never completed.

Soon after Bruce left, I found the Jim Lau Wing Chun Academy in West Los Angeles. Like Bruce, Lau was born in Hong Kong and began studying kung-fu as a youngster. Bruce's instruction was often monkey-see-monkey-do whereas Sifu Lau taught wing chun in the traditional manner. He was a stickler for proper form, breathing, balance, and coordination as well as correct hand and arm positions. It was while studying with Lau that I discovered many Chinese potions that supposedly healed bruising. Rarely did I return from a session with Lau's students that my arms and shins were not black and blue from blocking kicks, overhead strikes and punches.

Thanks to kung-fu training I learned to control the centerline that forms the axis for all attacks and defenses in wing chun. As long as the centerline is aligned directly in front of the attacker, a wing chun practitioner can charge straight-in with punches and low kicks, straight-up the opponent's middle. Now that I am nearly an octogenarian who has studied almost a dozen different martial arts styles over the past four decades, I realize more than ever the value of the economy of motion that I learned from kung-fu. With the passage of years my hand techniques and low kicks have become almost instinctive, therefore effective. Despite the ravages of age I keep my wing chun skills reasonably sharp with weekly workouts.

I still go on the mat from time to time at various martial arts studios where I am kindly invited to train. It pleases me when young black belts come charging in on "the old man" only to find themselves immobilized or hit by simple and effective kung-fu techniques passed down to modern times from ages past.

Since Chinese kung-fu is not merely a fighting system or philosophical discipline but a way of life, the art will not only improve the texture and quality of your life but also lead you to many unexpected benefits such as confidence, self-understanding, tranquility, and a more realistic approach to your existence. The secret is to let the art go deep inside you without forcing yourself to change. Let it quietly work on you until you find your own way.

The masters in this book are living repositories of Chinese martial arts culture and history, and exemplify kung-fu's most important moral and ethical principles. Each master is a bridge to kung-fu's glorious past and a springboard to its unlimited future. Contained within these pages is an enormous amount of philosophical and technical information that will help you to unravel the deepest secrets of the world's most mysterious and deadly fighting system. Enjoy.

About the Author

Born and raised in Madrid, Spain, Jose "Chema" Fraguas began his martial arts studies with judo, in grade school, at age 9. From there he moved to taekwondo and then to kenpo karate, earning a black belt in both styles. During this same period he also studied shito-ryu karate under Japanese masters Masahiro Okada and Yashunari Ishimi, eventually receiving a fifth-degree black belt. He began his career as a writer at age 16 by serving as a regular contributor to martial arts magazines in Great Britain, France, Spain, Italy, Germany, Portugal, Holland, and Australia. Having a black belt in three different styles allows him to better reflect the physical side of the martial arts in his writing: "Feeling before writing," Fraguas says.

In 1980, he moved to Los Angeles, California. His open-minded mentality helped him to develop a realistic approach to the martial arts. Seeking to supplement his previous training, he researched other disciplines such as kali, jiu-jitsu and muay Thai. His training in the Chinese martial arts for more than a decade mainly included hung gar kuen and wing chun kung-fu, although he occasionally trained in northern Shaolin methods as well. In his first struggling years he managed to meet numerous martial arts greats such as Jun Chong, Wally Jay, and Dan Inosanto.

In 1986, Fraguas founded his own book and magazine company in Europe, authoring dozens of books and distributing his magazines to 35 countries in three different languages. His reputation and credibility as a martial artist and publisher became well known to the top masters around the world. Considering himself a martial artist first and a writer and publisher second, Fraguas feels fortunate to have had the opportunity to interview many legendary martial arts teachers. He recognizes that much of the information given in the interviews helped him to discover new dimensions in the martial arts. "I was constantly absorbing knowledge from the great masters," he recalls. "I only trained with a few of them, but intellectually and spiritually all of them have made very important contributions to my growth as a complete martial artist."

However there were some drawbacks to his position as a publisher, Fraguas acknowledges, that directly affected his personal martial arts development. "Of course, some people taught me because of my position as a publisher and not because who I was as a person. Even though I recognize that, I'm still grateful for the knowledge they shared with me."

Steeped in tradition yet looking to the future, Fraguas understands and appreciates martial arts history and philosophy and feels this rich heritage is a necessary stepping stone to personal growth and spiritual evolution. His desire to promote both ancient philosophy and modern thinking provided the motivation for writing this book. "If the motivation is just money, a book cannot be of good quality," Fraguas says. 'If the book is written to just make people happy, it cannot be deep. I want to write books so I can learn as well as teach."

Originally from Madrid, Spain, the author is currently living in Los Angeles, California where he is the General Manager of CFW Enterprises, the world's leading martial arts publishing company.

Introduction

I've been both lucky and fortunate. Some of my best days were spent interviewing and meeting the masters appearing in this book. There is little I enjoy more than "gnawing" on a great interview while time slows and sometimes even seems to stop. Having the opportunity to meet and interview the most relevant and prestigious martial artists of the past four decades is something that every martial artist doesn't have the chance to do. Hopefully, in some small way, this will help make up for that.

Meeting the masters and having long conversations with them that were published in magazines around the world allowed me to do more than simply "scratch the surface" of the technical aspects of their respective styles, but to also research and analyze the human beings behind the teachers. Some of the dialogues and interviews began by simply commenting about the superficial techniques of fighting, and ended up turning into a very uncommon spiritual conversation about the philosophical aspects of the martial arts.

Although they are all very different, considering their respective styles and backgrounds, they all share a common thread of the traditional values such as discipline, respect, positive attitude, dedication, and etiquette.

For more than 25 years I've faced the long odds of interviewing these martial arts masters, one-on-one, face-to-face, with no place to run if I asked a stupid question. Many times, it was a real challenge to not just make contact with them, but also to make the interview interesting enough to bring out the knowledge that resided inside them. In every interview I tried to absorb as much knowledge as I could, ranging from their training methods, to their fighting methods, and to their philosophies about life itself.

Their different origins and cultural backgrounds heavily influenced them but never prevented them from analyzing, researching, or modifying anything that they considered appropriate. They always kept an open mind to improving both their arts and themselves. From a formal philosophical point of view many of them follow the wisdom of Zen and Taoism—others just use common sense.

They devoted themselves to their arts, often in solitude, sometimes to the exclusion of other pursuits most of us take for granted. They worked themselves into extraordinary physical condition and stayed there. They ignored distractions and diversions and brought to their training a great deal of concentration. The best of them got as good as they could possibly get at performing and teaching their chosen art, and the rest of us watched them and, leading our "balanced lives," wondered how good we might have gotten at something had we devoted ourselves to whatever we did as ferociously as these masters embraced their arts. In that respect they bear our dreams.

It would be wonderful to find a single martial artist who combined all the great qualities of these fighters—but that's impossible. That, however, was one of the things that inspired me to write this book. I wanted to preserve some things that were said a long time ago, of which not many people today are aware.

If you read carefully between the lines, you'll see that none of these men were trying to become a "fighting machine" or training in order to create the most devastating martial arts system known to man. They focused, rather, on how to use the martial arts to become better human beings. There are many links that, once discovered, open a wide spectrum of possibilities, not only to martial arts, but to a better existence as individuals.

The interviews often lasted as long as three or four hours of non-stop talking. I would begin at their schools and finish the conversation at a restaurant or coffee shop. A lot of information in these interviews had been never published before and some had to be trimmed, either at the master's request or edited to avoid creating senseless misunderstandings later on. It is not the questions that make an interview. An interview is either good or bad depending on the answers given. Considering the masters in this book, I had an easy job. My goal was to make these masters comfortable talking about their life and training—especially those who trained under the founders of original systems. In modern time, there are not many who have had the privilege of living and learning under the legendary founders.

"The masters are gone," many like to say. But as long as we keep their teachings in our hearts, they will live forever. To understand the martial arts properly it is necessary to take into account the philosophical and psychological methods as well as the physical techniques. There is a deep distinction between a fighting system and a martial art, and a general feeling in the martial arts community is that the roots of the martial arts have been de-emphasized, neglected, or totally abandoned. Martial arts are not a sport—they are very different. Someone who chooses to devote himself to a sport such as basketball, tennis, soccer, or football, which is based on youth, strength, and speed chooses to die twice. When you can no longer do a certain sport, due to the lack of any one of those attributes, waking up in the morning without the activity and purpose that has been the center of your day for twenty-five years is spooky. Martial arts can and should be practiced for life. They are not sports, they are a "way of life."

A true martial arts practitioner—like an artist of any other kind—be they a musician, painter, writer or actor, is expressing and leaving part of themselves in every piece of their craft. The need for self-inspection and self-realization of "who" they are becomes the reason for a journey in search of that perfect technique, that great melody, that inspiring poetry, that amazing painting or that Academy Award performance. It is this motivation to reach that "impossible dream," that allows a simple individual to become an exceptional "artist" and "master" of their craft.

Many of the greatest teachers of the fighting arts share a commonly misunderstood teaching methodology. They know the words that could be used to pass their personal experience to their students have little or no meaning. They know that to try "self-discovery" in quantitative or empirical terms is a useless task. A great deal of knowledge and wisdom (the ability to use knowledge in a proper and correct way) comes from what are called the "oral traditions," which martial arts, like every other cultural aspect, has. These oral traditions have been always reserved for a certain kind of student and have been considered "secrets." I believe these secrets are such because only few very special students have the minds to grasp them. As Alexandra David-Neel wrote: "It is not on the master that the secret depends but on the hearer. Truth learned from others is of no value, the only truth which is effective and of value is self-discovered...the teacher can only guide to the point of discovery." In the end "The only secret is that there is no secret," or as Kato Tokuro, probably the greatest potter of the last century, a great art scholar, and the teacher of Spanish painter and sculptor Pablo Picasso (1881–1973) said: "The sole cause of secrets in craftsmanship is the student's inability to learn!"

As human beings, we are always tempted to follow straight-line logic towards ultimate self-improvement—but the truth is that there are no absolute truths that apply to all. You have to find your own way in life whether it be in the martial arts, in business, or in cherry picking. Whatever path you pursue, you have to distill your personal truths to what is right for you, according to your own life. The quest for perfection is actually quite imperfect and is not in tune with either human nature or human experience. To have any hope of attaining even a single perfection, you have to concentrate on a single pursuit and direct all your energies towards it. In this sense, perfection comes from appreciating your endeavors for their own sake—not to impress anyone—but for your own inner satisfaction and sense of accomplishment.

Martial arts are a large part of my life and I draw inspiration from them, both spiritually and philosophically. I really don't know the "how" or the "why" of their affect on me, but I feel their influence in even my most mundane activities. It's not a complex thing where I have to look deep into myself to find their influence. All human beings have sources or principles that keep them grounded, and martial arts is mine. I believe that is when the term "way of life" becomes real. In bushido, the self-discipline required to pursue mastery is more important than mastery itself—the struggle is more important than the reward. A common thread throughout the lives of all the masters is their constant struggle towards self-mastery. They realized that life is an ongoing process, and once you achieve all your goals you are as good as dead. But this process is not all driven by action. Often the greatest action is inaction and the hardest voice to hear is the sound of your inner voice. You need to sit alone and collect your thoughts, free from all forms of technology and distraction, and just think. It is perhaps the only way to achieve mental and spiritual clarity.

I don't believe that great books are meant to be read fast. I've always thought that really good writing is timeless and that time spent reading doesn't detract anything from your life, but rather adds to it. So take your time. Approach the reading of this book with the Zen "beginner's mind" mentality and let the words of these great teachers help you to grow not only as a martial artist but as a human being as well.

The Uncompromising Dragon

CHAN KONG-SANG WAS BORN IN HONG KONG IN 1954, AND NEARLY SOLD AT BIRTH TO A BRITISH DOCTOR FOR $26 BECAUSE HIS NEWLY-ARRIVED HONG KONG IMMIGRANT PARENTS COULDN'T AFFORD TO FEED HIM. HIS FAMILY CAME FROM SHANTUNG PROVINCE, CHINA. AT THE AGE OF 7, WHEN HIS PARENTS IMMIGRATED TO AUSTRALIA, CHAN WAS ENROLLED IN THE CHINA DRAMA ACADEMY, A FLOURISHING CHINESE OPERA SCHOOL UNDER THE DIRECTION OF YU CHAN-YUAN. IT WAS THERE THAT CHAN LEARNED BOTH NORTHERN AND SOUTHERN KUNG-FU STYLES. ALTHOUGH CHAN CONSIDERS HIMSELF AN ENTERTAINER FIRST AND A MARTIAL ARTIST SECOND, HIS EMPTY-HAND MARTIAL ARTS SKILLS AND ABILITY TO USE SEVERAL TRADITIONAL KUNG-FU WEAPONS HAVE BEEN PUBLICLY ADMIRED BY HIGHLY-QUALIFIED MASTERS FROM CHINA AND HONG KONG. RATHER THAN FEEL SLIGHTED BY THOSE WHO TRY TO COPY HIM, JACKIE CALL THE IMITATION A COMPLIMENT, "IT FORCES ME TO BE MORE CREATIVE," HE INSISTS. NOW ONE OF THE MOST POPULAR ACTORS IN THE WORLD, JACKIE CHAN STILL KEEPS A MARTIAL ARTS HUMILITY THAT ALLOWS HIM TO KEEP HIS FEET ON THE GROUND, WHILE HIS STARDOM CLIMBS EVER HIGHER.

Q: Is it true you were almost sold to a doctor and you changed your name several times?
A: Yes. I like to look at it with a little bit of humor. I was a fat baby, so they give me the Chinese nickname "A-Puo" which means "Cannonball." Because I couldn't pronounce it well enough, I was called "Steve." When I was working on a construction site my friend thought that was not a good name so he introduced me as "Jack Chan." I added on the "y" because "Jacky" had a better rhythm. Later on Raymond Chow changed my name to "Jackie"—and so here I am.

Q: What was your training at the Chinese Opera like?
A: It was very tough. If you are 13 to 16 years old, you are already too old to be taught—and if you are a young child, it may appear far too tough to go through. Everything was my father's idea because I was very active as a child, always moving and doing things. I went to the school and I

Kung-Fu Masters

"After a couple of months I was not so thrilled with the idea of being there for ten years, and many of my friends began to escape. They used to say they had to go shopping for shoes or something like that, and just leave. But they never came back."

saw some kid doing kung-fu. I liked it, so my father signed me up for ten years. The teacher said to my father that the contract could be for five, seven or ten years. My father decided to sign me up for ten.

After a couple of months I was not so thrilled with the idea of being there for ten years, and many of my friends began to escape. They used to say they had to go shopping for shoes or something like that, and just leave. But they never came back. My problem was my family went to Australia so I had nobody in Hong Kong. I could find excuses to leave the school but I had no place to escape to. It was impossible for me to quit. In fact, the teacher adopted me and this made things worse for me because all the other kids used to call me "The Prince." Whatever mistake was made, I got the worst of it because the master would use me as an example. I really had to bear the whole burden myself. The atmosphere there was very difficult to deal with; it is like a juvenile reform school in America. It was very strict, too strict for little kids. For us, it was like a prison.

Q: What kind of training did you receive there?
A: We had many subjects to study under many different teachers. We used to wake up at 5 AM and dress with white shirts and black pants. We used to do handstand training that would last from one minute to one hour. Then, up to the roof where we would run for 100 laps, and after that kung-fu practice which included punching, kicking, forms, et cetera—you name it. We trained until lunchtime. Then, more study and

more training, this time with weapons and tools. After dinner, we studied some more until midnight. Then we went to bed. The boys and girls all shared an enclosed space—we didn't have regular beds to sleep in. We slept until 5 AM and then the whole routine started again. When it was time to go to regular school the next day, we were so tired that we all slept through it. Everybody loved school time. We'd all fall asleep while reciting the alphabet! Honestly, I wouldn't recommend this kind of life to anyone, and I would never send my own kids to something like that. But I have to recognize that it helped me be who I am today. So in some ways, I'm very grateful for the training and the experience.

Q: What styles of kung-fu did you learn at the Opera?
A: It was mixture of Northern and Southern styles. As you know, in kung-fu there is no ranking or graduation system like in Japanese karate or Korean taekwondo. The progress is very personal. We learned a combination of several systems that made us very complete as far as technique goes. After years of training we could perform different styles with proficiency and skill. We could start using techniques from Southern styles and combine them with movements and application of Northern methods. I truly believe this training was very valuable because once you have that particular base and foundation, you can expand and focus yourself on any particular system and become very good at it. Because I learned both styles—Southern and Northern, my cinematic style has a lot of jumping and footwork. The Southern style emphasizes hands over feet. I learned both, so I use both

"Honestly, I wouldn't recommend this kind of life to anyone, and I would never send my own kids to something like that. But I have to recognize that it helped me be who I am today."

Kung-Fu Masters

"A director came to our school and said he needed a child actor. I was a child, so I became an actor. It was that simple. I was really happy because it meant I was able to avoid regular training at the school."

when making martial arts movies. Bruce Lee used mostly the Southern style, so he didn't use much of the acrobatics that are used today.

Q: How did you get involved in movies?
A: When I was 7, I entered the movie business. A director came to our school and said he needed a child actor. I was a child, so I became an actor. It was that simple. I was really happy because it meant I was able to avoid regular training at the school. I fell in love with the movies. But when I was around 10, I wasn't so cute anymore, so the offers didn't come, which meant I had to stay in school all the time and go to regular training. Then, as I grew up, I saw how some of my schoolmates became stuntman in the movie circuit, so I thought I would become a stuntman. For that, I really didn't need any training. I literally fell into the movie business. By the age of 15 or 16, I had become a stuntman and began working regularly. I was not making much money then—and everything I made I was giving to my teacher who would give me a dollar back. But for me, that was very good.

Q: What was your first experience as a stuntman?
A: I remember that I had to jump from a high wall. I was the first one to climb up so I could take the jump down, but the martial arts choreographer asked me to come down. I felt very hurt, and I vowed that day that

one day I would be a great stuntman. I went and started to learn all the falls. I used the trampoline to sharpen my reactions and spatial awareness.

Q: What happened next?
A: In Hong Kong all the choreographers have their own stunt team, and if you don't belong to one, it's hard to get a job. I joined a choreographer's team and as time went on I became his assistant. This position gave me the opportunity to learning more and more about the movies. I used to stay close to the director and carefully observe his orders, how to organize the people, how to guide the cameraman, et cetera. Then one day I was offered the job of choreographer. Needless to say, I grabbed it. From that moment on, I had many opportunities to get better at what I was doing. I tried to improve my work and I took every chance I had to show I could do more difficult things. I always tried to incorporate more dangerous and difficult actions to give the director his money's worth. The directors always trusted my decisions and my judgment of how to approach a fight scene. In Hong Kong martial arts movies, the whole scene is the responsibility of the choreographer. In a certain way, you assume the position as the film's director.

"I always tried to incorporate more dangerous and difficult actions to give the director his money's worth. The directors always trusted my decisions and my judgment of how to approach a fight scene."

Q: In Hong Kong you used to work in many different aspects of production, even those that didn't have anything to do with directing. Why?
A: In Hong Kong, directors are number one. They do almost everything. Producers are nothing. In the United States it is the opposite. When I was directing in Hong Kong, I liked go to the set early in the morning. I enjoyed that system and the feeling I was in control of everything. Even when we finished shooting for the day, I used to stay there editing and

Kung-Fu Masters

"The films that followed after Bruce's death were known as 'Bruce Lee style' films. I was not planning to become 'Bruce Soo' or 'Bruce Woo.'"

watching other aspects of the production—the script, the other actors, their performances. I never got much sleep that way, but I enjoyed every minute of it and I truly believe that I became knowledgeable about movies because I spent extra time in other aspect besides what I was being hired for. I also realized that the system used here in America has a lot of value. You have the director, the editing director, music director, lighting director, casting director, everything. For me, in the beginning, it was very funny. Because in Hong Kong a director is like a *xing gong*—a general laborer. They do everything, and that's probably too much for one person.

Q: How did you deal with the post-Bruce Lee era in Hong Kong movies?
A: When Bruce Lee was big star, I was a martial arts stunt director. After his death, producers in Hong Kong said they wanted me to be a star. I didn't know what to do. Kicking? Punching? They are not really for me, not my style. Then I realized that doing those things would make me a second Bruce Lee and that was exactly what I didn't want. I admired and respected Bruce Lee, but I couldn't successfully try to copy him. I realized that I had to go in another direction. If Bruce punched and stay strong, I knew I had to punch and scream because I hurt my hand. I had to go in the opposite way—introduce comedy to what I was doing and find a way to express myself on screen. The films that followed after Bruce's death were known as "Bruce Lee style" films. I was not planning to become "Bruce Soo" or "Bruce Woo." I wanted to be Jackie Chan. I wanted to make people happy. Every martial arts movie has a serious fight and I was adding some comedy to it. You have to be careful because you don't want the film to

"In America, personality is more important than fighting. First come the stories and personality, then the fighting. In the Far East, fighting is more important than the storyline."

appear totally comedic. You have to put a serious fight in it to let the audience know that you are a serious actor. It's at the end of the movie where you need comedy, because the audience should leave the film happy. If you come out laughing, then you have something to talk about.

Q: How do you compare the Hong Kong way of making films to the American way?
A: In America, personality is more important than fighting. First come the stories and personality, then the fighting. In the Far East, fighting is more important than the storyline—both the story and the personalities are

Kung-Fu Masters

"For me to be successful, I had to incorporate more comedy and character development so I could bring a format that the American audience could identify with. It took time though."

secondary. In Hong Kong, a two-hour movie may have an hour-and-a-half of fighting. America is a big market where everybody wants to be. For me to be successful, I had to incorporate more comedy and character development so I could bring a format that the American audience could identify with. It took time though.

Q: Did the difficulty expressing yourself in a different language affect your acting?
A: Yes. In my first American movies my acting suffered because of the language barrier. In my native language, Cantonese, my expression is natural, my acting comes out in a natural way. In English, it is a different story. I have to study the lines and try to absorb the essence of it, so I can't act. When I started to improve my English I began to receive better offers and my career took off in America.

Q: What is martial arts training for you now?
A: Martial art training is for fun now, for enjoyment, not for fighting like in the old days. Training is something that can bring a lot of joy to your life if you learn them first for what they are and not just for fighting. They improve your mind and help you to develop qualities that will be impor-

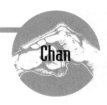

Author Jose Fraguas with Jackie Chan

"Education and knowledge are very important in life. You can do kung-fu for many years, but the education you gain as a young man will be with you forever and you'll never regret having it. Education is the most important thing in life and all martial arts instructors should help their students understand that."

tant for the rest of your life. You may train in martial arts for 30 years and never have to use it in a real fight. But you will always have them even if you don't need them. It's important that instructors teach the right way and educate the student to not look for fights. It's kind of a paradox that you are learning fighting techniques but you shouldn't fight. That's something that doesn't match in a child's mind. The teacher has to educate the student. This is very important. But the martial arts teacher has one more important thing to pass on to the student than mere physical techniques; the appreciation of an education. Education and knowledge are very important in life. You can do kung-fu for many years, but the education you gain as a young man will be with you forever and you'll never regret having it. Being able to speak and understand different languages will very helpful in the adult years. You'll be capable of getting information published in different languages—not only from books or magazines of your first language. Education is the most important thing in life and all martial arts instructors should help their students understand that. My

Kung-Fu Masters

"My advice to kung-fu practitioners is to be humble and stay out of trouble. Never use kung-fu to attack somebody. Defend yourself if the occasion arises but don't overuse it to do great harm."

strength and speed are not the same as when I was 25, but I'm a more complete human being and actor now than I was at 25. In life, your education will go up, whereas kung-fu skills deteriorate with age.

Q: What advice would you give to kung-fu practitioners?
A: Well, I'm not a grandmaster, but you can certainly say that I have used my skills professionally. I remember that when I was 17 years old, my body was very strong because of all the training I was doing—no discos, no women, and no nonsense. I was getting in fights because it was fun, but that was not right. My advice to kung-fu practitioners is to be humble and stay out of trouble. Never use kung-fu to attack somebody. Defend yourself if the occasion arises but don't overuse it to do great harm. As far as training, they should practice hard to train one's reflexes, and use it as a self-defense to improve their health. A healthy body is truly priceless. It's important that a martial arts student chooses the right school then puts himself into it, practicing with dedication and persever-

ance. I don't feel that a student should stick woodenly to any style or tradition but be flexible and tactful. Schools and styles are not really important; they are all very similar in their goals, although they have different way of doing things. What it is really important is the practicality of the art.

Q: So do you think kung-fu is a method of pure self-defense?
A: I consider kung-fu an art form. There are many different styles, but no matter what your style is, it can never fight a gun. Of course, you can attack and hurt somebody if you have the tools, but that's not the goal and real meaning of kung-fu training. Offensive and defensive actions are two sides of the same coin. In general, as much as I can, I would use the defensive. I was taught by my

"Schools and styles are not really important; they are all very similar in their goals, although they have different way of doing things. What it is really important is the practicality of the art."

teachers that if an aggressor has a knife on your back and asks for my money, I'd give it to him. Or if someone was pointing a gun at me, I would give him everything, regardless of how much kung-fu I may know and how fast I was. If I can control the situation without fighting, I will. Only when the attacker decides to hurt me physically would I use my skills to survive. An offensive is mandatory in that case. In actual fighting, I don't move before the opponent moves, but before the opponent tries to move. However, I do feel that kung-fu is good for self-defense and helps to maintain your body and your health. It's an excellent training for the

Kung-Fu Masters

"Owing to professional needs, my way of practicing martial arts falls into two categories. I practice practical techniques so as to increase my ability in real fighting, but I also do a lot of supplementary exercises because they are more suitable to the needs of actions in the martial arts movies."

body and the mind. But you need to know how to control your mind so your body will do the right things.

Q: What kind of training program do you follow now?
A: Owing to professional needs, my way of practicing martial arts falls into two categories. I practice practical techniques so as to increase my ability in real fighting, but I also do a lot of supplementary exercises because they are more suitable to the needs of actions in the martial arts movies. I'd say that the supplementary exercises take up two thirds of my time. I also consider warm-up exercises extremely important; they increase your potential, physical strength, and coordination. I also practice non-stop footwork, coupled with defensive and offensive moves. This

is an effective training method for both increasing strength and mastering techniques instinctively. At my current age, it is important to keep a good cardiovascular training program because that's the engine of the car. I focus primarily on that.

Q: Do you still do your own stunts?
A: Every time I can! My body is always in pain. I've had too many injuries over the years! In Hong Kong I was doing all kinds of dangerous stunts. But in America, for insurance purposes, they don't let you do the extremely dangerous ones. There is too much money involved. If I try to do a dangerous stunt and I get hurt, the company will lose a lot of money because I won't be able to work the next day. They can't allow this to happen and I understand. I'm realistic and I know that I won't be able to do some things when I am 62—but I will keep going as long as I can, as long as I enjoy it.

"I just love what I do. It is not money that drives me. I make films because it is my hobby and my passion and I will keep doing them as long as my fans want me to."

Q: How would you like to be remembered?
A: Remembered? I'm too young for that (laughs)! But I would like to be known as a smart man. There is a Chinese saying: "Smart men move mountains, stupid men just move." I believe that.

Q: Why does Jackie Chan still work so hard?
A: I just love what I do. It is not money that drives me. I make films because it is my hobby and my passion and I will keep doing them as long as my fans want me to.

William Cheung

The Terror of Wing Chun

WILLIAN CHEUNG (CHUK HING) BEGAN HIS WING CHUN TRAINING UNDER GRANDMASTER YIP MAN AT THE AGE OF 10. A MEMBER OF THE HONG KONG SWIM TEAM, CHEUNG DECIDED TO JOIN YIP MAN'S *KWOON* AFTER A CONVERSATION WITH A FRIEND OF HIS, THE LATE WONG SHUN LEUNG. FOUR YEARS LATER HE DECIDED TO MAKE WING CHUN HIS WAY OF LIFE AND MOVED TO MASTER YIP MAN'S HOUSE TO STUDY FOR ANOTHER FOUR YEARS UNTIL 1959, WHEN HE LEFT FOR AUSTRALIA. TRAINING UNDER YIP MAN, HE BECAME ONE OF THE THREE "TERRORS OF WING CHUN" IN THE STREETS OF HONG KONG—WONG SHUN LEUNG AND BRUCE LEE BEING THE OTHER TWO. THEY ACCEPTED AND WELCOMED EVERY CHALLENGE, SPREADING THE WING CHUN REPUTATION FAR AND WIDE.

IN 1964, CHEUNG ENTERED THE AUSTRALIAN NATIONAL UNIVERSITY IN CANBERRA, WHERE HE OPENED THE WING CHUN KUNG-FU CLUB. TEN YEARS LATER HE FOUNDED THE AUSTRALIAN WING CHUN ACADEMY, IN MELBOURNE, AND ALSO THE AUSTRALIAN KUNG-FU FEDERATION. LATER, HE WAS ALSO APPOINTED AS A CHIEF INSTRUCTOR FOR UNARMED COMBAT AT THE U.S. NAVY BASE IN YUKOSUKA, JAPAN. HE CAUSED A HUGE CONTROVERSY IN THE WING CHUN WORLD WHEN HE OPENLY PROCLAIMED HIMSELF TO BE THE ONLY MASTER WHO LEARNED FROM GRANDMASTER YIP MAN, AND THEREFORE TAUGHT THE ONLY ORIGINAL AND TRADITIONAL VERSION OF WING CHUN. HE HAS AUTHORED SEVERAL BOOKS ON THE WING CHUN SYSTEM AND ALSO STARRED IN MANY INSTRUCTIONAL TAPES.

Q: When did you begin your training?
A: Well, in the early '50s, Yip Man began accepting formal students. Wong Shun Leung and myself were both swimmers. Wong Shun was practicing a different kung-fu style. He decided to visit Yip Man's kwoon and challenge him. After being beaten up, he signed up for Yip's classes. He mentioned to me how good Yip was, so I signed up too.

Q: Why did you move in with Yip Man?
A: Some of us at Yip Man's kwoon began to accept every challenge issued to us from other schools. My reputation as street fighter became very big

Kung-Fu Masters

"Yes. I needed a place to go, so I told Yip Man that I would do the house chores if he let me stay at his house. He said that I didn't have to do anything, just move in."

and my family was not happy with that. I didn't feel very comfortable being at home—I couldn't find much warmth in the house.

Q: Did you tell Yip Man?
A: Yes. I needed a place to go, so I told him that I would do the house chores if he let me stay at his house. He said that I didn't have to do anything, just move in. I slept in the corridor in a canvas bed and ate whatever he did.

Q: How long did you live with him?
A: It was around three years. He used to teach me before or after the classes and I used to help teach other students.

Q: Was Bruce Lee one of them?
A: Yes. Wong Shun Leung was my senior and I was Bruce's.

Q: Why is your wing chun different from other wing chun teachers?
A: Yip Man learned wing chun from two different masters. The first was Chan Wah Sun. This version was based on the centerline and it is the wing chun version that you see in most schools today. But there's an older version of the art that is not based on the centerline, and this is the version the late Yip Man learned from Leung Bik, his second master. This is the one I learned from Yip Man while I lived with him. This simple but relevant concept changes the whole art. The wing chun system was developed by a woman, so it

"In the traditional version of wing chun, the practitioner deflects rather than stops a blow. This is the reason that positioning and footwork are so important. Wing chun specializes in close-quarter combat. I teach three stages of combat: the pre-contact stage, the contact stage, and the pursuit and retreat stage."

avoids meeting force with force. In the traditional version of wing chun, the practitioner deflects rather than stops a blow. This is the reason that positioning and footwork are so important.

Q: Did Yip Man tell you not to teach that version?
A: He said to me that what he was going to teach me I shouldn't teach to anyone. That was his secret and his knowledge. The day he passed away that knowledge would be mine and only I had the right to teach it.

Kung-Fu Masters

"Bruce always looked on me as a role model in wing chun. This can be a problem because you don't let your own potential come out naturally. You're always thinking about somebody else."

Q: What are the strengths of wing chun?
A: Wing chun specializes in close-quarter combat. I teach three stages of combat: the pre-contact stage, the contact stage, and the pursuit and retreat stage. For the first stage, the most important aspect is to focus on the opponent's elbow. For the second stage we use *chi sao* techniques, and for the third we focus on special footwork for pursuing and retreating.

Q: Do you think full contact sparring is important?
A: You can learn a lot of good things from it, but it's not necessary. Also, you have to wear gloves and that limits the versatility of empty-hand techniques. In sparring, you need to know how to improvise—that's why I use the most advanced innovations to upgrade the training methods I teach.

Q: You mentioned focusing on the opponent's nearest elbow. Can you elaborate?
A: People do not know that they cannot see a punch coming because it moves so fast. With a fast punch, the fist is so close to the eyes that you cannot focus. But you don't have to stop the punch by blocking the fist, you stop the elbow. Then you don't have to worry about the fist, just the elbow because it travels much slower than the fist. Also, if you stop the punch at the elbow, the force is less, so it is easier. The elbow is easy to watch and block and will always indicate the movement of the punch.

Q: How were your training sessions with Bruce?
A: Bruce always looked on me as a role model in wing chun. This can be a problem because you don't let your own potential come out naturally.

You're always thinking about somebody else. Also, I was his senior, I had more experience at that time and it was easy for me to play with him. I was bigger than him and I knew the original version of the art as well.

Q: What was Bruce Lee like at that time?
A: He was a little bit of immature and I'll dare to say that he had more or less some kind of inferiority complex. This is the reason why he trained so hard. He was constantly practicing and very hungry for wing chun knowledge.

Q: Did Yip Man tell you to teach Bruce?
A: Master Yip told me to take care of Bruce because we were always involved in fights and I was his senior. I had the responsibility of leading him a little bit.

Q: Did you see his evolution over the years?
A: He became very analytical, very scientific. If something doesn't make sense with scientific logic, it must be wrong. He also did a lot of research on physical conditioning. Just look at the screen—he had a great physical appearance. He realized that if you're not in shape then you're out of business in martial arts.

Q: Do you think he was ahead of his time?
A: Bruce was 100 years ahead of all other martial artists. Read his notes and look at what he was doing. Even today, people don't understand things he said a long time ago. Big principles, approaches, or revelations that are "in" these days, were things that Bruce was studying 30 years ago! You can see his influence in almost everything related to martial arts and physical fitness. I really think this is his greatest contribution.

"Bruce was 100 years ahead of all other martial artists. Read his notes and look at what he was doing. Even today, people don't understand things he said a long time ago."

Kung-Fu Masters

"You can discard and simplify when you already have something. Probably some people have oversimplified some things and the art is getting too thin. You might have Bruce's physical technique but lack the knowledge he had to make it work. So what's the use of trying to copy him?"

Q: What do you think about his art, Jeet Kune Do?
A: Bruce found what it was useful for him and he used certain logical philosophy. I don't think the name "Jeet Kune Do" is that important.

Q: Would he have kept evolving?
A: He was very clever and knew that when you're young you have to use speed, but when you're older you have to find something to compensate for the speed you're losing. That's nature. I'm sure he'd be doing research to find new ways to improve his ability and gain more knowledge.

Q: Do you think his art and philosophy was simple?
A: You can discard and simplify when you already have something. Probably some people have oversimplified some things and the art is getting too thin. Bruce had a lot of knowledge and there are certain things that won't work unless you have that knowledge too. You might have Bruce's physical technique but lack the knowledge he had to make it work. So what's the use of trying to copy him?

"Wing chun has solutions for some of the problems Bruce had. Maybe he didn't know that wing chun had a way of dealing with those tactical fighting problems he struggled with. If you know them, you don't have to go outside of wing chun to look for solutions."

Q: Do you think Bruce would have created Jeet Kune Do if he had known the complete wing chun system?
A: It's hard to tell. Bruce Lee left Hong Kong when he was 18 years old and he only knew part of the modified version taught by Yip Man. Perhaps Bruce had to look for answers and solutions outside wing chun because he didn't know enough wing chun and had to fill the gaps. Wing chun has solutions for some of the problems Bruce had. Maybe he didn't know that wing chun had a way of dealing with those tactical fighting problems he struggled with. If you know them, you don't have to go outside of wing chun to look for solutions.

Q: What were his biggest qualities as a fighter?
A: I think his speed. He was very fast. He trained for that speed but it was very natural. However, I'm sure he'd change his training regimen because after 30-35 you have to change the way you train, because your body

Kung-Fu Masters

"My philosophy of fighting is that if you can avoid a fight, do it. I don't recommend that anyone fight. But if you have to do it, watch your opponent's nearest elbow."

changes too. You can't go against nature. Speed and power were his greatest assets but even the level of those would decrease over the years and he would definitely compensate with other attributes in order to keep his level up.

Q: Who do you think would be a good fight for Bruce?
A: I really think that there was no one his size in the world who could have beaten him. But if I have to pick one person I guess I would say Benny Urquidez. He could give Bruce a good fight. But who knows what the outcome would be.

Q: What's your philosophy of fighting?
A: My philosophy of fighting is that if you can avoid a fight, do it. I don't recommend that anyone fight. But if you have to do it, watch your opponent's nearest elbow.

Q: Do you think it is good for students to analyze different fighting systems?
A: Definitely, I encourage students to get out of the system and come back so they know the others.

Q: These days there are many jealousies, not only in Wing Chun, but also in Jeet Kune Do and many other styles. What do you think about this?
A: As far as wing chun goes, I personally felt this problem. I'm sure that people like Yip Man, Bruce Lee, and other legendary masters would be very upset seeing people and students inside their families fighting and

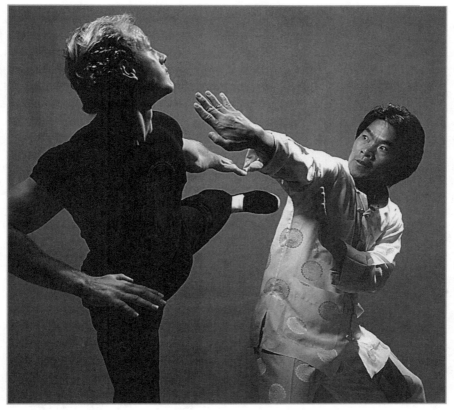

"The discipline in martial arts comes from respect and integrity. Unfortunately, some people seem to have forgotten what those are all about."

bad-mouthing each other. A junior must always respect his senior. And if the senior does wrong then the teacher will correct him, not the junior. The discipline in martial arts comes from respect and integrity. Unfortunately, some people seem to have forgotten what those are all about.

Masters Techniques

Master Cheung squares off with his opponent (1). As his opponent launches a front punch, Cheung deflects with his front hand (2). The attacker then spins and throws a spinning back-fist which Cheung blocks and then simultaneously counters with a left punch (3). Cheung follows with a downward push to open the line (4), then traps the attacking arm and finishes with a strike to the face (5).

From a ready stance (1), the attackers starts a high roundhouse kick (2), that Master Cheung blocks (3), and immediately counters with a low sidekick to the knee (4), followed by a hand control and right punch (5), and a new trap and left punch to the face (6).

Masters Techniques

Master Cheung squares off with his opponent (1). As his opponents begins to punch (1), Cheung simultaneously blocks with his right hand (2), and kicks to the ribs with his right leg (3). He uses this to close the distance and trap the lead hand while punching to the face (4), and follows with a left-hand trap and a right-hand punch (5).

From a ready stance (1), the attacker throws a sidekick that is deflected by Master Cheung (2). Cheung follows with a left punch to the head (3), and a left-hand control and right punch (4). Cheung then controls the opponent's lead arm and punches to his face with his right hand to finish (5).

Masters Techniques

Master Cheung squares off with his opponent (1). As his opponent throws a haymaker, Cheung steps out and blocks the attack, simultaneously punching with his left hand (2). Cheung then scoops the opponent's attacking arm and brings it down (3), opening a line for a new punch to the face (4). This allows him to trap and attack with a new left punch (5).

From a ready stance (1), Master Cheung blocks his opponent's lead-hand punch (2), and uses **biu sao** to deflect the second attack (3). Controlling the attacker's arm, Chueng counters with a succession of right punches (4), and finishes with **pak da** (5).

Robert Chu

A Perfect Balance

ROBERT CHU (CHU SAU LEI) BEGAN PRACTICING THE MARTIAL ARTS IN THE EARLY 1970S. HE SPECIALIZES IN COMBAT APPLICATIONS AND HEALTH ASPECTS WITH A FOCUS ON THE YIP MAN WING CHUN KUEN SYSTEM AS TAUGHT BY HAWKINS CHEUNG AND THE YUEN KAY-SAN AND GULAO WING CHUN KUEN SYSTEMS AS TAUGHT BY KWAN JONG-YUEN. A WRITER IN HIS OWN RIGHT, HE IS THE CO-AUTHOR OF COMPLETE WING CHUN AND HAS WRITTEN NUMEROUS ARTICLES FOR SEVERAL MARTIAL ARTS PUBLICATIONS. IN ADDITION TO HIS WING CHUN TRAINING, SIFU CHU HAS INSTRUCTOR RANKINGS IN HUNG GAR KUEN AND LAMA KUNG-FU. ALSO A LICENSED ACUPUNCTURIST/CHINESE HERBALIST, ROBERT CHU CURRENTLY TEACHES WING CHUN PRIVATELY IN THE PASADENA, CALIFORNIA, AREA.

A FACULTY TEACHER AT SAMRA UNIVERSITY OF ORIENTAL MEDICINE AND A FACULTY PROFESSOR OF TAI JI QUAN AND QIGONG AT LOYOLA LAW SCHOOL, AND CHIEF INSTRUCTOR OF TAI JI QUAN AND QI GONG AT THE ST. VINCENT HOSPITAL CENTER FOR HEALTH AND HEALING IN LOS ANGELES, ROBERT CHU IS ONE OF THE MOST RESPECTED INSTRUCTORS IN THE MARTIAL ARTS COMMUNITY, NOT ONLY FOR HIS INSIGHT IN THE COMBATIVE ARTS BUT FOR HIS DEEP KNOWLEDGE OF THE HEALING TECHNIQUES AS WELL— A PERFECT BALANCE.

Q: How long have you been practicing the martial arts?
A: I started martial arts during my youth, about 7 years old. My grandfather was a practitioner of Shaolin martial arts and *tai ji quan* and several times when I acted up, I was punished by having to stand in a corner in a horse stance. Little did I know that was basic training in the martial arts.

I trained primarily in Shaolin, *hung gar*, and *wing chun kuen* in my youth. As I matured, I became interested in *xing yi*, *tai ji quan* and *ba gua*, and *Mi Zong lama quan*. I was also one of the last disciples of the late master, Lui Yon Sang, the grandmaster of the *fei lung fu mun* (Flying Dragon/Tiger System). I was fortunate to have received the complete transmission from him personally. Despite all my cross training, I view my personal style as wing chun. I practice and teach tai ji quan also, but I feel wing chun is more closely suited to my personality.

Kung-Fu Masters

"I thought all systems had their good and bad points, and I thought to cross train and improve myself with the various systems. Some masters in Chinatown were masters of legitimate systems, some masters just made things up."

Q: Who were your primary instructors?

A: I studied with many teachers in New York Chinatown, and wanted to explore the Chinese martial arts as extensively as I could. I thought all systems had their good and bad points, and I thought to cross train and improve myself with the various systems. Also, as young man, I was also seeking a system that suited me best personally, and I wanted to sample what I could. New York Chinatown had all systems—7 star praying mantis, white crane, Lion Fist, *hung gar*, *bak mei*, *lung ying mor kiu*, *hung fut*, Northern shaolin kung-fu and many other systems. Some masters in Chinatown were masters of legitimate systems, some masters just made things up. At age 14, I studied some wing chun basics with a friend of mine, Jeung Ma Chut, who studied the Jiu Wan system. Later another friend, Eric Kwai, who was a student of Moy Yat, and I had a *gong sao* match, and although I beat him, his close quarters fighting skill was apparent, so I wanted to learn some of his basics in exchange for some fighting techniques. Eric suggested I continue my studies with one of Moy Yat's top students, so I learned from Lee Moy Shan. Because of a falling out with Lee Moy Shan, I left to study the Gu Lao and Yuen Kay Shan systems of wing chun under Kwan Jong Yuen, a good friend and generous teacher. I later went to seek out Master Hawkins Cheung in wing chun and have been with him since 1988. He is truly a master and an honorable man and it is his methods that I primarily use.

I trained in hung gar under Yee Chi Wai (Frank Yee). Yee is the successor to the Tang Fong system of hung gar, and I studied the major forms

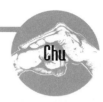

and weaponry of this system with him. He also introduced me to *mi zong lama pai* master, Chan Tai Shan, with whom I studied.

I studied Yang style tai ji quan and *hebei xing yi* under Kou Min Tang General and Chiang Kai Shek's personal bodyguard, Wang Shin Liu. Wang Lao Shi was a General in the KMT army and studied military science in Japan. He was a student of Yang Cheng Fu's disciple, Zhu Gui Ting. When the Japanese invaded China, Wang led many troops to do battle with the Japanese. Wang was also a master of Xing Yi which he learned from Zhu Gui Ting, who studied with Li Cun Yi, so I am proud to have learned these martial arts from a man who used the arts in the battlefield. Wang went to Taiwan when the Communists took over China, then later retired in New York City.

"I was very interested in the internal power that was cultivated in xing yi. Master Gong influenced me to seek internal power in all the arts I studied."

I also studied briefly under the late Kenny Gong, exploring his *xing yi*. Master Gong taught me the Five Elements, *za shi chui* and 12 animal forms, and I was very interested in the internal power that was cultivated in xing yi. Master Gong influenced me to seek internal power in all the arts I studied.

I was one of the last disciples of *fei long fu mun* under the late Lui Yon Sang. Master Lui was 83 years old at that time and many of the top young masters in New York Chinatown studied with him. He was interesting because his art primarily consisted of weaponry, most notably the pole and the spear. His fist art came from one of the greatest Southern fist masters of all time—Leung Tien Chiu. Lui taught primarily *san sao* and two man work when it came to empty hands. His art was simple, yet very devastatingly effective.

Kung-Fu Masters

Since most of Lui's students were experts in other systems of martial arts, I was introduced to *yin fu ba gua* under my fellow training brothers, Chan Bong and Thomas Lee, who studied under Wang Han Zi. I later continued more studies of *yin fu ba gua quan* under He Jing Han of Taiwan.

Q: Would you tell us some interesting stories of your early days in kung-fu training?
A: New York Chinatown was a mecca of Chinese martial arts and it was always exciting to meet other practitioners. I would often go and visit my friends from other schools and we would engage in "gong sao" (fighting matches) and exchanges with others. Most of the time, we would want to see the forms of the people we fought against—this led to comparison and trading arts. For example, I would fight a guy and if I didn't do so good, then I would study fighting methods and a set with him so I could improve my weakness. In this way, I became familiar with the strong points of many styles, and saw how each approached their training from. It was real exciting and fun. Also, there are a lot of family associations in Chinatown—Oak Tin, Jung Shan, Chinese Restaurant Worker's Association which sponsored spaces for visiting or local masters and I might have some friends who were studying or practicing there. I would often go and visit other martial artists and try to pick their brains on how to improve, or just to compare how their martial arts were practiced.

Q: Were you a natural at martial arts—did the movements come easily to you?
A: I was no natural—in fact, I was rather skinny and uncoordinated when young. I was tall and lanky compared to the average Cantonese. I did have one advantage—I had great flexibility with my legs, and usually beat most Southern fist practitioners with my legs. In martial arts, natural athletes rarely last. The martial arts are an acquired skill; they have to be learned. Some people learn things quickly and just burn out quickly. I also think if you have a burning desire to learn, then you will excel and continue practicing. There's a saying in Chan (Zen)—"No doubt, no attainment; little doubt little attainment; big doubt, big attainment." I'm a firm believer in that. Today's experts and masters all had to study real hard to get where they are today. No one just gets it handed to him. Some think they can buy martial arts knowledge. I think money may open up the doors, but when it comes to using it, you have to have it in your body, so hard work is essential.

Q: Has your personal martial art changed over the years?
A: I think it develops as you mature. For example, in my youth fighting was something that was natural—you did it for survival or for the sake of ego. Martial arts were something that led to big delusions—jealousy, hatred, ignorance. I see most practitioners still stuck there today. I saw a lot of guys get involved with the secret societies and with underground activities, and saw many lives ruined. I think that ultimately in martial arts, a small Dao (Way) should lead into a big Dao (way)—you use the arts to temper yourself and as a method to cross over from greed, anger, stupidity. This way you can be more in harmony with yourself and your world.

"Martial arts are both an art and a science. In wing chun, the art is scientific because it gives you tools and if you properly replicate them, you can have the same results. The art is flexible in that it allows for personal expression."

Physically, one has less time to train when he gets older, so one has to continue to practice basic "gung" (work)—that is, basic exercises to maintain strength, flexibility, and timing. Nothing leaves the basics. Advanced work is just the basics applied.

Q: With all the technical changes, do you think there is still a pure system of kung-fu?
A: Pure? I think there is no such thing as "pure"—it's an illusion. For example, everyone has his/her own personal style—you eventually express it when you reach the highest level where art and personality match. Martial arts are both an art and a science. In wing chun, the art is scientific because it gives you tools and if you properly replicate them, you can have the same results. The art is flexible in that it allows for personal expression. Personal expression is the art part. You learn the tools, then apply them; you don't learn the fighting forms of your master to

Kung-Fu Masters

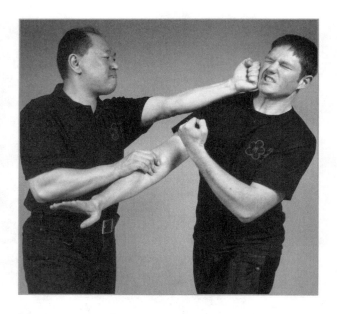

"Too many Chinese people are hung up with pure lineage, authentic transmission, from the grandmaster. You study martial arts for you—not for what names you can drop. All those names and credentials don't help when you're being attacked."

copy their style. For example, no one in Yip Man wing chun fights exactly the same as Yip Man did—it is not a style that you learn to fight with and duplicate your master. The system is based on the most effective use of human body and proper timing and positioning. Everything is dependent upon the moment and the energy that the opponent gives us. People are not entirely correct when they think that wing chun is only scientific and based on physics—the basics are the science, but the expression in application is the art. In wing chun, nobody teaches you step by step what to do in "chi sao" (sticking hands) or what to do when attacked spontaneously—you have to develop yourself to utilize it. We're not a paint by numbers system.

All of the founders of the above martial arts must have had some training elsewhere in order to create their system, so only people under that rigid thought of "lineage" try to be pure. Ed Parker said it best—"When pure fist meets pure flesh—that's pure." Too many Chinese people are hung up with pure lineage, authentic transmission, from the grandmaster. I see Americans buying into that also, because they were trained in that way. I think it's rigid. You study martial arts for you—not for what names you can drop. All those names and credentials don't help when you're being attacked. This is why I have a motto, "Let application be your sifu; let function rule over form." In that way, you really weed out the non functional and learn to use your core system.

Q: Would you talk about different wing chun styles or methods?
A: Sure. There are many schools of wing chun. There's Yip Man, Yuen Kay Shan, Gu Lao, Pao Fa Lien, Chi Sim Weng Chun, Pan Nam and others. Of

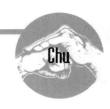

course, the best known is the school of Yip Man, and within it, there are many branches based on what the first generation students of Yip Man interpreted. For example, Leung Ting's association is known worldwide and reflects his teachings. William Cheung is also very famous and teaches his interpretation of what Yip Man taught him. I was lucky and was able to study many wing chun systems in the Yip Man family, but I concentrated on studying more of what Hawkins Cheung taught me. Hawkins' style I feel is unique, his wing chun emphasizes body structure and stresses combat applications. When I went to him, I already knew the entire system and had practiced wing chun for over 11 years. Hawkins told me that knowing forms wasn't enough—I had to concentrate on application. I thought, who is this cocky guy? Later I found out that he could back up everything he said.

When I studied with Hawkins, I found that the real DNA of wing chun is body structure, and this is what permeates in the application of it. What I was lacking in my previous study was how to use body power. When I learned this, it made sense, for after all, Yip Man was a small man—how could he beat bigger, huskier people like Leung Sheung, Tsui Sheung Tien, Lok Yiu and Wong Shun Leung, unless he had a mastery over body structure?

Some have speculated special or secret techniques, or another secret system, but this is not so. The truth is one either develops body structure or doesn't. With advanced practitioners of wing chun—the lineage isn't important—what I noticed was only a small handful of people had body structure. Most didn't. Even experts with 10 or 20 years practice still topple over during "chi sao" or go flying around the room. It's a shame.

Anyway, I also went to Hong Kong and Taiwan visited the elders of the system, including Wong Shun Leung, Tsui Sheung Tien, Lo Man Kam, Koo Sang and others. I also studied with William Cheung for a while. So my grounding is based mostly on the Yip Man system. I've also had the opportunity to study the Yuen Kay Shan system thoroughly, under my Sifu, Kwan Jong Yuen, and through my co-author, Rene Ritchie. I think the Yuen Kay Shan system is very rich in teachings and tradition. I was also fortunate Kwan Sifu also passed on the Gu Lao wing chun to me, a system that was brought to Gu Lao village by Leung Jan, wing chun's most famous fighter. The Gu Lao system, as you might expect, lays emphasis on combat application. Through the years I met people open and willing to share their systems. For example, the outstanding exponent of Chi Sim wing chun, Andreas Hoffman, taught and showed me his version of *weng chun*, which is a completely different system than wing

Kung-Fu Masters

chun. His stances are wider and deeper, and their body and pole work are excellent. I was fortunate to learn his applications of throws and joint locks first hand.

Through Hendrik Santo, I have been fortunate to study completely the Yik Kam *siu lien tao* system, which in my opinion, is probably the fore-runner to today's version of wing chun. This system is unique because it emphasizes the body structure, much as I do in my wing chun, and that it is composed of one set that embodies the three forms in Yip Man wing chun. The siu lien tao system is comprised of movements from Fujian White Crane boxing as well as Emei 12 Zhuang—an esoteric Buddhism health/combat/meditation system. Yik Kam Siu Lien Tao emphasizes the 36 Tian Gang hands which can be used to cure or injure. The system also has a short dummy set, pole and knives sets and features sticking hands, although from a different platform than what is seen in the Yip Man and Yuen Kay Shan systems.

Q: Do you think different schools of the same method are important?
A: Not really, as I think it is the practitioner who cultivates his martial art is most important. In the end, everyone develops his own personal style and if he has followers, a "school" ensues. For example, one of my early wing chun teachers was a very mediocre teacher, but I persevered and studied real hard and was not afraid to experiment with what suited me. Of course, I also consulted with other practitioners, seniors, and elders. Hawkins taught me something great, he said, "Yip Man would tell us not to believe him regarding application of the art, but to test out our wing chun for ourselves." I think this statement had a profound effect on me. Prior to studying with Hawkins, I was always concerned if I learned some-thing correctly, but Hawkins said it's the application that counts the most. In other schools people always care if they were passed down the art cor-rectly, but I find even if it is transmitted "correctly", but if one cannot make it work, it's worthless. This is why I laugh at all the claims of "origi-nal" wing chun—if you can make it work, then it is "original". If you can't make it work, then it is BS. Even wing chun has a saying passed down from our ancestors, *"Sao Gerk Seung Shiu, Mo Jit Jiu"* (hand and feet defend accordingly, there are no secret unstoppable techniques.) When people come out with secret lineages of wing chun, I question their inten-tions.

One thing I must say is that in the United States, many come out of the woodwork with secret family systems which claim to be "original" or the most "traditional". Often these claims are just a form of puffery, based

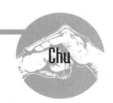

on greed or ignorance. In China, we used the marketing claim, "Old, original, or traditional", whereas here in the US, we say "new and improved". Often these individuals claiming their wing chun is the first or oldest is a load of crap—people just want to gain money or fame through the "secret lineage." There are a lot of giveaways and contradictory statements when people come up with this stuff, but often, people are gullible and want to really believe in this fake stuff. I guess some people can't tell the difference between chop suey and Peking duck. I guess unless one is scholarly and actually takes the time to look things up, one can fall for the tricks and advertising.

Wing chun probably developed most in the 1850's, although some say that it has it's roots are connected to events in Southern China to overthrow the Qing Dynasty that began 150 years earlier. In my opinion, all historians are speculators, since they weren't there. The late Dharma Master Hsuan Hua, the 45th Dharma successor to Chan (Zen) Buddhism said, "Historians are just people having nothing to do and looking for something to do." They want to investigate history, in other words, to discover what era this person lived in and what period that person lived in. It is like having eaten one's fill, one has nothing to do, so one putters around with meaningless things. In my opinion, these kinds of people are undesirable. The more they research, the more trouble they create, saying, "This is counterfeit, that is real." What is real in the world? What is counterfeit? Nothing! If you think it is counterfeit then it is counterfeit. If you think it is real, then it is real.

I think this scolding is full of Chan flavor. If you want to believe your lineage is real and you cultivate it and develop it to a high level, then it is. Who is to say something is legitimate or not? What historians try to do is

"Often these individuals claiming their wing chun is the first or oldest is a load of crap—people just want to gain money or fame through the "secret lineage." I guess some people can't tell the difference between chop suey and Peking duck."

Kung-Fu Masters

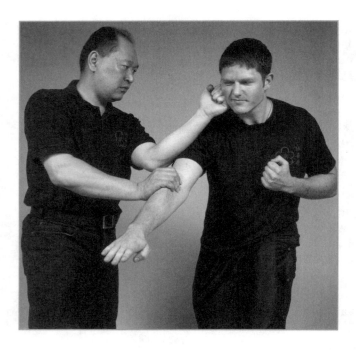

"If you want to believe your lineage is real and you cultivate it and develop it to a high level, then it is. What historians try to do is to prove their hypothesis based on facts they gather and create a paradigm for you to believe in. Pay your money and take your pick!"

to prove their hypothesis based on facts they gather and create a paradigm for you to believe in. Pay your money and take your pick! When I looked into the history of wing chun with Rene Ritchie, the first thing I told him was every branch will say they're the first, most original and best. You can't avoid the politics. And practically every branch of wing chun has said they are the oldest, most original. This is all human nature.

They all say that to bolster their egos or want fame, after all, Chinese think the most original is best. So in a sense, this is just a marketing ploy. Chinese knew and understood the power of myths and legends, knowing that the Chinese mind enjoys a mystery and likes to find things out if they are real or not. In fact, in Chinese culture, it is often a custom to exaggerate a friend's credentials when introducing him to another friend. It's a kind of puffery—the only thing is you have to find out whether it is real or not and in what context. It's the same with wing chun or any other martial art. For example, the origins of the Shaolin Temple—Damo (Bodhidharma) went to shaolin, he didn't found the temple; it was already there. Nor did he create Zen or Chinese martial arts. People (usually retired warriors and generals) brought the arts to the temple. The saying "all martial arts are from Shaolin" is an exaggeration. The secret society origins are also fables, popularized through myths and powerful images of Chinese culture. I think even the average Chinese knows the fables and take them with a grain of salt, but the average American has no idea of the culture and lore of the Chinese, so take things as fact. And you know what? You can tell when these people are try-

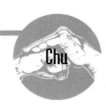

ing to say their style is special and most original exclusive of every other related style, after all, they're the ones trying hard to promote that lineage. If a person says that wing chun is over 300 years old, then it is true for all the branches as well, not just one branch, after all, they all are linked through one important period of time—the time of the Red Boat Opera people of the King Fa Hui. I realize what I say might be offensive to some, but if we have our differences, then I salute you! I can only say these things after I have looked into so-called secrets revealed and researched the history of China from the Ming to the Qing Dynasty period.

Personally, I think it is despicable when people lie and talk about their made up origins as real, but if a style has merits, then I try to focus on that. I think some people just want to fill their rice bowl with food and make a living, keep their business open, attract more students, keep their wives happy and put their kids through school.

Q: What is your opinion of sport competitions like kickboxing and fighting events such as the UFC? Do they represent the real martial arts?
A: I think these events are still basically sports, because the level of contact is agreed upon and there are rules. I would call these events "martial sports," just like boxing, but they do not reflect martial arts. I think these sports produce superb athletes with excellent condition and good all round skills, but the intent to kill someone is not there. True martial arts deal with a life or death situation and it also looks to heal the body, mind and spirit. Too many are practicing to be brawlers or fighters, but a true martial artist develops the soul of a Jun Zi—Confucius' idea of a nobleman—not necessarily in prestige or rank, but rather in character.

Q: Do you think that kung-fu in the West has caught up with the East as far as skill level?
A: Yes. We've probably even surpassed them. The best people always come over here as this is the land of opportunity. I also think that people in Asia struggle to make a living and have less free time to cultivate and develop themselves. I used to think the skill in Hong Kong or China must be superior to here, but after I visited in 1987 and later saw people who trained on the mainland, I was not impressed with the level of skill. Basically, if you're good here, you're also good there. I think one can always improve. The most important thing is to maintain my level and improve daily. One can get better in timing and positioning and with

Kung-Fu Masters

regards to experience, and in this way, intuition can take over. But it must be grounded in logic, and mastery of your arts.

Q: Martial art are nowadays often referred to as a sport. Do you agree with this definition?
A: The way most people practice is a sport, a recreation. I think martial arts is not a sport, but rather an art form. It is in a unique category. Martial arts is still the best name, rather than being classified as a sport.

Q: Do you think weapons training helps kung-fu physically?
A: Definitely. The weapons skills are a complement to the empty hand skills. They teach you how to move with weight and how to dynamically apply your power and momentum through an apparatus. Few people train today with the intent to fight with a weapon. Most wing chun people use the pole as a form of weight training, and the knives as an exercise with weights; I think this is wrong in a way, as it does not develop the thought of application with the weapon—how to really cut, or disarm an opponent, and how to finish him with your weapon. In essence, the martial intent behind the weapons is lost. Weapons skills in the United Sates have degraded into a show; basically everyone wants to dazzle people—but it's empty. In Southern China, one had to be proficient with a pole—to really protect oneself.

Q: Do you think a practitioner's personal training should be different than his teaching curriculum as an instructor?
A: Yes. But I do think teaching is also a form of training. When you have learned your art inside out and spent enough time, you begin to move within the context of the art—therefore, everything you do is training. You stop just using arm power when you use a wrench or hammer—your body, your intent—everything is behind your movement. I change my son's diaper, I have to use a 'wu sao' (wing chun guard hand) to protect myself from his squirting me. I use my steps to walk through crowds, I time my entry into a revolving door. All of these are daily activities that train us.

Q: Do you have any general advice you would care to pass on?
A: Yes, don't fall for Chinese marketing BS of "original" this or that! But seriously, everyday is training and find ways to train in everything you do. Try to study with as many people in your field as possible and concentrate on that. Then, get perspectives from outside your area of expertise. I

would also say the core of real skill, the DNA of wing chun, is body structure. A person wanting to really master the art ought to get some real instruction in that.

More information is available today, and slowly, all the secrecy is going away. Andreas Hoffman said something good to me, "In the future, there will be no secrets, all that people have to do is train hard and they will have it all". I think that is very true. More and more, teachers today are willing to share their fine points with you through books and videos. Of course, the majority of the stuff out there is mediocre.

Q: Whom would you like to have trained with?
A: Yip Man, mostly because he was such a character. I could also ask him whether or not he really taught some of today's people, especially the knives forms I have seen. I'd also like to have studied with Yuen Kay Shan because he had a great mind and he was always trying to improve. I've often thought of Leung Jan, because he was an expert in Chinese medicine, as well as a fighter and teacher. I regret not having enough time to visit with Si Bak, Wong Shun Leung, who's passing has left a hole in the wing chun family. I would also like to travel back in time and meet with the founders of wing chun, so I could really discern who was the real founder of system.

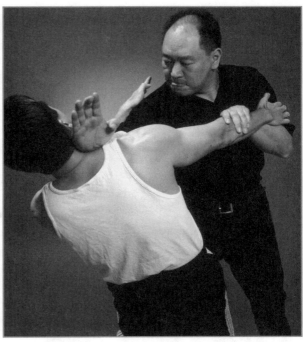

"Try to study with as many people in your field as possible and concentrate on that. Then, get perspectives from outside your area of expertise. I would also say the core of real skill, the DNA of wing chun, is body structure. A person wanting to really master the art ought to get some real instruction in that."

Kung-Fu Masters

"Find something that you like and stick with it. Try to get much advice from elders and seniors. Always think of how to improve and you eventually will attain a high level of skill."

Q: What would you say to someone who is interested in starting to learn martial arts?
A: Find something that you like and stick with it. Also, don't be afraid to try something else new if you don't like it. Try to get much advice from elders and seniors. Always think of how to improve and you eventually will attain a high level of skill. You have to leave techniques and theory behind and really dig deep to reveal the principles and concepts behind your systems. That is real training.

Q: What is it that keeps you motivated after all these years?
A: I believe that the wing chun method I practice is a very complete system. It has stimulated my mind to working out the variations, changes and combinations for many, many years. It stimulated my sensitivity to touch and pressure, with timing and directions so that I can develop my tactile sense. The guiding principles always kept me motivated, as this was advice from our ancestors. The spiritual, moral aspects of the art made me want to study Chan (Zen) deeper. The health aspects led me to study Chinese medicine and acupuncture and the body better. Johnny Wong, a fellow Yip Man wing chun practitioner once said to me that Yip Man told him, "The great secret in wing chun is that it develops your mind and makes you smarter."
I think that comment is very telling. If you can apply that mind set to anything else you study, you can be very successful. Speed, strength, accuracy, timing and cruelty are the basic requirements to get the job done, and a student has to learn how to apply things under stress. I think free fighting is just a means to develop proficiency under stress, but it is not everything.

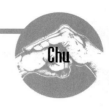

For a student to excel, students need to master timing positioning, concepts and principles. That they need the method, as well as the training behind it. Teachers shouldn't teach you theory, but rather they should teach you principles that work. Instructors shouldn't just teach techniques, but the concepts needed to create techniques. The difference is whether a person has gone through the experience or not.

Q: What is your personal training schedule now?
A: I do a little something every day. I generally practice the wing chun basics—stance work, form, stepping, and basic combinations. For me, wing chun is very natural. All movement I do embodies wing chun. For example, if I have to change a flat tire, I use body structure, not my shoulders. This is the way it ought to be. I also train a lot with the long pole, as I feel it is the best way to train for power in wing chun.

Q: What is your opinion about mixing styles like karate with kung-fu and kickboxing with jiu-jitsu? Does the practice of one nullify the effectiveness of the other?
A: I am a big advocate of cross training, but I believe you have to have a strong root and basis in one system you identify with. I firmly believe that you win with your basics and what you trained in the most. Not try to be a jack-of-all-trades, simply because you've studied a bit in all of them. For example, in wing chun, we finish a guy with our intercepting strikes. They try to strike us, and we intercept their attack with our own attack. Once we land, the opponent's reaction time is off, and we can further strike him to further slow his reaction time. This allows us time to win with multiple blows. If we can't win with that basic requirement, then our training in basics is crap.

Q: What is the philosophical basis for your martial arts training?
A: Since I am a Chinese doctor, I believe very much in Taoism and the harmony of *yin* and *yang*. The philosophy of yin and yang extend into the *si xiang* (4 corners), and later the *ba gua* (8 trigrams), and within this, all of the balance of body, mind and spirit are embodied. The core of this philosophy is balance. This is what wing chun stresses—neutralizing and balancing, and adjusting to fit in with your opponent. That is the highest skill. I also think very highly of Chan/Zen Buddhism. I find myself reading the Sutra of the Sixth Patriarch (Hui Neng) quite a bit, as I find that the essence of Zen is there, and it is the core of the Chinese martial arts. One of the passages in the Sutra that sticks with me is when Hui Neng was

Kung-Fu Masters

confronted by Hui Ming, he taught Hui Ming the essence of the Dharma in one sentence, "Not thinking of good or evil, where is your original face?" Hui Ming became enlightened at these words, and asked, "What other secrets did our master give to you?" Hui Neng said, "If you look into your heart, you know there are no secrets." I think these words can alleviate the frustration one encounters when trying to master a martial art. I also think that Zen is the root of the wing chun mind.

Q: Do you have a particularly memorable martial arts experience that has remained with you as an inspiration for your training?
A: I have been so fortunate to see many unique things and study with some real masters. I guess I can share some rather unique stories. For instance, when Yee Sifu practiced the hung gar system, you could really see the expression of the five animals come out. When he did the Tiger form, he looked like a tiger. When he did the crane form, he really looked like a crane. Yee was fast and explosive and extremely talented. In my opinion, he was the best hung gar man I have ever seen. His ba gua Pole was fantastic! Yee displayed all the strong, flexible and explosive power and deep stances of Hung Gar.

Lui Yon Sang at 83 asked me to attack him with a pole, but no sooner than I attacked him with a Biu Gwun (Darting staff), he disarmed me and struck me five times before the 8 foot staff hit the ground. He was amazing!

Kwan Jong Yuen always encouraged me to learn medicine, as he felt that martial arts knowledge was never complete unless you knew Chinese medicine. He felt you had to learn the body, the weak and strong points, the range of motion, and how to cure. Kwan Sifu taught me Dim Mak, and how to really injure a person striking their vital points, but he was also balanced, as he taught me how to treat someone if you injure them. This influenced me to study acupuncture and herbology, and I am a Licensed Acupuncturist with my own clinic today. In fact, most of my teachers were expert at acupuncture or herbs, including Yee Chi Wai, Chan Tai Shan, Lui Yon Sang, and Kenny Gong.

One time, Hawkins Cheung and I were discussing fighting techniques and I threw a punch at him. With one crashing slap, he used "pak da" on me and left an incredible expanding welt on my forearm. I was literally stunned at the power of this small man!

Wang Shin Liu was very accomplished in internal cultivation and stressed the internal feeling and movement of Qi in the practice of martial arts. But he was more than a warrior, he was always soft spoken and a kind gentleman. I was always impressed by his humbleness. He was truly

"Kung-fu means to cultivate. Every day cultivate a little and improve a little. Soon all will be clear."

a balanced warrior cultivating *wen* (scholarly) and *wu* (martial). All in all, I have been fortunate to meet so many talented individuals.

Q: After all these years of training and experience, could you explain the meaning of the practice of kung-fu?
A: Kung-fu means to cultivate. Every day cultivate a little and improve a little. Soon all will be clear.

Q: How do you think a practitioner can increase their understanding of the spiritual aspect of the arts?
A: I think a person has to get away from all the violence and worry about kicking butt and really have to find the inner wisdom. Avoid three things—greed anger and stupidity. Don't ever think you're a master or a Buddha. You have to always be a student of life. One thing I don't get is why people want to be teachers—lawyers and doctors have to be practitioners, so should martial artists. What's so great about being a teacher? It's hard

Kung-Fu Masters

"You have to always be a student of life. A martial artist can't be too smart, or else they won't persevere. If a martial artist is close-minded, they will never have greatness in their expression of the art."

work! Perseverance and an open mind are very important for improving in the arts. A martial artist can't be too smart, or else they won't persevere. If a martial artist is close-minded, they will never have greatness in their expression of the art.

Q: What advice would you give to students on the question of supplementary training?
A: I think all training is good, but you have to have a goal in mind. For example, if you train with weights, it may enhance your strength, but it doesn't really enhance your knowledge of body mechanics and application of strength in martial arts. I also think supplementary training is to overcome boredom in martial arts training, so I think if a student can cultivate something, then it's good. One of my students in Long Island once asked me of the peripheral equipment in wing chun like the sand bag, wall bag, iron palm, bag, and spring arm. I told him, basically, this is for dumb students—when a sifu doesn't like someone or really doesn't want to teach him one on one, he directs a student to a piece of equipment to get him out of his hair! Of course, I'm joking, but there is a truth to what I am saying.

I think because students are of a fickle nature they tend to stop training after few years. In our modern society, things come easy. We all study broadly and not deeply. So it is with studying martial arts. But I also think it is the fault if the instructor for not being a partner with the student and helping a student achieve his goals. I think the secrecy of the Chinese mar-

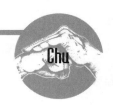

tial arts is also a detriment and causes much student drop off. When sifus have a scheme of withholding secrets or levels of training until a certain ceremony is held or a certain sum of money is ascertained, I think this is also a big turn off. Most Chinese know that Chinese hold secrets, and would prefer to study foreign martial arts like karate do, judo and tae kwon do in Asia. I think this is a laugh for people who hold too many secrets. I think also, it is a fault of commercial schools offering belts, certificates, testing, phony titles—they're all geared to make a teacher money and inflate the ego. People look at that and can see right through it. Of course, some people love that external accomplishment, but real martial arts training is better than that commercialism and money making scheming. Wouldn't something that preserves your health and offers you peace of mind be better than all of that commercialism? Of course, student can always choose with whom they want to study.

Q: Have there been times when you felt fear in your training?
A: I don't think fear is something you have while training—most training never escalates to a point where one is in danger. As long as an instructor teaches a student confidence, I think it will permeate in their demeanor. Fear is something good when you are in a dangerous situation—it heightens the senses and makes the body ready for fight or flight, so I think it is a good thing to be introduced to during training.

Q: What are your thoughts on the future of the martial arts?
A: I hope martial artists can study the martial arts to avoid delusion, stupidity, greed, envy, anger and hatred. It's a good medium to develop friendship and understand more about life. I'd like to see secrecy abolished and the ego and puffery of stylistic superiority be rid of. I think martial artists need to see others and try to understand people from their context, and avoid the negative politics, which breeds negative thoughts that lead to destructive actions.

Masters Techniques

Sifu Chu squares off with his opponent (1). As his opponent throws a punch, Chu blocks with both hands (2), which allows his opponent to attack with a left punch which he blocks again (3). Chu then counters with a right straight vertical punch to the face (4).

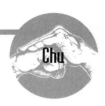

From a **by-jong** stance (1), Sifu Chu blocks his opponent's punch with a **kwan sao** (2). He then redirects the attacking arm to the opposite side (3), to set-up a counterattack (4), allowing him to deliver a finishing strike to the groin (5).

Masters Techniques

Sifu Chu squares off with his opponent (1). As soon as the opponent initiates the attack, Chu steps in and hits the aggressor with a **palm** *strike to the face* (2), followed by a **lap da** (3), and a final trap and backhand strike to the neck (4).

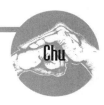

Sifu Chu faces his opponent (1). As his opponent begins to move the leg to kick (2), Chu intercepts by kicking the attacker's groin (3), disrupting the potential attack (4).

Masters Techniques

Sifu Chu, armed with a long pole, faces an opponent who is armed with a similar weapon (1). As the opponent thrusts, Chu blocks the attack (2), and circles the pole to the outside (3). This opens an angle (4), for a hit to the aggressor's lead hand (5), and allows Chu to finish with a new attack to the leg (6).

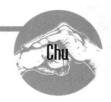

Chu

Sifu Chu faces his opponent (1). As the aggressor attacks, Chu blocks with his pole pointing downward (2), and counterattacks with a thrust to the instep of his opponent's lead foot (3).

Sifu Chu, armed with a spear, blocks his opponent's long-pole attack (1). Scooping the pole with his spear, Chu opens the angle (2), and delivers a finishing thrust to the aggressor's neck (3).

Vincent Chu

The Quest for Knowledge

As sixth generation lineage practitioner of the Yang style of tai chi chuan and the second of Gin Soon Chu's three sons, Vincent Chu learned the art directly from his father's hands, beginning his training very early. It was at the age of 16 that he began to help his father at the Gin Soon Tai Chi Club in Boston.

In an quest for increasing his knowledge, he went to train under Master Ip Tai Tak and Professor Fang Ning, obtaining his teaching credentials from both instructors. Lecturing to his students, Master Chu instills a philosophy which is very much a part of him: "The difference between a good kung-fu man and a poor one is paper thin." A regular on the seminar circuit not only in the United States but in Europe as well, Vincent Chu is a frequent contributor to martial arts magazines around the world and has authored several books and videos that explain the techniques and tradition of the gentle art of tai chi.

Q: How long have you been practicing martial arts?
A: I have been practicing tai chi chuan for over 30 years. I have only practiced Yang style tai chi. My father was my first teacher and was responsible for my introduction to the martial arts. He is the 5th generation Yang style tai chi chuan successor. In the '70s, our school was located on the 3rd floor in Boston's Chinatown. It was next to a bar so the landlord locked the door after 7 PM. The student had to ring the bell and I would drop the key down. The key was attached to a parachute and no student was able to catch it. Therefore, no matter how hard the student tried to catch it, the key always dropped on the ground or into the student's face. My father would always inspect the wall at the end of each class, where we put the board for dynamic push hands exercise. The impact of the students hitting the board was so strong that my father was afraid the wall might collapse!

As far as my technical evolution, I would say that I was a natural and learned the movements quickly, without any kind of trouble. However, my father always said I made many mistakes, I'm sure that I was doing a

Kung-Fu Masters

"Every martial arts system has good things. I don't like the attitude of some people who disrespectfully make statements putting down certain styles or artists. In the very end, it's up to the practitioner to decide what's best for him."

lot of things wrong but since his nature was to be a perfectionist, even if I was doing something right, I'm sure he wanted me to do better. In retrospect, I believe I benefited from the fact my father was never satisfied with my skills, so I was always trying to get better.

Q: How has your personal martial art developed over the years?
A: I think the most obvious change is my perception. As you get older, your goals change and also your idea of what a martial art is. I realized that no one style is better than others. Every martial arts system has good things. I don't like the attitude of some people who disrespectfully make statements putting down certain styles or artists. In the very end, it's up to the practitioner to decide what's best for him. Some people may get into martial arts because of the fighting aspect, others for training and personal enjoyment. Their goals are different and it's logical that the style they choose will be totally different. It's a mistake to think that everybody has the same goals and is going in the same direction.

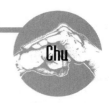

Q: Do you think there are still pure styles of kung-fu?
A: I strongly believe that there are—it just takes a little longer to find them. My father only practiced tai chi chuan and his teacher, Yeung Sau Chung, also only practiced tai chi chuan his whole life. There are people in the martial arts world who haven't been affected by the commercial and eclectic approach that is so common these days. Some martial artists want to preserve the ancient techniques and philosophies without adding

"There are people in the martial arts world who haven't been affected by the commercial and eclectic approach that is so common these days. Some martial artists want to preserve the ancient techniques and philosophies without adding and modifying things just for the sake of modernism."

and modifying things just for the sake of modernism. There are many approaches to the arts, and there are masters and practitioners willing to keep the authentic traditions of kung-fu.

Q: What is your opinion of sport competitions and full-contact fighting events?
A: I think these give people a false perception of what a martial art is. Definitely, this kind of competition is not what we could call true martial arts. It's simply a brawl involving two people who have fighting ability. They don't display any of the real and traditional values intrinsic to the martial arts. Only the fighting aspect can be seen, and in the very end it's not about true self-defense at all but about making money. Martial arts often involve life and death situations and I don't think this kind of competition is providing this type of reality. It makes martial arts seem not that serious.

Q: How close is the skill level in the West to that in China?
A: With many new immigrants and cultural exchange programs in the past few decades, the West has caught up with the East as far as the technical level. However, many people in martial arts still think that you can only learn authentic kung-fu in China. Let's face it, there are many excellent instructors outside China, so you can learn the art from them perfect-

Kung-Fu Masters

"I understand that regardless of how much knowledge a person may have, there is still a lot to be learned. No matter how skillful and knowledgeable you are, there is always more room to grow. If you don't think so, you are limiting yourself in the martial arts way."

ly. It is true that there is something you cannot duplicate outside China, and this is the cultural atmosphere and the training environment. To have this kind of first-hand experience, you have to go there and train.

Q: Do you feel that you have further to go in your studies?
A: Of course. I understand that regardless of how much knowledge a person may have, there is still a lot to be learned. I went to the Wudan Mountain, the birthplace of tai chi chuan, in 1992. Every time I though I have reached the summit, the route went onward. This happened three times. It took me two hours to finally reach it. This experience gave me better understanding of the Chinese saying, "When you have climbed a mountain, there will be a higher mountain behind to climb." No matter how skillful and knowledgeable you are, there is always more room to grow. If you don't think so, you are limiting yourself in the martial arts way.

Q: Do you like to train with weapons?
A: Yes. Although most of the Chinese martial arts weapons are not carried on the street today, I believed their training can definitely improve skill in other aspects. Since each weapon emphasizes a different aspect and technique, and require specific execution, this can improve one's overall martial arts skill. It's very important to know how to use the weapons in the right way because their use is related to body mechanics—the true secret of kung-fu unarmed techniques lies in body mechanics. If you understand how the body works you'll be able to generate an immense amount of power.

Q: Do you train differently than you teach?
A: Yes. Those two things are completely different. Personal training is required to improve one's skill. You have to do personal hard work to keep improving and growing in the arts. On the other hand, teaching is based on sharing information with someone else. You can't approach those two aspects the same way. The goal is different and the focus is the opposite. The focus of personal training is on you; when you teach, the focus is on the students. If an instructor wants to improve his skill, he needs to schedule time to practice on his own. He can't fool himself thinking that teaching time is practice time. Don't get me wrong, if you teach three classes and you show your students a technique and repeat it 30 times, of course you have done 90 repetitions of that movement. But you, as an instructor, need to work on things that your students don't. Therefore you have to allocate time for the specific training that only suits your needs.

Q: What are the responsibilities of an instructor?
A: The man who leads his students along the road of technical and spiritual advancement, is the man who progresses the farthest. The instructor

"Personal training is required to improve one's skill. You have to do personal hard work to keep improving and growing in the arts. On the other hand, teaching is based on sharing information with someone else. You can't approach those two aspects the same way."

Kung-fu Masters

"Some teachers try to make of students tough guys. While that may be good, strength shouldn't be the purpose of the teachings. The true goal of kung-fu or any other martial art is the unification of mind, body, and spirit towards the final perfection of the character."

progress by teaching because it is the best way of learning. The teacher must do as he instructs other to do. If he tells the students to hold their tempers, he need to show that he can control his; if he corrects the student's kick or punch, he has to make sure his punch and kick are a good example. Some teachers try to make of students tough guys. While that may be good, strength shouldn't be the purpose of the teachings. The true goal of kung-fu or any other martial art is the unification of mind, body, and spirit towards the final perfection of the character. There are thousands of techniques in martial arts. The desire to master the physical techniques should not be the true goal—it is the mastery of oneself. That is a misconception that should be corrected by the instructor in the early stages of training.

Q: Can an instructor have too much influence on a student?
A: Yes, and that is not good. An instructor has to correct his students' mistakes but not halt their inner development as martial artists and individuals. He has to be totally fair and impartial and have the good of the student in mind. If an instructor has selfishness in his heart, then his teachings cannot be good. As I said before, teaching is learning and the instructor should provide the right example. They need to have an open mind, but respect and preserve the traditional principles at the same time. This not only applies to technical aspects, but also to spiritual guidance as well. The martial arts begin and end with courtesy and respect, not only inside the school but in life as well. The diverse aspects of the art should be pointed out to the students in order for them to understand and incorporate good values into their daily lives.

Q: Does martial arts teach violence?
A: Let me say that martial arts does not develop violence, cruelty, arrogance, egoism or emotional immaturity—although some who claim to be martial artists display these qualities. The true spirit of martial arts stresses

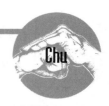

exactly the opposite—self-control, modesty, patience, humility, respect, integrity, discipline, and courtesy. Every martial art instructor has to insure his students' development towards these goals.

Q: What is the best way to improve technique?
A: As my father said, "Less talk and more practice." Nowadays, I see a lot of people talking and arguing about whether this or that technique would work in a real fight. There are too many philosophical arguments today that take us nowhere. In the very end those who really want to know the answers are the ones who train. The rest just want to talk and be in magazines all the time. Anyone interested in learning a true mar-

"Nowadays, I see a lot of people talking and arguing about whether this or that technique would work in a real fight. There are too many philosophical arguments today that take us nowhere. In the very end those who really want to know the answers are the ones who train."

tial art needs to first find a knowledgeable teacher—not necessarily a famous one. Fame and quality don't necessarily go hand-in-hand. Today, the majority of famous teachers are often involving with commercialism. Their main goal is to increase their income, not to produce top students.

Q: Do you think mixing styles is beneficial for students?
A: I have been traveling to Europe the past few years for workshops and seminars, and I have seen that cross-training is very popular there. In Chinese martial arts, a complete system often involves the student training in many different techniques and learning how to use these against other fighting methods. Of course, this fact is more obvious in the external systems than the internal ones. If one is already engaged in a complete system, I don't believe one has to keep jumping from one style to another without direction. Simply because someone can perform several forms from different styles, doesn't mean they are knowledgeable in kung-fu. Real mastery in kung-fu fighting skills are learned one step as a time and are very complete. You start with the solo form, then progress to the solo drill, then move to the partner drill. Free fighting is the final

Kung-Fu Masters

"If you only try to develop your technique and the physical side, then you are missing the point. The authentic kung-fu training is a full package: you should not take what you want and then leave the rest out. If you do that you'll never understand what the art has to offer."

piece of the puzzle and is the result of a consistent and diligent training in a proven method. A complete Chinese martial art system always trains student in these three areas. These areas take a lifetime to master—so how you can be a master of 10 different styles?

Q: What is the philosophical basis for your training?
A: Many students asked me what is the correct way to execute a movement and I often reply that there is no one single way to execute a correct movement. The process of learning what is best for you is on-going and never stop. The evolution is constant and we need to adapt to the circumstances in the right way. The philosophical basis of my martial arts training is that there is no absolute state. As explained in the tai chi symbol, everything changes daily.

Q: What single event most improved your tai chi?
A: I have many memorable experiences that have been part of my martial arts journey, but the most memorable was meeting my father's teacher. Growing up listening to my father talking about his experiences with his teacher, was something that captivated my curiosity for years. Finally, when I met Grandmaster Yeung, he personally explained to me how to improve my tai chi skill. I will never forget that.

Q: What benefits does forms training give?
A: It is a methodology that cultivates the body and mind. If you only try to develop your technique and the physical side, then you are missing the point. The authentic kung-fu training is a full package; you should not take what you want and then leave the rest out. If you do that you'll never understand what the art has to offer. You'll never discover all the great benefits that proper training can bring to your life. In some way, emerging victorious in a fight may be the goal of some martial artists—but that's not the real truth. To win fights only brings a relative victory.

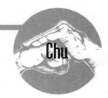

Not to fight and yet to be victorious, is the higher skill and brings absolute victory. It's important to learn how to fight, but it is even more important to learn how to avoid fighting. By learning how to not get carried away by winning, and by learning how to accept loss, the student will progress in the right direction for their life.

Q: How can practitioners increase their spiritual understanding?
A: It was said that Zhang San Feng, the creator of tai chi chuan, trained in the Shaolin system from his youth. Later, he reformed what he had learned by emphasizing the use of the body. He paid attention to all the changes inside the body not outside, moving into a more internal approach to what he was doing. Today, we understand tai chi chuan as a martial art as well as a health exercise. If a practitioner can truly think about the energy behind the movements, and not only learn and practice how to control the opponent in training, one will better understand the spiritual aspect of the arts and the internal energy behind the physical technique.

"Nowadays, too much emphasis is placed on the physical and technical aspects. Instructors and teachers are considered masters due to their skill level and not for their ethical and moral principles. You can teach a fighting system to students and create a legion of fighters, but true kung-fu is more than that."

Q: What are the most important qualities of a successful martial artist?
A: Chinese practitioners believe that martial spiritual and moral ethics are the most important aspects of training. In many Chinese martial art schools, the first lesson is in martial ethics. Nowadays, too much emphasis is placed on the physical and technical aspects. Instructors and teachers are considered masters due to their skill level and not for their ethical and moral principles. You can teach a fighting system to students and create a legion of fighters, but true kung-fu is more than that. It's a way of life and therefore, more important than simple physical movements. It is said that the legendary Yang Lo Sim earned the nickname of "Yang The Invincible"

Kung-Fu Masters

"Many students tend to stop training after a couple of years and I think there are several reasons for this. But it is mostly due to their perception of martial arts. Students do not expect martial arts training to be so difficult, and after a couple of years they get bored and decide to quit."

due to his internal skills and not only due to his physical skills. Many people wonder about the meaning of "pushing" in tai chi chuan. These people do not understand the philosophy of defeating someone without injuring them. If you have to defend yourself, then you have no choice; but you have to understand that there are moral issues and act accordingly.

Q: What do you feel about supplementary training?
A: I believe supplementary training is an important, but at the same time most boring, aspect of martial arts training. It definitely has a direct impact on skill because it makes the student reach a high level. By improving other aspects of the equation, your kung-fu will be better. It's very important, though, to not dedicate too much time to those supplementary drills and exercises at expense of real technical kung-fu training. Just because you punch the pad, lift weights, or run, your kung-fu skills won't improve. You need to know how to combine this type of training with you kung-fu in order to benefit.

Many students tend to stop training after a couple of years and I think there are several reasons for this. But it is mostly due to their perception of martial arts. Students do not expect martial arts training to be so difficult, and after a couple of years they get bored and decide to quit. We are living in a fast-paced society that has many temptations and demands short-term results. Unfortunately, it doesn't work that way with kung-fu. Kung-fu training is about patience and dedication—and the real benefits won't appear in two or three years. In order to avoid student burnout, the instructor has to educate students in the right way of training, and not lead them to have a wrong expectation of what they are going to achieve. The art of kung-fu needs students with true understanding and true spirit much more than it needs those who are only powerful experts.

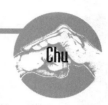

Q: Have there been times when you felt fear in your training?

A: Only the fear of change. I guess that is normal for all human beings. We try to stay within the boundaries of what we know and what we can control. But in life, you can only grow when you go outside of these boundaries—when you put yourself into a situation where you don't feel comfortable and need to adapt. Then you grow not only as a martial artist but as an individual as well. After I learned all the techniques my father taught me, I asked myself over and over what should I do next—in what direction should I take my martial arts journey? A lot of questions were banging in my mind and it took a long time to find the correct answers. Later, when I begin to teach, I realized that teaching was another step of the learning process for me. When you begin to teach and share with others, you have to analyze what you know from a different perspective.

"After I learned all the techniques my father taught me, I asked myself over and over what should I do next—in what direction should I take my martial arts journey? When you begin to teach and share with others, you have to analyze what you know from a different perspective."

Q: What is the future of martial arts?

A: It is very difficult to tell exactly what is going to happen to the martial arts in the future. I think it will be developed into more styles and that there will be more emphasis placed on sport competition. I really don't know whether to laugh or cry, because it's something I can't prevent or even effect. On the other hand, I am sure that a separate group of people will work hard to keep the traditions alive and develop them so they are useful to people for self-defense and in improving their everyday lives. There are many important reasons why I keep doing what I'm doing, and why I share the art with my students—but if I had to pick a single reason, I would say that the my desire to keep the teachings of my father alive is what keeps me going. It is my way of showing appreciation and respect to those who shared their knowledge and love with me.

Adam Hsu

A Modern Kung-fu Scholar

ADAM HSU IS THE LIVING EMBODIMENT OF THE CLASSIC KUNG-FU MASTER. HE IS AN EXCELLENT TECHNICIAN, A SCHOLAR, A QUIET MAN, AND ABOVE ALL, A GENTLEMAN. HIS DEEP KNOWLEDGE OF TRADITIONAL KUNG-FU MAKES HIM STAND OUT AS ONE OF THE FEW TRUE ICONS OF THE CHINESE MARTIAL ARTS IN MODERN SOCIETY.

THROUGH DECADES OF DEDICATION AND HARD TRAINING, ADAM HSU HAS GATHERED AN IMMENSE AMOUNT OF INFORMATION THAT TRANSCENDS THE PHYSICAL ASPECTS OF THE ART AND MANIFESTS IN THE MOST TRADITIONAL CHINESE PHILOSOPHY OF LIFE. HIS ULTIMATE GOAL IS PRESERVING THE TRADITION AND ENSURING THAT IT IS AVAILABLE FOR FUTURE GENERATIONS. A LIVING ENCYCLOPEDIA OF SEVERAL TRADITIONAL STYLES COMPRISING BOTH INTERNAL AND EXTERNAL METHODS, THIS KUNG-FU INSTRUCTOR DISPLAYS THE QUALITIES OF EVERY STUDENT'S DREAM TEACHER, NOT ONLY IN A PHYSICAL AND TECHNICAL SENSE BUT ALSO IN AN EDUCATIONAL APPROACH TO THE DEEP CHINESE TRADITIONS AND PHILOSOPHIES.

Q: Kung-fu is strongly related to the Chinese culture. How do you think these two aspects, martial art and culture, are perceived by the Western world?
A: In China, the purpose of education has always extended beyond acquiring knowledge. The long hours that a person spends at the kung-fu school are intended to develop not only intellectual skills, but perhaps more importantly, foster the cultivation and refinement of character and personality as well. Students obey instructors dutifully and without asking questions. This kind of discipline and obedience provides the student with the necessary foundation to lead a harmonious life. Only after a skill has become mastered through precise and repeated practice will creativity and originality eventually emerge.

Definitely this approach is completely different than what we find in the Western world. Westerners are less willing to accept the "just do it and one day you'll understand" answer and they need explanations for everything they do. There are some instructors who are a bit more flexible in adapting their kung-fu to the Western society without sacrificing the

Kung-Fu Masters

"The absence of ranking system in the traditional kung-fu makes everything more difficult to understand in terms of clear-cut levels of skill in the Western world. The instructor is seen as some sort of supernatural being with a skill the students will never have a chance to equal, much less surpass."

art's essential qualities and goals. But, unfortunately, others, mainly due to their upbringing and cultural background, can't effectively change their approach. This is understandable. The absence of ranking system in the traditional kung-fu makes everything more difficult to understand in terms of clear-cut levels of skill in the Western world. Because of this, many students feel unsure of their abilities and goals, and thus frequently become discouraged. The instructor is seen as some sort of supernatural being with a skill the students will never have a chance to equal, much less surpass.

Q: Students always try to imitate their instructors; could be this considered a mistake?
A: Yes, and it is very common one. They try to copy and imitate the instructor as closely as possible, not only in terms of the teacher's kung-fu, but also in style of dress, mannerisms, and even as far as likes and dislikes. A senior student becomes a carbon copy imitation and in many cases it gets worse because these students overdo it and become even more severe than their instructor.

Q: When do you think a person should start training?
A: Well, as soon as they get interested! I understand your question and I have to say that there is some controversy about what is the best age to

start training in kung-fu. I disagree with the idea that the best age is from five to ten years old. The reason is very simple, the child's body is nor developed enough to provide a strong foundation and perform the hard training that is required in the art. The tendons, the ligaments, the muscles and the bones are going through many changes and are not strong enough to deal with the proper training. The child's body must be more fully developed and balanced before you can begin to reshape it in a kung-fu way. I believe it's okay to train kids but it's important to always make the training fit their special needs and not represent an obstacle to their physical and mental development. Their training should be designed to develop coordination and balance and, at the same time, give them a basic understanding of what real kung-fu training is all about. Then, when they reach the proper age to start serious training, they already have a basic foundation on which to build.

"Reaching a high level on kung-fu mastery requires more than just physical ability. It's a mature sophisticated art and therefore youth is not a guarantee for it. A good kung-fu exponent is the result of many years of consistent and dedicated training."

The main problem I see is that when you teach a child the art of kung-fu you'll be facing problems not only found in martial arts but in every physical activity. The instructor tries to satisfy the parents' dreams for their children and this can be damaging for the student and eventually limit his-her potential because, quite naturally, training designed for adults is not necessarily suitable for children. And the value a child can get from a "watered-down" version of the true training is questionable. Reaching a high level on kung-fu mastery requires more than just physical ability. It's a mature sophisticated art and therefore youth is not a guarantee for it. A good kung-fu exponent is the result of many years of consistent and dedicated training and the essential element the students must acquire as they develop their martial arts is an

Kung-fu Masters

"Kung-fu training, like any other martial art or art form, cannot give "Superman" powers. There are neither 15-year-old instructors, let alone "masters," nor 100-year-old teachers who can defeat a 25-year-old fighter. Let's be realistic. Kung-fu is a practical art based on intelligence and combat experience."

inner understanding and maturity that goes beyond mere performance of the physical techniques.

Kung-fu training, like any other martial art or art form, cannot give "Superman" powers. There are neither 15-year-old instructors, let alone "masters," nor 100-year-old teachers who can defeat a 25-year-old fighter. Let's be realistic. Kung-fu is a practical art based on intelligence and combat experience. Only through extensive training and dedication can one achieve mastery and understanding.

Q: So what's missing in those teenagers who display amazing techniques and perfect forms in competition?
A: A long time ago I watched an Olympic gymnastic competition. It was a floor exercise division. I was truly impressed with the skill, power and technical proficiency of the competitors. However, I didn't see much meaning expressed in the form—only the polished veneer of the physical techniques. The same happens these days with the young competitors. The have a good command of their language (basic techniques) and they can create almost perfect sentences (reproduce a form) but the movements

don't contain the maturity and creative element and invest each movement (word) with meaning (as in poetry). What's missing and lacking is an understanding of what they are doing beyond technique and the ability to give a "personal and mature" interpretation to the physical movement. They are "performing" rather than "creating" or "expressing" the art. I haven't seen any teenager or young person display that special quality in the movements. The reason is he or she is still too young to have that level of maturity as individual and martial arts practitioner (regardless of his-her physical skill in performing the technique). He has not the understanding to bear the art with his-her personal stamp. In kung-fu or any other martial art, when one matures, his expression of the art matures too and it manifest in the way the forms (*kuen*) are done. Age greatly influences the way a kung-fu man does his kuen or a karate man does his *kata*. Unfortunately, when the practitioner ages, the very effect of aging becomes an obstacle to reaching a higher level. Contrary to some popular myths, you get physically weaker as you get older. You can

"Age greatly influences the way a kung-fu man does his kuen or a karate man does his kata. Unfortunately, when the practitioner ages, the very effect of aging becomes an obstacle to reaching a higher level. There is no way to hide from the inevitable physical and metal deterioration, except in the fantasy world of kung-fu legends and movies."

perform as you did in the younger days but you don't feel the same motivation for training. This situation is common to any practitioner of martial art, regardless of style and method and is the reason why many people get disappointed and stop training when they realize this fact. There is no way to hide from the inevitable physical and metal deterioration, except in the fantasy world of kung-fu legends and movies.

Q: Would you tell us about your early days in kung-fu, when and how you became involved in the arts?
A: I have to say that my introduction to the art of kung-fu just seemed to come about naturally. My grandfather, who studied modern military sciences in Japan, helped to overthrow the Ching dynasty during the early

Kung-Fu Masters

"I had three younger brothers and we used to make too much noise in the house. All the punishment we received didn't help at all, and the things just got worse. My father decided to teach us kung-fu to burn up our overload energy. Don't forget that was meant to be a 'punishment.'"

1900s. My father was also a student in the Army Academy, receiving great honors on the day of his graduation. My mother's ancestors are Mongolian and they helped Genghis Khan conquer China, establishing the Yuan dynasty. As a young kid I was attracted to any kind of fighting art, to the Chinese Opera and Chinese circus. I was always imitating whatever I saw at the plays and mimicking the actors. I had no idea how to tell apart the real kung-fu from the dance but it definitely put a seed in me. When we moved to Taiwan, my physical condition was very weak and I had to miss a whole semester going to the school only for the exams. This gave me the opportunity of staying at home and read a lot of my father's books. Because my father studied kung-fu before he went to Japan, he did have some real kung-fu books. I remember that what attracted me the most were the swordsman novels. I treated these books like my private treasure. Of course, before too long I found myself copying the movements from these books. Fortunately for me, this intent didn't work and I didn't improve much so I had to take into consideration the possibility of receiving real training. I knew that what I was doing was not right!

I had three younger brothers and we used to make too much noise in the house. My family tried everything to makes us calm down—but that just treated the symptom, because the source of the trouble was still there. All the punishment we received didn't help at all, and the things just got worse. My father decided to teach us kung-fu to burn up our overload energy. Don't forget that was meant to be a "punishment." My father was not a real martial artist, he practiced when he was very young but he forgot most of what he learned. The good thing is my father's original goal was achieved; the peace returned to our family and we became more tranquil

both in the house and around the neighborhood. With that limited background I decided that I wanted to pursue my training in kung-fu and I went to Han Ching Tang who taught me the systems of *chang chuan* and a variety of weapons and two-man forms. Sifu Han was famous for his Islamic and mei-blossom long fist. He was very easy to approach and he had a great deal to offer. At that time I still had a certain percentage of fantasies around, but his serious training put my feet firmly on the ground. I believe it was a great training because I got an excellent foundation for my later training in kung-fu. I always thought that a martial art should be more than just exercise and when sparring with my classmates I discovered the techniques differed only slightly from our "natural" way of fighting, so I had to try harder to do it the right way. I could do forms beautifully and skillfully but at that time I couldn't use *chang chuan* for fighting. I lacked the maturity to realize that system is a formidable fighting system.

"I always thought that a martial art should be more than just exercise and when sparring with my classmates I discovered the techniques differed only slightly from our "natural" way of fighting, so I had to try harder to do it the right way."

Because of that feeling I went to train in praying mantis kung-fu, which is famous for its rapid and complex of succession of movements. I studied the eight-steps mantis style from Wei Hsiao Tang and later on the seven-stars style under Li Kun Shan. This training made me capable of applying not only the techniques of the mantis style but also those from my previous training in *chang chuan*. I began to understand the reason why I was winning or losing in sparring. At that time, I began my training under Chao Lien Fang in the style of *hsing-i chuan* because I thought I needed a more effective way of delivering power. Chao was a very traditional teaching and I couldn't help but sense that reverting to the "old-

Kung-Fu Masters

"Although I was satisfied with pa chi/ pi kua training I found myself training and studying more styles. After all this training I realized that any complete kung-fu system taught by a qualified instructor should contain the necessary aspects of training, usage and power."

fashioned" way would only help bring a quicker end to a style that was by then fighting for its life. Chao helped me to meet Liu Yun Chao, whom I consider my finest instructor.

Q: How was your training under Liu?
A: Liu had the opportunity himself of training under the best teachers of his time so he never insisted I quit all the previous styles, just that I forget everything I ever learned! I began with *pi kua*, which forced me to start from the scratch so I could learn how to develop the correct way of using power. All the stretching exercises helped me to relax and improve my flexibility, and believe becoming a beginner all over again was one of the most painful things I've ever had to do. Then he taught me the forceful style of pa chi chuan that created a great combination with *pi kua*. With his direction I learned how to issue power in the proper way. This type of old practice is endless, mirroring the old saying, "there is always another mountain that is higher."

Although I was satisfied with pa chi/pi kua training I found myself training and studying more styles. Liu Yun Chao introduced me to his good friends Chang Hsiang Shan, who taught me 'six harmonies' praying mantis, and Tu Yi Che, who schooled me in the original chen-style of *tai chi chuan*. In Chang's 30 years of teaching, I was his first six harmonies student. After all this training I realized that any complete kung-fu system taught by a qualified instructor should contain the necessary aspects of training, usage and power.

Q: So do you advocate a cross-training approach to the art of kung-fu?
A: I know it may sound like a contradiction but I believe that the serious kung-fu practitioner should limit himself to develop one style so his techniques rise to a mature level. Because someone practices many styles does-

n't mean he will be a better fighter or a more challenging opponent in a fight. Rather, he is easier to confuse and defeat. I know many people think that the more styles one learns, the more knowledgeable his kung-fu is. But how the ancestors used to say, "One hundred techniques you know cannot compare with one technique you have mastered." I guess that unknowingly and due to a desire and commitment to help erase the many kung-fu misconceptions, I perhaps misled the kung-fu people by training in different systems. Today after many years of experience I believe the student should stick to a chosen style and work hard to understand it and make it work in the right way.

Q: Japanese arts have spread very well in the Western world as compared to Chinese kung-fu, what do you think is the reason for that?

"I know many people think that the more styles one learns, the more knowledgeable his kung-fu is. But how the ancestors used to say, 'One hundred techniques you know cannot compare with one technique you have mastered.'"

A: It's true. I believe there are several reasons for that. After the WWII the Japanese introduced the Americans to the arts of *budo*. They didn't hold back things and started to openly teach the different systems. On the other hand, kung-fu became really popular in the 70s which means that people started to hear about the Chinese art almost 20 years later. But there are more important reason than these.

The Japanese and the Chinese cultures are very different. For instance, Japanese can be described as clean, neat, straightforward and well disciplined. Chinese are more individualistic, more complicated, indirect and resilient by nature. These two different personalities affect the way the teachers approach the art. Japanese immediately decided to structure the arts, create textbooks, ranking systems and examinations standards. If you

Kung-Fu Masters

"I personally value the old ways and consider them virtuous, but at the same time I understand that some steps need to be taken to make the art grow in an organized way. We need better organizational and promotional techniques for the masses feel comfortable to join not only the art of kung-fu but the Chinese culture as well."

want to spread something and have the masses to practice it, then you need these kinds of things so people can follow it. Chinese people never structured the art with all these rankings and standards. It's true that kung-fu has more than 100 styles as compared to Japanese arts but that's is not an excuse. Those kung-fu organizations that have set up standards and ranking have grown big in comparison to others.

Also, the Japanese arts are based on the code of bushido. The Japanese warriors always were different than the average person. They were a separate and highly respected class. They acted different from others, wore their hair and clothes differently, and affected distinguish habits such as their usual treatment of women. They stood out, and could be identified among thousands. Chinese have always been unlike the *bushi*. They were trained to act as other did. For old kung-fu practitioners, it was a high compliment when they were told that nothing in their appearance or behavior suggested their kung-fu mastery. So, if you consider all these facts, you'll sure understand why the kung-fu arts haven't spread as have the Japanese arts. I personally value the old ways and consider them virtuous, but at the same time I understand that some steps need to be taken to make the art grow in an organized way. We need better organizational and promotional techniques for the masses feel comfortable to join not only the art of kung-fu but the Chinese culture as well.

Q: How important is the aspect of fighting in the art of kung-fu?
A: Fighting is a natural and very instinctive human trait. It's not necessary to learn kung-fu or any other form of martial art to survive in a fight. Neither do you need an instructor to learn a few tricks and techniques to use in the street. In fact, you if watch carefully, you'll see that many of those who

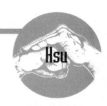

claim to be a martial artist are merely truly experienced street-fighters who rely in their natural combative abilities, rather than technique to defeat an opponent. Kung-fu is an art of fighting, not just a fighting art. The distinction implied here is that kung-fu emphasizes a special way of using the body to deliver not only power, but also complex and sophisticated strategies that utilize the knowledge gained from centuries of the battlefield experience. Learning kung-fu to fight is a very difficult and lengthy process and it's not something that you can learn from books and videos. You need a qualified instructor. During my early days my classmates and I concentrated on improving our skills, not on abusing them by hurting or taking advantage of other people. Fighting is a natural emotion and inclination in the human beings that's why I think the instructors have a great responsibility because they need to satisfy the student's natural inclination through real fighting in correctly supervised kung-fu training. It's a good way to effectively satisfy the youngster's curiosity and avoid him to be in the streets creating or looking for trouble. Kung-fu may help the young person to build up the correct idea about fighting.

"Kung-fu is an art of fighting, not just a fighting art. Learning kung-fu to fight is a very difficult and lengthy process and it's not something that you can learn from books and videos. You need a qualified instructor."

Of course, the purpose of any martial art is to win the fight but we can't forget the fact that the "natural" unschooled fighter is always defeated by the superior technician. A genuine martial art style is quiet different than a "natural" fighting form, just as poetry is different from more natural, conversational forms of writing. In both cases, poetry and kung-fu, you need a certain attitude and special training to learn such an art. The longer you practice the art, less you need to fight. Kung-fu teaches how to stop fighting in a broader and higher sense. As an old Chinese saying goes: "Learn kung-fu three days and you'll go anywhere; learn kung-fu three

Kung-fu Masters

months and you'll only wander around your own city; learn kung-fu for three years and you'll find hard to move a single inch."

Q: But it's true that some kung-fu practitioners love to fight.
A: Yes, it's true, but it's mostly young people. You change as the time goes by and your knowledge and maturity increases. I remember that my kung-fu brothers and I had a joke saying that the toughest guy in the world is the first-degree black belt. You ignore this guy unless you have to fight him because he will look for any reason to fight with you. But like I said when you increase your understanding and love for the art you don't really need to fight in the streets. Looking for fights is a simple sign of immaturity.

Q: As a martial arts instructor, how do you approach teaching both male and female students? Should practitioners of both sexes train together or in separate classes?
A: Martial arts classes are made of different kind of people and it's a big responsibility for the instructor to convey the art to them in a proper way. The reasons for them to join the school are varied. The first aspect for him to consider is that classes in composed of male and female students. The instructor will try to teach both in the same way but by doing this he will probably making a mistake. The fact of the matter is that men and women are different and therefore should be taught differently. For instance, men are physically stronger than women and women are less aggressive than men. These and other considerations and details should be taken into account when teaching a martial art. If possible I would recommend having some coed classes but mostly teach men and women in separate classes that the instructor specifically designed for each group. Men can be brought into female classes for sparring and self-defense aspects of the training, something that will be very helpful for the female students. You have to be careful because sparring is

"The longer you practice the art, the less you need to fight. Kung-fu teaches how to stop fighting in a broader and higher sense. Looking for fights is a simple sign of immaturity."

a dangerous situation and these sessions should be carefully supervised to avoid unnecessary injuries.

Each student is unique and the instructor must be able to judge each individual's potential and design the training more appropriate to his-her needs. The training regimen should act like a map, directing the student in a clear and definite direction. Kung-fu may be a traditional art but it doesn't mean instructors should be blind to some of the advances with modern training methods and teaching philosophies.

Some instructors are not motivated by the idea of teaching women and some women overreact to the current situation and give the instructor more excuses for not teaching them. These instructors should understand that there is a place for women in martial arts, and that place is different from men. And female student should understand the situation and help the process of change with patience, because in many ways the female students of our time are pioneers. It won't help matters if a woman quits her study because she is discouraged. The solution is a mutual understanding of the facts and of each other.

"Each student is unique and the instructor must be able to judge each individual's potential and design the training more appropriate to their needs. The training regimen should act like a map, directing the student in a clear and definite direction."

Q: The name of your kwoon is "Chih ke." What does it mean and what is the overall philosophy of the school?
A: It refers to the ancient Chinese military virtue: "To stop the fight is the goal of kung-fu." It is a basic Chinese military moral principle. Learning to fight can also teach the value of not fighting, of developing one's character and martial skill to control aggressive impulses. Chih Ke not only involves acquiring the skills to stop the external conflict and maintain a peaceful society, but also stopping the inner struggle, creating an inner harmony. We use our martial arts skills to face the enemy within and to

Kung-Fu Masters

"True kung-fu is not a matter of comparing styles, because no style is more special than any other. Kung-fu emphasizes a certain way to issue power, retraining the practitioner so that the whole body is used. It is not a supernatural power, but the full potential of human power."

keep our lives and the lives of those around us in harmony.

True kung-fu is not a matter of comparing styles, because no style is more special than any other. Kung-fu emphasizes a certain way to issue power, retraining the practitioner so that the whole body is used. It is not a supernatural power, but the full potential of human power. I believe that this idea, "tsan szu chin" (reeling silk energy) is the main difference between kung-fu and other styles. The art has been in existence a long time and styles have survived the test of time on the battlefield and have proven their worth in private matches. All the useless techniques have been thrown away already, so there is no need to try to improve or revise the art. As in other aspects of Chinese culture, kung-fu is a mature art and is best used with intelligence and discretion.

In Chinese history the utmost respect and credit is paid to those people who stopped conflict and brought peace. This is a very high ideal, and one to which all kung-fu men should aspire.

Q: Martial arts movies have popularized the art, but do you think they have been the right vehicle to spread the proper kung-fu mentality?
A: Definitely not. I believe that there was a time when it was a great help to popularize the name but we tend to forget that a kung-fu movie is not kung-fu, just as a hot dog is not a dog. The movies are purely for entertainment and although they can be good for having a good time seated in theater, they haven't portrayed the right morals and teachings of the true art to help people understand the real philosophy behind the physical techniques. It's amazing how much influence these movies can have over the real art, not only in people's appreciation but also in instructor's minds. I have seen instructors trying to learn techniques from the movies. Don't get me wrong—as a kid, I loved these movies but I wanted to learn the real art and I took the proper direction. Without the real philosophy

all that is left is just a bunch of crazy fantasies like walking on water, one man defeating a troop of 50 soldiers, et cetera. Kung-fu is the virtuous man's training. A true practitioner has to use discipline and judgement to control and govern the physical techniques learned through many hours of training.

Q: What final advice would you give to kung-fu practitioners and martial artists in general?

A: Kung-fu, like any other athletic skill such as tennis, football or basketball takes dedication and hard training. You can't become good just because some Immortal visits you during the night in a dream and gives you all the secrets so you'll be a master as soon as you wake up the next morning. It's impossible to gain a high level of skill because your sifu feeds you a special formula or teaches you a "secret" style of kung-fu that can be mastered with easy, slow and soft training at home. Necessary sacrifices must be made and unless you are ready to pay the price, you won't get the rewards. Kung-fu teaches you to face life with honesty and bravery, to live each day of your existence as if it were the only day, enjoying every minute of it completely and thoroughly.

"It's impossible to gain a high level of skill because your sifu feeds you a special formula or teaches you a "secret" style of kung-fu that can be mastered with easy, slow and soft training at home. Kung-fu teaches you to face life with honesty and bravery, to live each day of your existence as if it were the only day."

Masters Techniques

Sifu Hsu enters inside the aggressor's attacking arm (1), pulls it up and twists his body (2), places himself behind his opponent (3), and applies a finishing punch to the groin (4).

Sifu Hsu blocks the attacker's lead punch with his left hand (1), scoops the attacking arm (2), closes the distance to the opponent (3), and applies a palm strike to the lower abdomen (4).

Sifu Hsu faces his opponent (1), and scoops the attacking arm to open a line (2). Closing the distance (3), he places himself in a position (4), to control both arms (5), and applies a finishing blow to his opponent's midsection (6).

Masters Techniques

From a ready stance (1), Sifu Hsu blocks the attacker's first punch (2). As soon as he perceives a second attack (3), he lifts the arms to block the punch and steps forward (4), positioning himself behind his opponent (5), where he applies a finishing blow and sweep (6).

From a ready stance (1), Sifu Hsu blocks the aggressor's punch (2). As soon as the aggressor begins his second attack (3), Hsu lifts both arms to block the incoming punch and steps in with his left foot (4), placing himself on the opponent's right side (5), where he delivers a finishing blow to the chest (6).

Shi Xing Hung

Spreading the Shaolin Roots Around the World

Master Shi Xing Hung is one of the most celebrated monks to emerge from the Shaolin Temple. Because of his skill and ability in the Shaolin empty-handed forms and armed combat techniques, he was appointed the main trainer for the monks living in the temple. He is also the director of the Shaolin instructors training program. His knowledge and understanding of the technical and philosophical foundations of the Shaolin ways are second to none. After a long trip around the world giving numerous demonstrations and seminars, Master Shi Xing Hung granted this interview before returning to China. He explained the movement inside the temple to spread the word and fist of Shaolin to the four corners of the globe. According to Master Shi Xing Hung, the best of Shaolin kung-fu is yet to come.

Q: Why do you spend so much time traveling around the world?
A: It is a great opportunity to meet new people and it gives me a different way of looking at life—a different perspective. This process makes me grow as a martial artist and as a human being. It's important to see how other people perceive life. It's also very refreshing that in all these countries nobody knows me, so I don't need bodyguards. People are very nice to me.

Q: Why would a Shaolin monk need a bodyguard?
A: It's not so much a matter of self-defense. In Europe we are very popular, so it's almost impossible to walk in the street without creating a big problem. People know that we are monks from the Shaolin temple and they want to get closer to us and that creates some problems just crossing a street or taking a walk.

Q: Rumor has it that the Shaolin monks are planning to open new temples.
A: We opened a new temple in Japan quite some time ago and had a great turnout. We are also planning to open a new temple somewhere in

Kung-Fu Masters

"The only way to learn the real knowledge of Shaolin is in Chinese. I understand that this limits the total amount of students, but we are looking for quality not quantity. The student has to fulfill many requirements and he has to become a Buddhist."

Europe. The reason for doing this is to make the Shaolin arts available to the Western public without forcing them to travel to China. Of course, the person leading the temple has to be a one of our real monks. He has to uphold the Shaolin temple traditions not only in martial arts, but in philosophy and attitude as well.

Q: Is the training hard for those who want to be leaders of the new temples?
A: Yes. To begin with, they have to speak fluent Chinese because for that kind of training translators are not allowed. The only way to learn the real knowledge of Shaolin is in Chinese. I understand that this limits the total amount of students, but we are looking for quality not quantity. The student has to fulfill many requirements and he has to become a Buddhist.

Q: Why is speaking Chinese so important?
A: Basically because the old teachers only speak Chinese. The translators don't have permission for listening to the master's words. So if the student doesn't speak and understand Chinese the amount of knowledge that he will receive will be limited.

Q: Who supervises the training and teaching at the different temples outside China?
A: High ranking monks travel in order to keep high standards both in technique and spirituality. There's something that I would like to mention; some people think that because you're Chinese you are better than a

Caucasian as far as kung-fu is concerned. This is wrong. Some great students from the West have become very skilful in the martial techniques and have developed a very spiritual attitude as a Buddhist. Time and attitude are what's important—not if you're Oriental or Caucasian.

Q: Will each of these temples be independent from the headquarters in China?
A: They will be branches dependent on the central temple, and they won't become independent. The training, religious teachings, and martial testing will be supervised by the monks in China.

Q: Do the technical aspects of kung-fu and the Buddhist religious teachings go hand in hand?
A: For us, both aspects are very important—but the person which goal is strictly to learn the physical aspects of kung-fu will be able of learn it without being involved in the religious aspects of the temple. Of course, for those interested in obtaining a deep understanding of Buddhism there will be a way to do so.

Q: How many people are authorized by the Shaolin temple to teach the original arts?
A: Not many. As I said before, we look for quality not quantity.

"Some great students from the West have become very skilful in the martial techniques and have developed a very spiritual attitude as a Buddhist. Time and attitude are what's important—not if you're Oriental or Caucasian."

Kung-Fu Masters

"The real Shaolin is about peace, not about fighting. Of course, the physical aspect is important and I would say that from the technical point of view in kung-fu, everything boils down to few factors. These basic elements are very important, yet many people neglect to teach or practice them."

Q: What does Shaolin mean to you?
A: It means a lot of things, but it is more related to life and peace than to the violent aspects of kicking and punching. The real Shaolin is about peace, not about fighting. Of course, the physical aspect is important and I would say that from the technical point of view in kung-fu, everything boils down to few factors. These factors determine the level of understanding and skill that the student will have in their future years. These basic elements are very important, yet many people neglect to teach or practice them. One is led to believe that many instructors have taken these basics for granted. The result is that too many students do not have a clear understanding of their importance.

Q: What are they?
A: They are breathing control, relaxation, and the power of the waist. But let's take one at a time. As science has proven, breath control is fundamental to all forms of activity. Failure to control breathing results in a much faster rate of fatigue and the corresponding inability to execute moves with proper speed and power. In the temple we are fully aware of how important it is to have a surplus of energy. Such a surplus can only be generated by good nutrition and proper breathing techniques. The student must learn to control breathing during every movement, regardless of the duration of the activity he's performing. Continuous practice

will allow the breathing control to become automatic. Through proper breathing patterns, the muscles will be more effective because they are receiving a good supply of oxygen and because they will obtain a rich supply of blood from an efficient heart. In addition to that, proper breathing will increase the speed of a technique because exhalation is applied in the same direction as the force of the movement. Power is also heightened as impact is made when the power is most concentrated in the abdomen due to stiffening of the abdominal muscles during exhalation. In general, breath control will also result in stronger lungs and greater vital capacity.

Q: What about relaxation?
A: Relaxation is also essential for faster and more powerful punching or kicking. An arm without tension is light and flexible, and capable of greater

"Relaxation is also essential for faster and more powerful punching or kicking. An arm without tension is light and flexible, and capable of greater speed than a blow thrown from a tensed arm."

speed than a blow thrown from a tensed arm. Also, contracting the muscles as the fist approaches the target generates greater acceleration and, therefore, power in momentum. But despite the effects of breathing and muscle tension in increasing speed and power in a technique, it is also necessary to learn good waist movement to control the effects on your own body of the power generated by the technique. The waist is the mediator between the movement of the lower and upper limbs. It is the center of balance, power and speed, adjusting for movement in one hemisphere of the body to compensate for movement in the other half. The waist should rest in a state of equilibrium, balanced between the positive and negative forces which result from twisting the body. For exam-

Kung-Fu Masters

"Kung-fu is more than that, it is a science expressed through the human body. Once a thorough understanding has been accomplished, however, these principles must be practiced and experienced until they become natural and coordinated."

ple, twisting the upper body to the left results in a positive force counterclockwise and negative force clockwise. These forces work together to produce power in the body much like snap of a bullwhip. Power in punching comes from a quick twist of the waist rather than the swinging of the arm.

Q: So you need to combine these three elements to be fully efficient?
A: Yes, from a traditional kung-fu technical point of view, not necessarily to beat somebody up. Kung-fu is more than that, it is a science expressed through the human body. The unity of these three elements is the key to achieving perfection in your techniques. Obviously, these basic elements will be much easier to attain in simpler techniques than in more advanced ones; it is recommended that you begin practicing them one movement at a time before incorporating them into forms or sparring. Once a thorough understanding has been accomplished, however, they must be practiced and experienced until they become natural and coordinated. Once you master these principles so they occur automatically and instantaneously, you will be able to concentrate on fighting strategy rather than the proper execution of the movements. You can master position and timing so that each blow will be delivered effectively and with minimum of energy expenditure.

These three principles closely comply the restrictions placed on the human body by nature so that maximum effectiveness is achieved with a minimum effort.

Q: What is your opinion about so many different kung-fu arts even within the same style?
A: There are so many varieties of sub-styles in the different martial arts that it is difficult to talk of them in generalities. Actually, the different styles emphasize different things, some close-range fighting, some longer distances, and some wide or narrow areas. Each has its own merits according to the environment. Usually the styles are specially tailored for a particular situation.

Q: How do you reconcile tradition with the modern world?
A: Both halves of the whole have to live together. Tradition is what is passed on from the older generation to the younger. These things are not only physical techniques but respect, discipline, and other intangible skills. I would like to keep some tradition and use that as a base on which to build. We should keep the knowledge we have just like any other science, and then use what is already known and work from there to extend knowledge. If you want to pass the tradition from the older generation to the young and build knowledge, it has to be done in a way that is adapt-

"There are so many varieties of sub-styles in the different martial arts that it is difficult to talk of them in generalities. The different styles emphasize different things, some close-range fighting, some longer distances, and some wide or narrow areas."

Kung-Fu Masters

"Tradition is the life of martial arts. The codes, rules, and conduct expressed by the martial arts can guide its followers to superior levels of inner development and mastery of the naturally selfish ego."

ed to the society of the country were you are teaching. This is the only way a martial art tradition will survive outside of the country of origin.

Tradition is something that the individual instructor has to emphasize and explain in order to show the practical value of learning. One person can't change all that. It has to be a widespread effort. I try to emphasize that much can be realized from traditional values. But I think also that tournament rules can also be used to reinforce the styles. Tradition teaches all facets of strength, natural power, mercy, and discipline. Tradition is the life of martial arts. The codes, rules, and conduct expressed by the martial arts can guide its followers to superior levels of inner development and mastery of the naturally selfish ego. To understand the intense importance of tradition, you must first master yourself.

Q: People tend to believe that Shaolin kung-fu is a method that focuses more on form than fighting. Why?

A: I can't answer for the people who think that way, but I can say that's not true. The misconception probably comes from what we do in demonstrations, which is mainly forms and not much free-fighting. One problem is that the most of China is blocked from the outside world, especially the interior where the martial arts are the best. Most of the available kung-fu men are from Hong Kong in the south and are short-

range fighters. This represents a minority of the styles. In mainland China, in the north and central parts, there are more styles available but you can't see them anymore for political reasons. The government has greatly influenced the martial arts. They have lessened the emphasis for fighting. It is listed under the athletic department, so it is only a demonstration sport and just an exercise. They aren't doing it for fighting, they are doing for demonstration. The whole purpose is twisted. If the government emphasis were on something else it might be different. Kung-fu is a fighting method and a self-defense system—not simply an acrobatic skill.

Q: But some groups do focus on fighting.
A: Definitely, Usually the Westerner tends to ignore forms in favor of the free-fight-

"Usually the Westerner tends to ignore forms in favor of the free-fighting aspects of kung-fu. They don't realize that forms can help their fighting. They feel you have to hit something to score a point, so practice for free-fighting should always involve contact."

ing aspects of kung-fu. They don't realize that forms can help their fighting. Just practicing individual movements, even one straight punch or kick, is a form in itself. When you put together kicks and punches you get forms also—only longer. So, actually we are always practicing them, but they ignore the traditional forms because they think it is time consuming and unrealistic. They feel you have to hit something to score a point, so practice for free-fighting should always involve contact. Also, they don't think that they will actually move the same way in free-fighting as they do in a form.

One of the reasons people have lost interest in forms is that the traditional forms don't apply to modern circumstances because of the differ-

Kung-Fu Masters

"Once two men begin to fight in a tournament they clash and then separate. In a real situation, once they clash they rarely separate. So in tournaments the amount of time in combat at close distance is relatively short compared to a real fight."

ences between tournament rules and the attacking methods on the street. For instance, many of the old styles prefer punching close-distance. This is natural because many fights occur at close distance. Once two men begin to fight in a tournament they clash and then separate. In a real situation, once they clash they rarely separate. So in tournaments the amount of time in combat at close distance is relatively short compared to a real fight. You don't have the opportunity to realize the importance of close-distance techniques that many forms emphasize.

On the other hand, there are actually many people changing the forms to keep up with the environment and demands of competition. I have no objection to this because sometimes change is necessary Old forms are often changed by the way people practice them for purposes different than what the inventor designed. But I think it is also necessary to keep some of the old forms as they were. Some of the traditions should be preserved instead of changed.

"All efforts must be congruous with nature in order to succeed; martial arts against nature cannot exist. The way of nature is the way of success—this is the way of Shaolin kung-fu."

Q: So why are forms so important? What do they really develop?
A: What forms develop, other than the individual moves, is how to put the movements together—the transition from one movement to another—that particular coordination need to move your body properly in combat. All the balance and overall coordination ties things together. The more you practice the form, the more flexible you are in an unrehearsed situation. You become a more well-rounded fighter.

Q: What are your goals as one of the leading performers and young masters of the original Shaolin temple?
A: To help people to understand and appreciate the true art of Shaolin. As human beings, we should live in peace and in harmony with nature. All efforts must be congruous with nature in order to succeed; martial arts against nature cannot exist. The way of nature is the way of success—this is the way of Shaolin kung-fu.

Buck Sam Kong

Opening Doors and Minds

HE STARTED HUNG GAR KUNG-FU TRAINING IN HONG KONG AT THE EARLY AGE OF 6, UNDER GRANDMASTER LUM JO, AND LATER DECIDED TO LEARN ANOTHER SOUTHERN STYLE, CHOY LEE FUT. HE WAS ONE OF THE FIRST TEACHERS TO OPEN A KUNG-FU SCHOOL TO THE GENERAL PUBLIC IN THE 1970S IN LOS ANGELES. HIS WORK AS A KUNG-FU INSTRUCTOR HAS BEEN RECOGNIZED ALL OVER THE WORLD AND HIS REPUTATION IN THE CHINESE COMMUNITY IS SECOND TO NONE.

SOMETIMES HE REMEMBERS HOW "SPECIAL" HIS OLD HOLLYWOOD BLVD. SCHOOL WAS, WHERE A FEW CRAZY PEOPLE USED TO STOP IN TO CHALLENGE THE STUDENTS. HE CLOSED DOWN HIS *KWOON* IN 1987 TO OPEN ANOTHER BUSINESS, BUT KEPT TRAINING HIS OLD STUDENTS PRIVATELY IN HIS BACKYARD.

AS A PROMOTER, MASTER BUCK SAN KONG HAS PRODUCED SEVERAL SHOWS AND TOURNAMENTS, BRINGING IN PERFORMERS FROM AS FAR AWAY AS HONG KONG AND ATTRACTING MORE THAN 70,000 SPECTATORS. AUTHOR OF TWO BOOKS ON HUNG GAR KUNG-FU, SIFU KONG RE-OPENED HIS SCHOOL IN 1994 AND HIS SIU LUM PAI KUNG-FU ASSOCIATION IS GROWING AGAIN. THE FIRST MASTER TO TEACH NON-CHINESE STUDENTS, MASTER BUCK SAM KONG IS THE MAN WHO PUT THE CAPITAL "K" INTO THE ART OF KUNG-FU.

Q: When did you start your kung-fu training?
A: When I was 8 years old I began under Master Lum Jo.

Q: How was the training back then?
A: It was a long time ago so the teachers were very traditional. I remember that I used to be in a horse stance for over 45 minutes. And that was it! Master Lum Jo would light a stick of incense that lasted almost an hour to burn all the way down. When the incense was over then I was allowed to move.

Q: Do you agree with that kind of training?
A: The purpose is twofold. One of the reasons is to really know the student's intention and character. Don't forget that for the traditional mas-

Kung-Fu Masters

"I keep the kuen, or forms and techniques, as close as possible to those I have learned from my sifu. But I have incorporated new training equipment and a different approach to some traditional exercises."

ters, the knowledge they have is a treasure. They just don't give it away because you pay the monthly fee. A mutual commitment has to exist.

Q: Have you made any innovations to your Siu Lum hung gar kuen style?
A: I keep the *kuen*, or forms and techniques, as close as possible to those I have learned from my sifu. But I have incorporated new training equipment and a different approach to some traditional exercises.

Q: You are also a teacher in the choy lee fut style, correct?
A: Yes, I was very attracted to choy lee fut because it is much more aggressive than hung gar. I started choy lee fut at the age of 12.

Q: When did you begin teaching the art to the public?
A: After serving for two years as a hand-to-hand combat instructor for the US Army, I decided to return to civilian life in 1963. I located in Hawaii but it wasn't me who opened that school.

Q: Who did?
A: Well, some karate people opened it for me. One day they said, "Sifu, this is your school." In the beginning I was teaching to students from other styles like judo, karate, and aikido, but later on different people joined the school and I started to teach all kind of students.

Q: Do you consider yourself a traditionalist?
A: First of all, not every kung-fu style is good for everybody. Everyone has to find the right system for themselves. Then, the student should aim for perfection and try to keep the style as close as possible to the way it was

taught by his sifu. As you can see, tradition is a very important factor in my teaching.

Q: You mentioned that you were an instructor for the U.S. Army. How did you approach that?
A: I had to modify certain things. The people in charge found out that hung gar techniques were more practical that what they were using at that time. So they were very receptive. I also updated the bayonet use, modifying the old kung-fu spear and staff techniques for the training.

Q: What's your philosophy of fighting?
A: I always considered fighting a matter of self-control. You must analyze your opponent's strong and weak points. You have to know his advantages over yourself. Once you understand this, you select the right techniques to deal with that kind of opponent—applying the techniques best suited for the circumstances to overcome the challenger. In short, fighting is based on how well you know your adversary.

"I always considered fighting a matter of self-control. You must analyze your opponent's strong and weak points. You have to know his advantages over yourself. Once you understand this, you select the right techniques to deal with that kind of opponent."

Q: Were you criticized by the Chinese community when you decided to teach everybody?
A: Yes. It was a long time ago, in the early '60s, and the Chinese were much more traditional about this than they are now, so I had to face a lot of criticism from those who wanted me to only teach Chinese people. I didn't agree with that idea. Kung-fu is good for everybody, not only the Chinese. Therefore, I didn't have any problem teaching the art.

Kung-Fu Masters

"When you spar full contact, you realize the strong and the weak points not only of the technique but of yourself as well. To win or lose is not the important thing. What is really valuable is the understanding we get from this kind of experience."

Q: Why do some in the Chinese community feel that way, even today?
A: Well, you have to understand the kung-fu is part of the Chinese culture. There is a lot of Chinese tradition and philosophy in every kung-fu movement—it's a Chinese treasure. All this has been passed down from generation to generation, from father to son. They don't like to see people playing around with their cultural heritage. And please, don't misunderstand me, neither do I. But I know there are people out there who really appreciate and treasure the Chinese art and culture as we do, and they deserve the chance to study kung-fu.

Q: In the '70s, full contact kickboxing events revolutionized the martial arts world. What do you think of those kind of tournaments?
A: I guess that if we know how to use this kind of event properly, we can get a lot of benefits. Basically, until this kind of fighting came out, everything about the effectiveness of this or that technique was just pure conjecture. When you spar full contact, you realize the strong and the weak points not only of the technique but of yourself as well. To win or lose is not the important thing. What is really valuable is the understanding we get from this kind of experience. When you fight full contact, you discover that styles that look very different at first sight have a lot in common! Of course, you learn the weak points of your system also.

Q: Do you have a personal training program that you recommend to students?

A: Training programs change according to the person, but I do consider things like running, stretching, and weight training very important. They give you the basic foundation for kung-fu. I also believe in patience and endurance in kung-fu training, so I recommend doing horse stance training as long as possible. This can be done as a warm-up exercise. This will also discipline your mind to focus and concentrate as well as build the muscles in your legs for powerful stances.

Q: You said before that Chinese kung-fu tradition was passed down from father to son. What if a son wasn't interested?

A: That's sad, but then the father's kung-fu was lost. This is the main reason why a lot of kung-fu knowledge has been lost. All the secrecy around kung-fu caused a great loss of knowledge. That's why when I was challenged for teaching the art to Caucasians, I told those people that it was more important to preserve the art than to protect the traditions and lose the art. Teaching should both protect and preserve the old knowledge.

"All the secrecy around kung-fu caused a great loss of knowledge. That's why when I was challenged for teaching the art to Caucasians, I told those people that it was more important to preserve the art than to protect the traditions and lose the art."

Q: You have a new school in Los Angeles. What do you remember about your old kwoon?

A: There were a lot of good people there. It was a great group. They used to train real hard and their techniques were very good. I was very happy to pass my knowledge on because the students were at the school just for the training, and they truly appreciated everything I gave them.

Kung-Fu Masters

"Learning kung-fu forms is like having a dictionary. You can refer to it in order to find the answers, but you must work hard to achieve any results. You have to repeat the form thousands of times until they become second nature."

Q: Did anything change with you moving to China and then coming back to Los Angeles to open a new school?
A: No. The training is very similar. Of course, people's mind are different. They look at kung-fu in a different way.

Q: You also train students for full contact tournaments, right?
A: Yes, but kung-fu is much more than that. The idea is not to harm another, because the goal of kung-fu is self-protection. I like to say that when you're learning kung-fu, you're not only learning the fighting but the virtue as well. That virtue is to be humble because kung-fu is not meant to harm people but to help them.

Q: What are the strengths of your style?
A: The hung gar system is very demanding physically, and slowly works its way inward. The low stances are a trademark in the system so the student can be powerful on the ground. Power and speed in the arms are also important.

Q: How important are the *kuen* or forms?
A: Learning kung-fu forms is like having a dictionary. You can refer to it in order to find the answers, but you must work hard to achieve any results. You have to repeat the form thousands of times until they become second nature. Then a lot of hidden movements start to reveal themselves and give you new answers for different situations. This understanding comes only through hard training and practice. The most important forms in the hung gar system are *fook fu kuen, kung chi kuen, fook hok sup jin kuen*, and *tid sin kuen*, which is the most difficult set in the system and is designed

"When you learn kung-fu, you don't want to think and then react to an attack. The idea is to input the motions in your reflex system so your hands and feet will be automatically in the right place at the right time."

to improve the function of the internal organs. Of course, there are many other forms but these are very important.

Q: What do you mean by "second nature?"
A: When you learn kung-fu, you don't want to think and then react to an attack. That's too slow. It will be too late for you to defend. The idea is to input the motions in your reflex system so your hands and feet will be automatically in the right place at the right time. To be able to do this in combat you have to understand the very nature of fighting. Only then will this understanding become your strategy.

Q: What would be your last words to your students?
A: I would tell them to practice the basic things because they are the most important. Everything goes back to the basics. My goal is to help people and promote good will between martial artists all over the world.

Masters Techniques

From ready stance (1), a knife strike is delivered toward Sifu Buck Sam Kong's chest (2). Kong responds with a double claw (3-4), and then an elbow grab that pulls the attacker in (5-6). He finishes with a shoulder lock that forces his opponent down (7-8). Close-up (9).

From a ready stance (1-2), a bear hug attack from behind is thwarted when Sifu Buck Sam Kong steps out with his left foot and hits the groin of the aggressor (3-4). Kong follows with a back-fist to the face (5), a right elbow to the solar plexus (6-7), a claw-hand to the groin (8), and a same-hand uppercut to the chin (8).

Masters Techniques

From a ready stance (1), Sifu Buck Sam Kong is trapped in an attacker's headlock (2). Kong counters by stepping back with his right foot (3), grabbing his opponent's left leg (4) and breaking the hold by dropping the attacker over his knee. (5)

From a ready stance (1), an attacker delivers an overhead club strike to Sifu Buck Sam Kong (2). Kong sidesteps to the left and guides the hand to the outside (3). He then directs the weapon to the attacker's groin (4), and finishes with a right uppercut (5-6).

Brendan Lai

A Labor of Love

BRENDAN LAI BEGAN HIS KUNG-FU TRAINING IN HONG KONG AT AN EARLY AGE AND MODESTLY PLAYED DOWN HIS OWN MARTIAL ARTS ABILITIES. DURING THE LAST THREE DECADES, ON MANY OCCASIONS, HE SERVED AS THE HEAD JUDGE AT MAJOR KUNG-FU TOURNAMENTS AND HIS CREDIBILITY PLACED HIM IN DECISIVE POSITIONS IN SEVERAL KUNG-FU ORGANIZATIONS THAT RELIED ON HIS KNOWLEDGE FOR SUCCESS. HIS RECOGNITION IN THE CHINESE COMMUNITY WAS SUCH THAT MANY TOP KUNG-FU INSTRUCTORS OF DIFFERENT STYLES HAD INDIVIDUALLY APPROACHED HIM TO RECEIVE PERSONAL INSTRUCTION IN THE NORTHERN PRAYING MANTIS SYSTEM HE TAUGHT. IN SEARCH OF QUALITY, MASTER LAI ALWAYS LIMITED THE NUMBER OF STUDENTS IN HIS CLASSES. ALTHOUGH CONTRARY TO THE BASIC RULE OF COMMERCIALISM, THIS FUNDAMENTAL PRINCIPLE BROUGHT UP SOME EXCEPTIONAL STUDENTS THAT WILL EVENTUALLY BRING THE ART TO A HIGHER LEVEL. NOT WILLING TO COMPROMISE HIS MASTERS' TEACHINGS AND TRADITIONS, BRENDAN LAI SHARED EVERY DETAIL OF THE ART AS TAUGHT TO HIM WITHOUT RESERVATION. NOT ONLY WAS HE A TRUE GENTLEMAN AND A VERY CLASSY MAN, BUT A TRUE MASTER OF KUNG-FU AS WELL.

Q: How did you begin studying kung-fu?
A: When I was about 12 years old in Hong Kong, I had a schoolmate whose mother practiced a strange exercise she called tai chi. She was about to start teaching her son that form of exercise, and since I was his good friend she taught me too. I learned on and off for a year or two until my family moved to another part of the city and I had to stop learning from her. Though I didn't learn much, that short period made me a strong believer in the merit of such practice. I knew I wanted to continue to learn in whatever system I could find.

One day I chanced to pass a kung-fu studio in my neighborhood, and I noticed that a northern praying mantis kung-fu system by Master Wong Kwong Fung, president of the Northern Praying Mantis System Association, was taught there. I was a very young kid then and was too afraid to go in to ask for acceptance. So I went home and wrote a letter of inquiry and sent it to the master whose name appeared on the sign.

Kung-Fu Masters

"In order to learn the art well, we had to listen to everything our masters told us and accept it without question. In China this was very easy, because as children we were taught to have total respect for our elders. But in the Western world, the youth have the freedom to question everything and accept only those things they feel they are right for them."

I waited impatiently for a day or two—then to my greatest joy a letter was sent from the master, asking me to come for an interview. Not knowing what to do, I talked it over with my mother and she suggested that I take a box of noodles as a gift for the master when I went. It wasn't much of a gift, but that's all my family could afford at the time.

In order to learn the art well, we had to listen to everything our masters told us and accept it without question. In China this was very easy, because as children we were taught to have total respect for our elders. When our parents took us to our sifus, it was only natural that we were to obey their every word. But in the Western world, the youth have the freedom to question everything and accept only those things they feel they are right for them. There is nothing wrong with this, but you can't learn any kung-fu system as taught by the masters in this way—it is too hard. I'd rather teach a few well, than expose many to the art erroneously. If the art is lessened now, in a few more years it will no longer be an art. I'd rather run in red ink than spread the art too thin.

As a child I was exposed to a lot of martial arts. I saw a lot of people practicing these arts and I was very impressed with what they could do. I wanted to learn to do those things too. But most of all, I decided to take it because I was weakling, and people said kung-fu would help me gain strength. But no true disciple of kung-fu can hope to master the advanced disciplines of any system without accepting the traditional way. During my training days that discipline was stressed, and we had to obey every word of our masters without question.

Q: What happened at the interview?
A: I went to it as scheduled, feeling rather worried that I would be rejected. and was guided to the sitting room where Master Hon-Fan Wong was already waiting for me. I presented my box of noodles and said with my head down, "Master Wong, please accept this humble gift of mine as a gesture to wish you good health and happiness!" Master Wong replied, smiling "It is not necessary for you to bring me any gift, but since you have brought it, I am very pleased with it." Master then started asking me questions like how old I was, at which schools I was receiving my education, and so on. I answered each one carefully and politely. Then master Wong asked me why I wanted to study kung-fu. I answered that I was born weak during the war and that I was sick all the time. I told him that I wanted to learn kung-fu in order to strengthen my body so that I didn't have to be sick all the time. With a humble tone and head bowed, I asked, "Master, would you accept me as your student? Though I am not very bright, I will work hard to make up for it!" I will never forget that moment when master replied, smiling, "Yes, I will take you as my student!" I can't remember how many times I thanked my master, or what we talked of afterwards, but I can still remember that I went home with great joy. The excitement of knowing that I would become a praying mantis kung-fu practitioner was too much, and it kept me awake all that night. That is how I became involved with martial arts. From then on, I was a dedicated practitioner of the northern praying mantis kung-fu system.

Q: When you started teaching kung-fu, did you earn a living or was it a part-time activity?
A: Teaching kung-fu was not a way of supporting my family, so I took a job as a computer programmer. I worked with the same drive and dedication that characterized my involvement in the martial arts, but the environment was a far cry from what I expected. I wasn't satisfied with what I was doing. I worked like crazy and the other workers wondered why, since it was against common practice. I never liked that philosophy, I want to be valuable. My value, I feel, is to offer my knowledge to students who think highly of it. While I was still working at the computer firm, I maintained a small *kwoon* in a garage-like building; but when I quit for good I moved to a larger location to enable myself to teach the art to more people and bring in an income at the same time. My first few students remained with me, and together we rebuilt the new structure into a kwoon.

Kung-Fu Masters

Q: What is the history of the praying mantis system and its technical characteristics?
A: The beginning of the praying mantis style is in the Shaolin Temple in the northern Chinese province of Honan. Master Long accidentally found a little praying mantis fighting with a cicada, and from there developed the principle that goes along with the fighting of the praying mantis. This, however, wasn't sufficient because the footwork was missing, so he copied the footwork of the monkey's feet and the hands of the praying mantis. He combined 17 other arts and grouped them into the praying mantis and he had what was called the praying mantis section in the temple. This section was the most advanced category—so advanced that both the monks and the practitioners had to study the other sections first, step by step, until they were qualified to enter the mantis section. So you can see its position in the temple. The outsiders who later had a view of the system all agreed that it was fast, to the point, and very, very deadly.

From the technical point of view, our system uses a lot of claws, what we refer as a *dil*, which are like the claws of the praying mantis. We use the forearms likewise, imitating the forearms of the mantis, and we also use kicks. But the praying mantis is such that the movements are very speedy, yet very natural. It does not pretend to start with or attempt to gather up force, so that outwardly the opponent cannot see right away that the practitioner is about to start the offensive. You can call it very sneaky. We can look at you, and all of a sudden, we are behind you. There are no shoulder movements, and although the movements are very fast and jerky, they are naturally fluid.

We are called the "Seven-Star Praying Mantis" system. At one time, the first generation leader had three students. When the three students graduated, he wanted them to go out and catch a praying mantis and each identify his own system. My generation leader found a praying mantis with seven dots on its belly arranged like stars. Still the differences among the systems are very little. In all three, the force should come from the waist, up the back, and into the arms. It should not come from the muscle of the arms. This is a soft style because we don't use sheer force. The northern praying mantis requires strict coordination because the hands and feet all go out at the same time, thereby causing confusion in the opponent.

The system is known for its speed in both offense and defense, and is also most famous for its remarkably fast footwork. One of our requirements is to be able to reach our opponent first with either a punch, jab, or kick, even though our opponent might have already started the attack

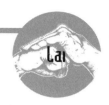

first. This requires extreme alertness and lightning speed. We learn how to intercept the opponent's actions. We are also known for our unique grabbing methods. This gives us the advantage of being able to trap and hold our opponents for our final deadly strike. It is unfair to try to make a comparison of the merits of one martial art to any other. After all, fighting is fighting, and any martial art that has remained popular through the years has proven itself a good fighting art.

Q: How has training in martial arts changed your life?
A: In all those years of training, I not only learned a physical skill that turned my weak body into a healthy one, but I also learned a gentle philosophy towards others. As I gained more and more self-defense knowledge which increased my confidence, I felt less and less the necessity to quarrel with anybody. In other words, I learned to co-exist with everybody and make friends despite the odds against me. This is how I benefited from kung-fu. During all my years of teaching kung-fu in the U.S., I tried to relay that philosophy to my students. I also tried to be an example of this by making friends with all types of martial artists. I was blessed with meeting some of the best in the country. A few years ago, I was asked to handle exhibitions for the kung-fu circle and as master of ceremonies. I also tried to convey the message of love, respect and honor to my audience.

Then in 1979, I was asked to handle an exhibition set up by Master Hak-Fu Chan, the famous white crane instructor from Hong Kong. In that exhibition, I had the honor to act as master of ceremonies for some of the best martial artists in the U.S. For that occasion, I designed an elaborate ceremony that was geared to show honor and dignity to those highly

"In all those years of training, I not only learned a physical skill that turned my weak body into a healthy one, but I also learned a gentle philosophy towards others. As I gained more and more self-defense knowledge which increased my confidence, I felt less and less the necessity to quarrel with anybody."

Kung-Fu Masters

"In kung-fu we use our bodies to engage in exercise to find out what we can do. The movements of the hands flow in accordance with the flow of the universe. But we are learning a deadly art."

respected performers. I don't have to elaborate on how satisfied the performers felt. They all became good friends of mine. In kung-fu we use our bodies to engage in exercise to find out what we can do. The movements of the hands flow in accordance with the flow of the universe. But we are learning a deadly art.

Q: What training program were you following then?
A: I used to train four hours a day and rarely missed a day's training. On the day I had to go to the studio, I would train two hours there and when I came back home, which was only about two blocks from the school, I put in two more hours training there. However, on the days that I didn't have classes at the studio, I would simply train a full four hours at home. That would be from 8 PM to 12 midnight.

One of the exercises I liked to do was around 11:30 PM. I would be sweating severely after hours of training and I needing a bath. Where I lived in Hong Kong, we didn't have much of a bathroom like what we have here in the United States. We simply bathed in the kitchen, which was roomy enough for us to pour water over our bodies. After the bath, I hung a towel on a rope across the kitchen, and started kicking at the towel. The idea was to kick so vigorously that one day I could send off all the water from my legs to the towel by a kick or two. Moreover, because of the strength of each kick, the towel would move back and fourth vigorously in correspondence with each kick—moving forward because of the wind sent off from the kick, and moving back towards me because of the suction created by the withdrawal of the leg. After practicing with the legs I would practice with my hands in a similar fashion.

Since I would be sweating again, I would have to take a second bath before leaving the kitchen for an hour or so of homework. It took me many years of practice before I reached the stage where I could send off almost all the water with a kick or two, and also cause the towel to fly back and forth. The praying mantis system requires extreme speed in both hands and feet. This is but one of the many methods to achieve speed, power, and accuracy.

Q: How did the art evolve in the United States?
A: When I landed in San Francisco in 1961, kung-fu was not yet a household word. Few Americans knew what it meant, and the majority thought it was some kind of edible Chinese dish! With the exception of few kung-fu studios located in the Chinatown areas of big cities like San Francisco, Los Angeles and New York, I doubt they could be found anywhere. As more immigrants arrived from Asia in the next few years, more studios were set up all over the country, adding force to the spread of kung-fu. After the first and second huge exhibitions in 1968 and 1969, both held in San Francisco, kung-fu officially went public. Those performances amazed the American audience, and for the first time demonstrated the benefits of kung-fu to the body and health. This further opened the door to probe the mysteries of its bottomless depth. With the birth of *Inside Kung-Fu* magazine in 1973, news of kung-fu activities was brought to every part of the country. Its reports on the various kung-fu systems and their teachers in the U.S., helped the masses gain a much better understanding of this Chinese martial art and thus greatly promoted kung-fu.

The early part of the '70s was a glorious time for kung-fu as Bruce Lee became an international superstar. His charismatic display of the speedy and powerful kung-fu actions on the screen fired-up the enthusiasm of the whole world. Thousands and thousands of students looked to enroll in whatever kung-fu studios they could find. In areas where no authentic kung-fu instructors could be found, the fly-by-nights took over, and many students with good potential never gained adequate knowledge in an art to which they were devoted. Therefore, although it was a time of great flourishing of the art, it is sad that kung-fu was unable to retain its usually high standard of quality. The untimely demise of Bruce Lee in 1973 shocked and saddened the martial arts circles, and started a gradual recession of the kung-fu economy. The dropout rate was severe in the next few years. However, those who continued to learn kung-fu proved to have sincere devotion to this art, and many of them have now become second-generation sifus.

Kung-Fu Masters

Then in 1974, we saw the new Chinese *wushu* introduced to the U.S. by the official wushu team of China. Their acrobatic forms captured the attention of many youngsters, and soon some were teaching after having studied it for only a short time. Many later found their way to China to have a more thorough study, and came back to help to spread the art. However, this half-breed of kung-fu, although rather beautiful to watch, was found to be lacking in martial arts content, and consequently did not threaten to replace kung-fu. Since 1975, I have been vigorously promoted huge-scale performances in which I have had the honor of presenting the true meaning of real kung-fu to audiences. Today, four decades after kung-fu's first public introduction in San Francisco, I am happy to say it has found acceptance in a society dominated by Western culture.

However, because the art was allowed to develop without the proper control, guidance, and education, certain unhealthy phenomena were fostered that clearly indicate a lack of understanding of the Chinese culture associated with kung-fu. I hope that our next generation learns not only a physical art, but also a philosophy that is very much a part of kung-fu. As far as memories and experiences go, I had many—but probably my greatest satisfaction came in 1980, when I was asked to design appropriate ceremonies for the 1980 Coliseum Martial Arts Expo held in Oakland, California. Because of the importance of this world-class event, I designed an "Eternal Flame" ceremony, for which 11 high-ranking martial artists were selected from different countries to participate. The ceremony was based on the theme of brotherhood and togetherness. Later, both participants and spectators agreed that the ceremonies brought home the message, and that they were deeply touched. I'm always looking for opportunities to expose the public to the good teaching of martial arts.

Q: Do you follow a particular diet?
A: I got used to eating everything. As a businessman, I have to host my clients regularly, and I don't have too much choice in selection. But in a nutshell, I don't eat fatty meats and favor eating vegetables instead.

Q: What is your philosophy of fighting?
A: When I was still learning in the studio I constantly sparred with my classmates. I felt it was necessary to spar in order to understand the usefulness of what I learned. No matter how heatedly we fought in the studio, we never ended in bad terms after the match. Instead, we learned to respect each other. However, once out of the studio, we never tried to fight with anybody. I don't mean that one should never use what one knows, but

when one does it better be the last resort—like facing someone who means harm you. Fighting which arises from disagreement, quarrels, or situations where one wants to prove fighting superiority are unnecessary and incorrect. When one is confident enough, one does not have to prove anything by injuring others. Empty bottles make the most noise. A lot of instructors argue that if you come in to learn, you want to learn to fight. This is appealing to the newcomer. You've got to make sure that you give the impression that your studio can really produce students who are capable of fighting, otherwise you won't be able to attract students. Then if the student gets the idea that even the instructor condones it, he will go out and look for trouble to prove how great his system is. This is against the kung-fu philosophy, and against general martial arts philosophy. In kung-fu and all martial arts we want to learn to be peaceful.

"I have yet to find one who is a non-traditionalist. Every bit of knowledge we have has a source in the past. The world of today is a beneficiary of all the knowledge of the world of yesterday. We are all traditionalists to a certain extent, even though we might be making continuous improvements; but these are still based on the knowledge of the past."

Q: Do you consider yourself a traditionalist?
A: I don't know what "traditionalist" means! If it means one who practices something that had always been practiced in the past, then yes, I am a traditionalist. I have yet to find one who is a non-traditionalist. Every bit of knowledge we have has a source in the past. The world of today is a beneficiary of all the knowledge of the world of yesterday. Likewise, my knowledge of the praying mantis system was given to me by my late master, who got his from his late master, and so on and so forth. Without all these ancestors, there would be no "me" with this knowledge, and without all those who have passed away from this world there wouldn't be the civilization we have today. We are all traditionalists to a certain extent, even though we might be making continuous improvements; but these are still based on the knowledge of the past. So when I hear some martial artists claim they are non-traditionalists, or "non-classical," I just wonder where their knowledge came from. Certainly, it didn't come to them from dreams! To claim one's knowledge did not come from the past is to disrespect one's predeces-

Kung-fu Masters

"Kung-fu is supposed to teach humility, for its bottomless depth makes us wonder how much we actually know. Those who are deep into its study no doubt feel how little they have learned. It is from this awareness that we develop a keen interest in the pursuit of knowledge and a humble attitude about ourselves."

sors, whether they are still living or not. One virtue we should learn from the martial arts is respect, especially to those who hand down the knowledge. Whoever is displaying that kind of attitude is a very disrespectful individual. Kung-fu is supposed to teach humility, for its bottomless depth makes us wonder how much we actually know. Those who are deep into its study no doubt feel how little they have learned. It is from this awareness that we develop a keen interest in the pursuit of knowledge and a humble attitude about ourselves. Yet there are some people out there who display a character of superiority, even to the extent of declaring it in magazines articles they write. They may be good fighers, but they are definitely bad martial artists.

Q: How are traditional values instilled into students?
A: It involves many different aspects and not only affects the students. When the first Chinese instructors came here they began teaching traditionalism. The new generation of instructors do not try to instill these values like the old teachers did. Some instructors will teach you whatever you want. If the instructor teaches in a traditional way and the student lis-

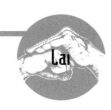

tens and practices as the teacher shows, then there is a better chance that the student will pass on the art as the instructor has taught him. The sifu must be an example to the student. If the sifu is respectful to others, then the student will be respectful to you. You cannot compromise this. You must be traditional so the student will be traditional. They will see you doing a movement and they will copy it—so you, as the instructor, must do it correctly. On the other hand, the student has to know how to address the instructor properly. The student is obligated to call his instructor "sifu." It is an insult to the instructor if the student does not address the teacher in this fashion. The student should always do everything with his best effort. That's part of a respectful attitude to his teacher. And this is the most important traditional value—respect.

Q: Do you think altering the traditional forms is wrong?
A: There is always a little modification, but the traditional forms supply everything the students need. To me, traditionalism is the forms and techniques with internal breathing and pure breathing. Each movement must always be done with full force and deep focus. But to most people, traditionalism is something that was taught 500 years ago by the founder. Don't get me wrong, I feel that's also correct. But if there is a move in a form that has no meaning or is not effective then I feel it should be modified to be effective. Does this mean the form is not longer traditional when a movement is changed? No, it still remains a traditional form. To me, if a person does a movement without purpose, that is non-traditional. But if that person makes that punch or technique effective and with purpose, then that is maintaining traditionalism. A person shouldn't think they must do the move exactly like it was done four centuries ago and pass it on from generation to generation to maintain traditionalism. Traditional forms will never go away or be replaced by modernization. To be traditional, you must be effective. That is why people in China are going back from wushu to traditional kung-fu. The concept of traditionalism is having effective punches and kicks, not simply acrobatics. In traditional kung-fu we place the majority of the emphasis on perfecting the forms and sets. This is what kung-fu is all about. When we teach, we teach to preserve tradition and to try to do better all the time. Kung-fu instills a way of life in a student. Authentic kung-fu focuses on truly learning the forms. Modern arts created by so called freestyle martial artists do not.

Kung-Fu Masters

Q: Are you against adding fancy movements to the forms?
A: The traditional kung-fu forms do not have any fancy movements. They were designed to fight and any fancy movement could be fatal. But now we train for other reasons than simply fighting. If you are doing a form and you spice a certain movement without losing the meaning of it, then that's alright. But if you do something without a purpose, just to make it appear fancy, that is not martial arts. If its effective, than its alright. If it has no purpose, than it's more like wushu. It must be useful, regardless of what it looks like. If the practitioner makes an aerial move just for show, and it is not effective, than that is pointless. If you do the form with purpose, then it's good.

Q: What is your opinion on modern combat sports like kickboxing?
A: I favor full-contact fighting or kickboxing because it offers an environment in which both fighters can fight to the fullest extent with all the techniques they know. In my opinion, although martial arts can be altered to become a sport in which two competitors engage in contact competition, it should never leave its role as an effective fighting art. In an actual fighting situation, he who knocks out his opponent comes out the winner. However, if his attack is just a little short or too slow, then his opponent will have just a split second to counterattack and knock the attacker out of action and become the winner. A split second can decide who the winner is. In order to gain this split-second control, one has to fight as realistically as possible. This realistic fighting situation can only be offered in this type of match.

In old China, every match was a life-and-death match. There was only one way to decide who the winner was—to have one competitor knocked to the floor without any ability to stand up again, whether he was still living or dead. Martial artists in old China therefore had to train extremely hard, because they knew they could not depend on lucky punches to win a match. They also knew the consequences of being a split second too slow. They couldn't afford that mistake.

That's not to say that I favor excessive violence on the stage—I don't. Instead, I favor fighting bouts that have control and purpose to demonstrate technique. I especially like Thai boxing matches, in which competitors are free to use all the techniques that are within the limits of the rules. These competitions should definitely be encouraged for those who favor them. They also have certain value as a spectator sport and I do not object to their existence at all.

Q: Have you made any innovations in your style?
A: As martial artists, we always strive to perfect our techniques, and therefore it is important to make improvements. I am no exception to this rule. Based on the knowledge that was passed down to me by my master, I've made many innovations which work for me and the times I am living in. In kung-fu training, we are learning what the body can do. Coordination of the body has a lot to do with the state of mind. If a person's mind is not functioning, he cannot have coordination. In our system, coordination connects to the head. Because we have many small movements in the system, the student has to think to understand why the small movements work as they do. If he doesn't, his hands won't move according to the person who he trained. If a student thinks, he will find that sooner or later his mind and head will be sharper.

Q: How would you sum up your overall philosophy as a teacher?
A: That is a very difficult question to answer. A true kung-fu practitioner prefers harmony over conflict but definitely needs to know when to take action. It is not so much the losing of face, as the saving of humanity and the showing of respect and kindness. When you are attacked and are forced to defend yourself or others, then you have to exercise technique to a point and we not hesitate. You owe yourself your life. There will be one strike and somebody will be down—either you or him. But this is used only to be used as a last resort.

Kung-fu is called the "unseen weapon." We, as instructors, give this weapon to the students. If the instructors say "go out and kill," the student will feel it's OK to hurt people whenever he can. Being instructors, we cannot let this happen. Kung-fu techniques and the kung-fu ethic

"Based on the knowledge that was passed down to me by my master, I've made many innovations which work for me and the times I am living in. In kung-fu training, we are learning what the body can do. Coordination of the body has a lot to do with the state of mind. If a person's mind is not functioning, he cannot have coordination."

Kung-Fu Masters

"In my studio I try to teach my students to tolerate and respect without yelling or fighting. Only under just conditions, to rescue their own life or the lives of others, should they use their techniques."

must go side-by-side. The students must understand this ethic before they get the technique. That's why in the past, the masters were so careful in screening their students. The students had to go through many humiliation test before they were accepted by the masters. And even after that, they were constantly played down to the point where they showed true humility towards others.

In my studio I try to teach my students to tolerate and respect without yelling or fighting. Only under just conditions, to rescue their own life or the lives of others, should they use their techniques. The student has to come in and I have to talk to him. He has to come in and observe a few classes to make sure this is how he feels. I'll explain the good points of what he will see, and then let him decide. If, in his conversation, I detect that he is on the aggressive side, someone who want to learn in order to beat people up, I tell him politely that there are other studios more suitable to his desires.

Q: What is your opinion about the ranking system in the West?
A: That's a very difficult and touchy question to answer because there are different answers. I have seen people promote themselves to an exceptionally high rank, and I must say that is very harmful for the art. I have never seen as many "masters" in the Orient as there are in the West. I grew up in a society where the title "sifu" had to be earned, and the title "grandmaster" was even more difficult to earn. It had to be awarded by those in the kung-fu circle and also recognized by the public. Usually they need to fulfill these requirements: he must be the head of his system; he must be of senior age; he must be exceptional in his kung-fu abilities as recognized by those in the circle; he must have contributed a great deal to the promotion of the art; and above everything else he must be recognized as one who achieved high standard in moral character, thereby having great influence

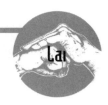

on the next generation by his good behavior. By the code of humbleness, those whose sifus are still living can never be addressed as "masters," and those who themselves are addressed as "masters" by others will never introduce themselves as such in speech or in writing. But in the Western world, unfortunately, things are different. As if the title of "sifu" is too low a rank, many simply promote themselves to "masters." When there are too many masters, which cheapened the title, many advanced themselves to "grandmasters," and then to "great grandmasters," and "super grandmasters." This stupid competition for a better titles goes on and on and sometimes I wonder where this spiral will end. This behavior is certainly damaging to the image of kung-fu around the world. Students are striving for vanity instead of pursuing the essence of the art. This attitude not only shows a lack of humbleness, but also shows a lack of understanding of the Chinese terms and Chinese culture. As I look back to all these years in which the popularity of kung-fu rose and fell in cycles, I can't help but ask whether we who brought the art into the Western world have done a good job in promoting it. The answer is an apparent "no," for if we did, the above title inflation could not have existed.

Q: What is the number of training years needed to reach instructor level under you?
A: There is no definite time in my system when a student can become an instructor. Customarily, it falls into the master's hands to decide if the student is eligible or not. Usually, it takes place after eight years of constant practice. In some cases, it might even be earlier. A lot depends on the student's ability, how hard he practiced, and most importantly, whether he has a good character so that his students can benefit from him. That's the real test. In the past I have dismissed a few students who did not learn how to be grateful. In the front they would say "yes," and in the back they would something contrary to what I taught them. With the students who possess the right attitude I have to be tough—because someday, kids like these will be teaching others. If I allow them to be imperfect and don't impress on them how important it is to get the movements exactly right, in a few generations the art will be destroyed. I cannot see how an instructor will pat one of his students on the back and say "good job" and then have to turn around and throw up because the movements are so bad. I just can't do that. I will not degrade my art, and I don't want my students to either.

Masters Techniques

Master Lai faces his opponent (1). As the aggressor attacks (2), Lai covers the angle, deflects the punch, and counters with a back-fist to the head (2). When the strike is blocked by his opponent (4), Lai sees an open line, directs a finishing low kick to the groin (5), and assumes an on-guard position (6).

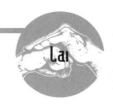

From a ready stance (1), an attacker delivers a punch to the midsection of Master Lai (2). Lai counters by blocking and punching to the face simultaneously (3). When Lai's punch is blocked by his opponent's left hand (4), Lai traps the hand, pulls it down in a crossed angle (5), unbalances the attacker, and delivers a finishing sweep (6).

Jim Lau

The Intelligence of Wing Chun

JIM LAU'S OPINIONS ARE SUPPORTED BY LONG YEARS OF EXPERIENCE AND BY CONSIDERABLE THOUGHT. A FORMER COLUMNIST ON THE ART OF WING CHUN FOR *INSIDE KUNG-FU*, THE WORLD'S LEADING KUNG-FU MAGAZINE, LAU'S WRITINGS WERE CONSIDERED TO BE AMONG THE MOST THOROUGH TO EVER APPEAR IN A MARTIAL ARTS PERIODICAL. HE HAS APPEARED ON THE COVER OF SEVERAL MAGAZINES, AND HIS TEACHING METHODS HAVE BEEN THE SUBJECT OF ARTICLES FOR MORE THAN THREE DECADES. HE BEGAN HIS STUDY IN HONG KONG, WHERE HE WAS BORN AND RAISED, AND HE HAS BEEN LIVING AND TEACHING IN THE UNITED STATES FOR MORE THAN 30 YEARS. JIM LAU IS AN APPEALING COMBINATION OF CALM EASTERN PHILOSOPHY AND EFFICIENT WESTERN PRAGMATISM, EXEMPLIFYING THE LOGIC AND PHILOSOPHY OF THE ART THAT, AS A CHILD, HE CHOSE TO PRACTICE IN HONG KONG. "THAT CITY IS AN VERY SPECIAL PLACE TO GROW UP," LAU RECALLS. "LEARNING MARTIAL ARTS IN HONG KONG IS LIKE LEARNING BASEBALL IN THE UNITED STATES—EVERYBODY PICKS UP SOMETHING, SO IT IS NO BIG DEAL. THE PEOPLE THERE CAN BE A VERY TRICKY AND YOU DEFINITELY NEED TO KNOW YOUR WAY AROUND TO SURVIVE!" SIFU LAU IS ONE OF THOSE RARE AND TALENTED PEOPLE WHO FOUND THEIR WAY IN THE "TRICKY" STREETS OF HONG KONG, AND WHO HAS NOW BECOME ONE OF THE MOST SOUGHT-AFTER WING CHUN EXPERTS IN THE WORLD.

Q: How did you get involved in wing chun?
A: I began when I was 11 years old with the study of various styles of kung-fu. At 14, I started my study of the wing chun system. Like most other boys of that age, I did not understand the significance of such an experience. The seeds of my appreciation for wing chun as an intelligent and practical art were, however, planted. During this period I also made what eventually turned into a close friendship, as well as an ongoing learning relationship, with one of Master Yip Man's first and most capable students, Sifu Wong Shun Leung.

At the age of 20 I immigrated to the U.S. to join my family. Settling in Los Angeles, I attended Pasadena City College where I began teaching wing chun as a means of arousing local interest and perfecting my own talents. It was after I moved to America that I began to feel the true strength and

Kung-Fu Masters

"I believe that only through teaching can one practice and reach the highest goals of martial arts understanding. Today, I still live by the ancient Chinese proverb that says, 'The person who teaches will learn himself, and the person who learns will always be the teacher of himself.'"

intensity of my desire to explore the potential of the art, and I studied and practiced over the ensuing years with uninterrupted intensity. The value placed on directness and efficiency in America provided me with an unusual appreciation for those characteristics as exemplified in the wing chun system of kung-fu. The physical separation from my homeland left a void which developed into an insatiable appetite for Chinese literature. Those factors have provided me with the basis for a unique, personal method of analysis which utilizes the simple, economical, direct, and complete characteristics of the wing chun system, complemented by numerous organizational concepts found in Chinese literature.

After my graduation from college, I devoted a lot of my time and effort into professional teaching, training, researching, and promoting the true value of this ancient art. I believe that only through teaching can one practice and reach the highest goals of martial arts understanding. Today, I still live by the ancient Chinese proverb that says, "The person who teaches will learn himself, and the person who learns will always be the teacher of himself."

I am also the owner and chief instructor of the Jim Lau Wing Chun Academy which was founded in 1975. After all these years, I don't like to speak of any achievements other than those which are more personal in nature. Certainly, the friendships I have made along the way are the most important to me. My travels and years of study and teaching have led to a number of close friendships which are particularly special.

Another personally satisfying achievement has been the growth of my abilities to communicate verbally, and in written form, both in Chinese and English. As my desire to progress in wing chun grew, my need to develop precision in both forms of communication had to be expanded. Communication is a form of influence, and the ability to properly influence someone without having to use physical capabilities is an art within

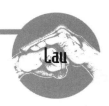

martial arts. I also have grown to know myself more intimately than I would have thought possible. In order to really study kung-fu, you must study what it means to be a human being. This entails a great deal of personal introspection and it is certainly not a simple or painless process, but for me, it has been a major personal achievement up to this point in my life.

Q: What are the main principles of the art?
A: Wing chun is essentially an art of maneuvers, specifically those designed to deal with practical fighting situations. Hence, formal bowing, artistic forms of dancing, symbolic imitations of animals and showy movements of any kind are not a part of this art. In theory, wing chun stresses simplicity, directness, economy and completeness. These terms are almost self-explanatory. Simplicity means that movements and techniques should be clean and uncomplicated. Directness implies immediate effectiveness. Economy is the conservation of energy and effort. And completeness signifies the use of all possible body tools like hands, arms, feet, legs, body, et cetera.

"Wing chun is essentially an art of maneuvers, specifically those designed to deal with practical fighting situations. Hence, formal bowing, artistic forms of dancing, symbolic imitations of animals and showy movements of any kind are not a part of this art."

At the core of wing chun maneuvers is the concept of the centerline, the imaginary vertical line running down the center of the body—in front and back. A wing chun practitioner must preserve and protect his own centerline while, at the same time, breaking and invading the opponent's centerline. This maxim of combat is accomplished by constantly pushing forward, controlling the opponent's arms, and narrowing the distance between you and him.

Once contact is made with the opponent's arms, he can be effectively maneuvered by adhering to the wing chun motto: "When hands approach, withhold. When hands withdraw, follow. And when hands slip from control, strike." With this motto in mind, the wing chun practitioner must put his whole body to work, systematically executing maneuvers and attacks. The techniques for maneuver and attack fall into four categories: strikes, kicks, throws and holds.

Kung-Fu Masters

"Theoretically, wing chun forms serve as a reference guide which articulates all the basic movements and fighting techniques within the context of the centerline. Learning the forms properly, practicing them diligently, and understanding them thoroughly are the three essential steps towards a successful wing chun experience."

The wing chun system has a very precise method for preparing a student for combat. This training method includes three empty-hand forms, a set of 108 wooden dummy techniques, *Muk Yan Jong*, a long pole form, *Luk Dim Bun Gwun*, and a short knives form, *Bot Jeom Do*. But the real trademark and focus of wing chun training centers on sticking-hands practice, *Chi Sao*, which is exclusive to this art.

Q: Are the wing chun forms flashy?
A: In contrast to other styles of kung-fu, wing chun forms are not always graceful or entertaining. The reason is that wing chun forms are designed to practice maneuvers. The three empty-hand forms of wing chun are *Sil Lum Tao*, "The Little Idea," *Chum Kil*, "Searching for the Bridge," and *Bil Jee*, "Thrusting Fingers." These three maneuver forms are relatively simple and short, yet refined and sufficient. Each form has its own specific purpose, theory, and techniques. At the same time, each one represents a specific level of learning. In order to learn the forms efficiently, practitioners are advised to master each one individually, in the proper sequence of sophistication. Theoretically, wing chun forms serve as a reference guide which articulates all the basic movements and fighting techniques within the context of the centerline. Learning the forms properly, practicing them diligently, and understanding them thoroughly are the three essential steps towards a successful wing chun experience.

Q: Do you have a personal training program?
A: I do not subscribe to the theory that each individual quantity of labor or effort produces a directly proportional quality of result. For maximum result one must put forth maximum quality of effort. Quality cannot be

measured in raw terms such as the number of hours in which routine physical labor is performed.

The art of wing chun, particularly through its three empty-hand and, one wooden dummy, and two weapons forms can represent an essentially complete overview of human kinesiology. Regardless of the style, individual practice should be based upon personal motivation, desired result and precise physical and mental work to achieve that result. Because of this, I do not follow a personal training regimen which prescribes specific physical exercises to be completed over a determined length of time each day. Such training would produce mental and therefore, physical rigidity. And this is not what I am looking for. I vary my training to fit my own desired results. Regardless of the type of exercise, I always have a precise concept of the desired result when I train. This is not to say that some individuals do not need the type of discipline found in a more materialistic kind of training structure particularly in the early stages. Such training throughout one's lifetime, however, produces a rather static and labor-oriented individual in my opinion.

"Regardless of the type of exercise, I always have a precise concept of the desired result when I train. This is not to say that some individuals do not need the type of discipline found in a more materialistic kind of training structure particularly in the early stages."

Q: Do you follow a particular diet?
A: One of the elements of wing chun centerline theory is moderation. Much like one uses a compass to check his direction, if one knows moderation it is safer to deviate and still find your way back. I do not consider my normal diet to be special. I eat food just like most people, hopefully of reasonably good quality. When I find my diet beginning to vary towards an extreme, for instance junk food, I am simply aware that this represents a deviation that may not produce satisfactory results if continued in excess over long periods of time.

Kung-Fu Masters

"The more educated and pragmatic students of today care only very briefly about the names of one's instructors, conflicting claims concerning who is a master or successor of a style, or other such irrelevancies. A teacher can only guide you. He cannot work or think for you."

Q: Do you consider yourself a traditionalist or a modernist in your expression of the art?
A: I believe that the type of thinking which allows for either/or answers truly limits our ability to progress. The more educated and pragmatic students of today care only very briefly about the names of one's instructors, conflicting claims concerning who is a master or successor of a style, or other such irrelevancies. They generally seek instruction from those with obvious personal ability who can communicate as well as actualize that ability. This modern attitude can be productive for the student if properly channeled.

The current non-traditionalist trend was actually fostered by the rigidity of some of the so-called traditionalists. In fact, everyone follows an established tradition. In spite of learning from the same teacher, practitioners of many different traditional martial arts disagree about what is authentic. Such insistence often leads to retrogression and failure to explore the potential of the art's original concepts. What turns out to be practiced and preserved is merely their interpretation of their teacher's interpretation of the art— an honorable achievement but certainly not a guarantee of authenticity or a benefit to the art. In their attempt to escape the obvious limitations of such a myopic perspective on a truly dynamic human condition, many people simply end-up confused. Certainly a number of kung-fu styles offer the basic framework by which one may achieve far greater understanding of these dynamics. This requires one to pursue his study far beyond the simple repetition of the physical mechanics in fond hope of some mysterious personal transformation. A teacher can only guide you. He cannot work or think for you. Guidance, however, should not be underestimated. Without truly comprehensive study, which entails far more than casual study of a multitude of styles over a period of years, the non-

traditionalist goal of attaining sophisticated analytical abilities is simply a myth.

Q: What is your attitude towards full-contact karate and the UFC?
A: Although it is referred to as "full-contact," in a true sense it is certainly not. It is actually a protective, though admittedly rough, contact sport which permits one to employ only a limited number of specialized fighting methods in a controlled environment. Because it allows for the general safety of the participants I believe it has a legitimate place in our modern society much like boxing, football or other contact sports.

Q: Have you made any innovations in your style?
A: Innovation implies "new"—and if one seriously studies the past he will find that we are generally rediscovering our potential. Realization and understanding of our commonality rather than searching for the unusual provides the greatest insight. Did I answer you question?

"I prefer not to make comparisons between styles. Each individual merely expresses to the best of their ability their own understanding of a style. It is somehow inappropriate to make public comparisons since they are of such a purely personal nature."

Q: I'm not sure. What are the special strengths of the wing chun system?
A: I prefer not to make comparisons between styles. Each individual merely expresses to the best of their ability their own understanding of a style. It is somehow inappropriate to make public comparisons since they are of such a purely personal nature. I believe it is sufficient to say that my style is wing chun and I enjoy practicing it.

Q: How many years of training are necessary to reach instructor level?
A: There is no formal ranking in wing chun kung-fu. Teaching is part of any complete learning process and as a result a few of my more advanced students assist with instruction. As I mentioned earlier, given quantities of individual time and labor don't automatically produce proper results. I

Kung-Fu Masters

"Chi sao, or sticking hands practice, is the final wing chun training method. This drill is used to sharpen and condition one's instinctive fighting responses. If the forms are the textbooks of wing chun, then chi sao is probably best described as a 'living laboratory.'"

assess students by the quality of their output not the quantity of their inputs. My students are taught to assess their own abilities in the same manner.

Q: Chi sao is considered the key factor in the art of wing chun; how do you describe this aspect of training and how important is it to the overall structure of the style?

A: *Chi sao*, or sticking hands practice, is the final wing chun training method. This drill is used to sharpen and condition one's instinctive fighting responses. There are two forms of chi sao practice. Single chi sao, in which one sticks to only one hand at a time, prepares the novice for double chi sao. And double chi sao, where one sticks to both hands simultaneously, is the preliminary to actual combat.

If the forms are the textbooks of wing chun, then chi sao is probably best described as a "living laboratory." Within the laboratory, practitioners of this style of kung-fu may experiment and analyze all the technical movements previously learned in the empty-hand or the wooden dummy forms. Because chi sao is practiced at close range, practitioners gradually build confidence and fearlessness in confronting an attack. They also become acquainted with combat situations, and develop a calm presence of mind and relaxation of body under stressful situations.

During chi sao practice, the three pivotal hand techniques of wing chun are ingeniously interlinked through the theory of the yin and the yang. Since the hand techniques of *bong say* and *tan sao* produce one another, through a twist of the arm, they represent the yin principle. But *fook sao*, which opposes them, represents the yang principle. From this peculiar relationship which exists between these techniques during chi sao, hundreds of other patterns, positions, and mutations of hand techniques are generated. Through the *lin sil die dar* principle, simultaneous attack and

defense, a punch or finger jab could be used for blocking and neutralizing. The latter principle is best expressed by the motto: "A striking hand is a neutralizing hand, and a neutralizing hand is a striking hand."

Once chi sao is mastered, all that remains to prepare a student for combat is an adjustment in the basic stance. In wing chun, there is a technical distinction between the fighting stance and the training stance. The training stance is governed by learning demands, and tends to be more open to the opponent. However, both the training stance and the fighting stance are designed to enhance the qualities of stability and mobility.

Actually, chi sao serves many purposes. During the initial training period, chi sao provides a lot of different benefits. It develops a certain sensitivity and a certain kind of muscle tone. Before most people train, their arms are not flexible—and so through chi sao they develop flexibility. So those are some of the basic training functions of chi sao, but of course there are many more. During the practice of chi sao a person is gradually getting used to the feel of the range. When you fight you have to get in close—if you can't touch, you can't hit. And if you can't hit, you can't finish. The overall idea is just really getting used to something. Like

"The muk yan jong is made from a tree trunk and has two wooden arms and a wooden leg, attached to resemble a man. This "hypothetical opponent" is probably the most advanced apparatus in existence for kung-fu training."

trained race car drivers—they have no fear. They see a curve and they turn; they see a slope and they go up. A normal person cannot achieve that simply because they are not trained. There's no secret or magic to it. If you train your hands, you know they can do something for you, and you are confident enough to relax. You see that street-fighters are always very calm and relaxed. That is because they've fought many times and been in a lot of situations like that. In wing chun, the training is also that way—you practice getting used to confrontation so you no longer have fear.

We have another term for free sparring—we call it *lut sao*. This is a situation where there will be a defender and an attacker, and the attacker

Kung-Fu Masters

"I think some people get confused nowadays; they cannot differentiate what is for training and what is for actual application. This is something that a lot of people don't understand about wing chun."

will attempt to keep the defender near his range, while the defender will make every attempt to keep him away. In other words, one will practice how to get away, and the other will practice learning how to pursue their prey.

Q: How does it apply to real fighting?
A: When you talk about fighting, your eyes, your ears, your nose are not as important as your sense of touch. You could say that chi sao is a very limited kind of sparring, as opposed to free sparring, which would be unlimited. But the difference is that in an unlimited situation, you cannot go back to pick up what you did wrong. With chi sao, it's more productive in a sense. You get hit if you don't do it right, and right away you know if your elbow is off center. Wing chun is constantly hitting, and where there is an empty gap, you hit. The saying in wing chun that, "when the hand slips off, straight lunge." Chi sao helps you build hand sensitivity—and that's basically the idea, to develop that instantaneous reflex to reach without thinking, because when you talk about movement, your eyes cannot be as fast as your mind. So you have to be able to let things happen by themselves. I think some people get confused nowadays; they cannot differentiate what is for training and what is for actual application. This is something that a lot of people don't understand about wing chun. A lot of wing chun students think that to develop the chi sao ability is the highest expression of combat. They think that if you can do chi sao, you can fight. This is not true. The competence at self-defense is only partly a product of chi sao practice. Also necessary for development of real fighting ability is training in footwork, free sparring, and in strategy or tactics. The time spent practicing on the wooden wing chun dummy is very much related to development of self-defense ability.

Q: Is it correct to say that chi sao is the common thread for all wing chun techniques?
A: To a certain extent. The practice of chi sao remains one of wing chun's trademark training methods. And like I said before, there are enough variations on the exercise to make it appropriate for both beginners and advanced students. Other variations include *pak sao*, "slapping hand," and *lop sao*, grabbing hand. In these versions of the exercise, the students learn open-hand and grabbing techniques. Proper chi sao, the two-handed pushing exercise, is usually the final step before a student spars live. Chi sao is like learning a song. You learn the notes and lyrics, and then you put the song together. Also, when you practice in a school, there are always people of different sizes and different characters, and you get to practice with each one. Some are artistic, some are chicken, and you get used to the feel of each one. So after a while, chi sao becomes a way to study characters.

Q: Some people are trying to create a formal chi sao competition. Do you agree with this?
A: I honestly don't believe in chi sao competition, because I think the martial arts should be something more than that. There are good things, of course, in the sticking hands, but the sad fact is that some people have the tendency to think that they have reached the highest goal when they win a sportive championship of some kind. There is more to the art than just chi sao.

Q: How is a typical wing chun class structured?
A: It depends of the instructor but typically my students spend an equal amount of time on the dummy and at chi sao. If they practice chi sao for 15 minutes, then they work on the dummy for another 15 minutes to get balance. The dummy has special qualities—consistent drilling in the dummy allows a practitioner to correct the alignment of his hand positions and to go full blast with the hand and foot techniques. Human part-

"Chi sao is like learning a song. You learn the notes and lyrics, and then you put the song together. Also, when you practice in a school, there are always people of different sizes and different characters, and you get to practice with each one. So after a while, chi sao becomes a way to study characters."

Kung-Fu Masters

"I think some people get confused nowadays; they cannot differentiate what is for training and what is for actual application. They think that if you can do chi sao, you can fight. This is not true."

ners sometimes get hurt, or tired, or overcompensate for their sparring partner. But the dummy never changes, can't be hurt and never tires. Practice of the 108 movements on the dummy is a good workout and develops a certain amount of toughness as well.

Q: Speaking of the *muk yan jong*, what can you tell us about training with this piece of equipment?
A: The muk yan jong is a training device. Translated literally, muk yan jong means "wooden man pile," but is better known in English as the wooden dummy. The muk yan jong is made from a tree trunk and has two wooden arms and a wooden leg, attached to resemble a man. This "hypothetical opponent" is probably the most advanced apparatus in existence for kung-fu training.

Since the wooden dummy cannot be physically injured, one may actually practice techniques with full strength, and thus feel the power of one's internal energy. At the same time, the wooden dummy allows one to practice striking and kicking techniques individually, or simultaneously, in a manner which builds power. There are a total of 108 movements in the wing chun wooden dummy form. These movements are considered to be techniques of the higher levels of learning. This ingenious device also comes in handy whenever a real sparring partner is absent.

Q: What is the importance of footwork in the wing chun system?
A: It's a very important part of the whole package. The role of footwork in wing chun is the reason why there are few, if any, blocks in the system. The footwork is our way of blocking. Blocks are unnecessary when your opponent can't touch you.

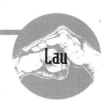

Q: So do you think that realistic self-defense depends upon awareness of a given situation?
A: You have to have sensitivity—when you know what your attacker wants, then you can decide what to feed him. For example, a person who is only trying to steal your wallet would be treated differently from a person who has decided to beat you up because he doesn't like you. Different kinds of motivations require different responses. Drunks are usually just evaded. Muggers, bullies, or persons who are just in a bad mood are other types of attackers who would require different responses. The one general rule is to stay calm and be reasonable. Always try to reason with your aggressor, even though you may be dealing with someone who is not quite rational. I think the most important thing is studying the motivation of the aggressor, to find out why he's doing what he is doing. If you can focus on that, then your response will come naturally, and you can choose the right tool for the job."

"In wing chun, there is a technical distinction between the fighting stance and the training stance. The training stance is governed by learning demands, and tends to be more open to the opponent. However, both the training stance and the fighting stance are designed to enhance the qualities of stability and mobility."

Q: What is the essence of wing chun training?
A: Although wing chun emphasizes individuality as the ultimate ideal, it is impossible to learn the art by oneself, or through a book. Just as a child needs guidance in learning to walk, so too does the novice need instruction in learning to fight. Only after years of practice can one comprehend the theories and practice of wing chun. And only with a proper foundation can one venture out on their own to discover new dimensions in the art by themselves.

Q: What is your opinion on the growing number of unqualified wing chun instructors?
A: It's funny, but is seems that as soon as anything becomes popular it becomes corrupted. Too many people want to be the chief and nobody wants to be an Indian. I'm still an Indian.

Masters Techniques

From a ready stance (1), an attacker moves in to take down Sifu Lau (2). Lau lowers his center of gravity (3), and redirects the force. As the opponent starts to grab his knees (4), Lau pivots to the left and grabs his hair (5), pulls up (6), and finishes with a palm strike to the chin (7).

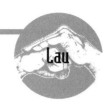

*From an on-guard stance (1), an attacker closes the gap and grabs the wrist of Sifu Lau (2-3). Lau flows from a **tan sao** (palm-up hand) to a straight arm-lock (4), to a back hook on the opponent's left leg (5-6), and takes him to the ground (7).*

145

Masters Techniques

From an on-guard stance (1), an attacker throws a right cross at Sifu Lau. Lau counters by sidestepping to the right with a **tan sao**, and delivers a straight punch to the opponent's face (2). He follows with a side kick (3), then finishes with an arm-twist takedown (4, 5, 6).

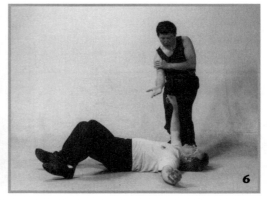

From an on-guard stance (1), Sifu Lau is attacked with an overhead club strike (2). Lau meets the attack with a **bil** sao (darting hand), which pulls the enemy closer for a groin kick (3). This allows Lau to follow with a knee to the chest (4), and finish with a low knee kick (5), that brings his opponent to the ground (6).

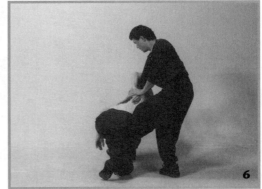

Masters Techniques

From a ready stance (1), an attacker comes at Sifu Lau with a front kick (2). Lau applies a *gaung sao* to the inside of the kick and a *dao sao* to the leg (3). He then steps forward and delivers a right side-kick to the opponent's left knee (4), while applying a *fak sao* to the opponent's face (5).

From an on-guard stance (1), an attacker clamps down on Sifu Lau with a headlock (2). Lau raises both arms to slip the hold (3), circles his right foot behind the attacker's left leg (4), and finishes with a left palm strike to the groin (5).

Eric Lee

The King of Forms

AS A COMPETITOR, HE SET AN EXAMPLE FOR ALL MARTIAL ARTISTS TO FOLLOW. HIS DYNAMIC AND POWERFUL PERFORMANCES IN THE KATA AND SPARRING DIVISIONS MADE ERIC LEE ONE OF THE TOP COMPETITORS EVER AND ONE OF THE ALL-TIME SOUGHT AFTER INSTRUCTORS AROUND THE WORLD. WITH AN INCREDIBLE PHYSIQUE AND REMARKABLE TECHNICAL SKILLS, LEE AMAZED NOT ONLY STUDENTS BUT ALSO WELL-KNOWN INSTRUCTORS OF DIFFERENT MARTIAL ARTS STYLES WHO CAME TO HIM TO IMPROVE THEIR FORMS FOR COMPETITION. ALTHOUGH STRONGLY ROOTED IN TRADITION, HE REPRESENTS THE ECLECTIC APPROACH TO THE MARTIAL ARTS. IN HIS MIND, THE SEARCH FOR KNOWLEDGE IS MORE IMPORTANT THAN AN ALLEGIANCE TO ANY ESTABLISHED SYSTEM OR METHOD. HIS PHILOSOPHY OF LIFE IS BASED ON BALANCED AND "HAPPY THINKING," AS HE LIKES TO SAY. EVEN THOUGH HE IS VERY MODERN IN HIS APPROACH TO MARTIAL ARTS, HE DISPLAYS ALL THE TRUE SPIRITUAL QUALITIES OF A WELL-TRAINED AND WELL-VERSED TRADITIONAL KUNG-FU MAN. HE IS A TRUE AMBASSADOR OF THE ANCIENT SHAOLIN TEMPLE WHO WALKS THE ROADS OF THE 21ST CENTURY.

Q: How long have you been practicing martial arts?
A: For over 40 years now. The first few years I wasn't that serious about my training, it was simply for fun. I become serious when I got beaten-up by some bullies. They had fun pushing people around and one day it was my turn. It was a very bad experience because I stayed laying in the field almost choking! I practiced different methods of fighting but I don't believe in one style. Every style is a personal view of several different principles. Mainly I have trained in Northern Shaolin, kajukenbo, wun hup kuen do, wing chun and tai chi. I'm not proficient in all the styles I practiced, but I studied them and learned a great deal.

Many years ago I was living in Oakland where Bruce Lee had his school. I trained under James Y. Lee in the '60s. At that time the method Sifu James Lee was teaching was called Jun Fan Gung-Fu. Sifu James Lee was very direct. He didn't hold to any tradition and he wanted to be effective above everything else. The techniques at that time were very simple, *pak sao, lop sao* and straight blast with a few kicks added. I wish I

Kung-Fu Masters

"At this moment, I'm really interested in learning about the healing arts, and surprisingly, due to muscle memory, your body opens the meridians that you used many years ago in training the forms—the techniques feel different."

had the opportunity to train under Bruce Lee because he was an innovator and a pioneer in many ways, not only physically but also philosophical as well. My teachers also were Al Dacascos in wun hop kuen do and sifu Ken Chong in wing chun gung fu. I trained in chi kung with Share K. Lew in San Diego, medical chi kung with Dr. Hua Huang and I'm currently training qi qong under Wen Mei Ju, who I consider one of the top instructors in the world in this method of Chinese martial arts. During one of my visits to Hong Kong, I studied tai chi and hung gar kuen, the style of the tiger and crane. This system is a very powerful kung-fu style and it is interesting that I am re-assessing the practice of some of the traditional forms. It amazing how you body uses the energy a different way when you get older. At this moment, I'm really interested in learning about the healing arts, and surprisingly, due to muscle memory, your body opens the meridians that you used many years ago in training the forms—the techniques feel different. I also training in AG Matrix System with grandmaster and founder Mr. Al Garza.

My father is a herbalist in Hong Kong and I learned a lot about how to use the herbs to improve your physical health and to recover your body after intensive training sessions. This knowledge helped me a lot in my martial arts career.

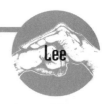

I enjoy learning movements that I can adapt and modify when you reach a high level in the martial arts. You need to know different methods so you can face different opponents and situations. For instance, if you face a judo man, you don't want to grapple with him because he is going to defeat you easily. Then you need to have another method that you can use to balance the situation. The old one-system approach is not good enough these days. You need to look and learn different techniques so you can use those that are appropriate a particular moment. I'm fascinated by knowledge and not by styles.

Q: Did you have any memorable experiences when you were competing?
A: When I was competing I had a great time. I was one of the top competitors back then. I remember I had a friend who was a magician. I was teaching him kung-fu and he was teaching me magic. It was a good trade and fun also. But I'd love to tell one story that still is

"The old one-system approach is not good enough these days. You need to look and learn different techniques so you can use those that are appropriate a particular moment. I'm fascinated by knowledge and not by styles."

very much alive in my mind. Due to my obsession with kung-fu it, many nights I couldn't go to sleep and relax. One day I learned a double-sword form so I went to the park very early in the morning to practice. Then a little baby bird fell from a tree. I picked him up and suddenly dozens of birds appeared from nowhere and started to attack me. It was like the Alfred Hitchcock movie "The Birds." I was so scared that I began to use the swords to defend myself. In fact, I chopped a few birds! They poked at me and I ended up bleeding. I put the bird in the shirt pocket and ran to my car. The birds chased me all the way to the car and once there I

Kung-Fu Masters

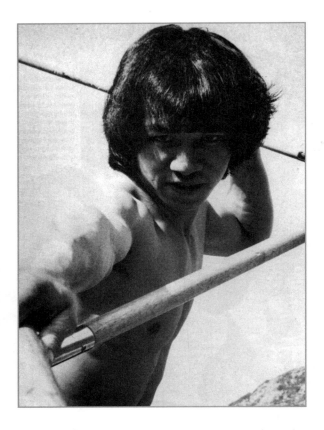

"The old movies display a lot of the great traditional values found in the Chinese martial arts. They were black and white movies and they inspired me very much—you know all the traditional stories and adventures."

couldn't find the key. Then, I put the bird down to look for the key in my pockets and most of the birds stopped attacking me. I finally made it inside the car and to my surprise some of them got into the car with me! Finally, I got rid of them. It was crazy. I promised never to pick up a bird again. Now If I want to have a bird, I go and buy one!

Q: Is it true you were inspired by old kung-fu movies?
A: Yes, it is. The old movies display a lot of the great traditional values found in the Chinese martial arts. Kwon Duk Hing was an actor in the old kung-fu movies from China and he strongly impressed me. He always played the part of the great hung gar master Wong Fei Hung. They were black and white movies and they inspired me very much—you know all the traditional stories and adventures. In fact, when I started to compete, other competitors used make fun of me because I was wearing the traditional kung-fu uniform. I remember a lot of things these characters did in the movies and I decided to compete in the sparring division to prove I could fight too. Later, I ended up taking home trophies for both kata and sparring!

Q: Has your personal expression of the art changed over the years?
A: My father was very influential in my training. When I was very young I went to Hong Kong to live. Everything in my early training was very traditional—very formal. I spent time in the Chinese Opera and this really made an impact on me. Today, I'm not that traditional as far as the tech-

niques go, but I'm traditional in the moral and ethical aspects of the art. You need the traditional way to develop a good foundation, but after years of traditional training you can expand your horizons and taste different arts. This is called "cross-training" today. I enjoy looking at several arts and absorbing different methods. Even if you are on a diet, you still can read the menu. All these elements have definitely changed the way I express kung-fu.

I believe that having an open mind is extremely important. Fortunately, teachers have an open mind for students too, otherwise we couldn't have as many kung-fu schools as we have today. Don't forget that in the old times, the sifu hardly accepted any students. They were very interested in your character first, not your money, and this made the schools packed with students as we can see today.

Q: Were you a natural, or did you work hard to get to a good technical level?

A: I don't think I was very natural. I had to train really hard for competition and to improve my technique. The science of training those days wasn't as advanced as today. We basically stayed in the school all the time and repeated the movements over and over. I remember that we used music to spice our training, but it wasn't like what we know today as tae bo. We used the music to develop the necessary rhythm for kata competition. At this moment health is my priority. The arts gave me a lot of things. I'm a successful person. Sometime people think of success in terms of monetary rewards, but there are many other ways of being successful in martial arts—you meet great people and you have the opportunity to travel

"You need the traditional way to develop a good foundation, but after years of traditional training you can expand your horizons and taste different arts. This is called "cross-training" today. I enjoy looking at several arts and absorbing different methods."

Kung-Fu Masters

"A good instructor, regardless of being Caucasian or Chinese, should have patience with the students. Patience is the most important aspect; this is followed by setting and teaching by example. A teacher should be physically fit because he is the example for his students."

around the world and meet other masters and learn from them as well. All these things—when you are no longer interested in competing—are truly priceless. These are the things that stay with you forever.

Q: How is the Western kung-fu level compared to the technical level in China?
A: Don't forget that for many years kung-fu was prohibited in China. In America, when people take something and break it down and re-structure it, they create a new format. I'm a product of an American mentality, I'm an eclectic martial artist. I don't have any limitations or boundaries that prevent me from absorbing knowledge from different sources. In China, this wouldn't be possible because the environment is more traditional. A good instructor, regardless of being Caucasian or Chinese, should have patience with the students. Patience is the most important aspect; this is followed by setting and teaching by example. A teacher should be physically fit because he is the example for his students. I remember that in the beginning of my teaching days I was expecting my students to perform the techniques perfectly right away, but they didn't. I learned that different students learn and absorb the material at different speeds. You, as their instructor, must be sensitive to that and help them to improve accordingly. Kindness and patience are the keys.

Q: Do you consider yourself a traditionalist or a modernist?
A: For many years I tried to develop a system with explosive techniques; but as I got older I found out that you have to strive to be deceptive and capable of flowing with your opponent's movements. It's not about what

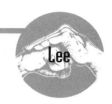

you want to do but how you react to what is given to you by your aggressor. To some extent, I consider myself a modernist because I truly believe in the approach that allows the student to incorporate principles and techniques from different systems. I don't think students should be limited by any external boundaries that prevent them from achieving their potential as martial artists and human beings. I like to experiment and exchange ideas, concepts and strategies with other martial artists because it helps me to improve and to express myself through the arts. On other hand, I feel that I am a very traditional martial artist because I strongly advocate for the traditional values of martial arts like respect, humility, and honor.

Q: What can you tell us about the self-defense aspects of kung-fu?
A: Self-defense is a very tricky aspect of the martial arts. For me,

"Self-defense is a very tricky aspect of the martial arts. For me, self-defense falls in a whole different category because it involves a series of external factors that are not present in the average martial arts school. You may be a great kicker, forms performer, and very skillful in all the techniques—but not be able to teach self-defense."

self-defense falls in a whole different category because it involves a series of external factors that are not present in the average martial arts school. You may be a great kicker, forms performer, and very skillful in all the techniques—but not be able to teach self-defense. You can win many tournaments and be great in sparing and it won't mean anything in a street fight. I would advise to those interested in self-defense to research and find the right school for this purpose. There are five basic elements necessary to build a good self-defense system: simplicity—complex or elaborate techniques can easily fail through lack of proper execution; surprise—try to catch your assailant unaware; speed—move fast and with determination; impact—work to develop power; follow-up—don't stop after the first hit— keep hitting until you are completely out of the situation.

Kung-Fu Masters

"Diet is an important part of your life because your body operates with what you put in it. Without the proper nutrients in the body, you simply cannot perform your best. It's that simple. My basic advice is to keep your nutrition clean and simple, covering all the basic elements. The right foods and proper exercises will bring health to you."

Q: How does diet and nutrition affect martial arts?

A: Diet is an important part of your life because your body operates with what you put in it. Without the proper nutrients in the body, you simply cannot perform your best. It's that simple. It's like being a machine that doesn't have the necessary fuel to run or the raw material to repair itself. I eat a lot of fresh fruits and vegetables, stay away from sugar and greasy foods, and have a good sources of protein. It is advisable to supplement that with vitamins, minerals and Chinese herbs. They will improve your energy levels if you work and train hard. My basic advice is to keep your nutrition clean and simple, covering all the basic elements. The right foods and proper exercises will bring health to you.

Q: Do you recommend a specific personal training program?

A: It is hard for me to recommend a specific training program because I have changed mine so many times. It all depends where you are going and what your goals are. There are some general principles you should always include, though. Endurance training with exercises such as running; isometric exercises for power and strength; explosive drills with or without a partner, using bag work and focus mitts; and stretching using both dynamic and static stretching exercises. Don't forget to include sensitivity drills, such as sticky hands training. The mental aspects should be cultivated through meditation and visualization training. As far as weight

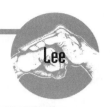

training, I recommend using light weights and high number of repetitions with a slow steady pace, then add a quick burst. This simple technique will help you to develop the capacity for sudden, explosive power. If you put all these elements in your training routine, you'll have a complete package. Vary your training schedule every once in a while to focus on different aspects of the whole picture.

Q: How do you approach physical training in the martial arts?
A: From the very beginning, my approach to competition was to make it part of my life, without upsetting the natural processes of my day-to-day existence. Diet, physical training, mental discipline and recreation—all these elements of life are equally important factors in the presentation of forms. There is absolutely no way I could have been successful without attending to each of these elements individually, every day. The music, the lights and the dramatic presentations were merely part of a whole. It is very important to understand that training is a whole

"Diet, physical training, mental discipline and recreation—all these elements of life are equally important factors in the presentation of forms. There is absolutely no way I could have been successful without attending to each of these elements individually, every day. It is very important to understand that training is a whole process."

process. The entire body and mind must benefit from that process. Now, I don't pretend to be able to tell other people what sort of conditioning program they should abide by, but for me the practice has to begin with diet. For being in shape for competition, training hard is about 50 percent of the job and nutrition is the other 50 percent. You can't perform at your best, no matter how much you train for an event, if your body lacks essential nutrients. Also if you train hard every day—do a lot of running and so on—but your body doesn't have the right nutrients, then you are just using your body up.

Kung-Fu Masters

Q: Do you like to run?

A: It's better to run every other day than to make a religious daily regimen out of it. The body needs a certain amount of time to recuperate. Sure you can run more than that, but it gets to be a case of diminishing returns. Besides, there are other things to do in training that work on the aerobic system. I like to combine running with a program of isometrics and limited weight training. I lift weights on a very light schedule two or three times a week, working on specific muscle groups that are important in martial arts techniques. The idea is not to build too much muscle tissue, which doesn't really help in performing forms, but to build strength. I lift the weight very slowly most of the way through its arc, and then speed-up suddenly, concentrating on strengthening the ligaments.

Q: You were known in your competition days for having extremely deep concentration when performing. How did you reach that level of concentration?

A: In exercise, concentration is most important. I can spend 15 minutes working on a particular exercise, and if I'm concentrating well I can get more out of that than I would in two hours otherwise. I use the same pattern of exertion in doing calisthenics as I do in weight training—slow, steady effort, then a quick burst. This helps to develop the capacity for sudden, explosive energy, which is a crucial aspect of martial arts technique. It's important to do the right kind of exercises and do them in the way that is most rewarding and applicable to the purpose you have in mind.

Q: Can you give an example?

A: In upper-body work, when I'm doing push-ups, rather than trying to do as many as I possibly can, I prefer to do several rapid sets of 25, and rest for a minute or two between sets. Again, that helps develop the kind of explosive power I want. Then from there I'll pump a few weights and then go into some isometrics. Exercise cannot be seen as a purely physical activity. To gain the greatest good from it you also have to work on concentration and breathing. I breathe steadily during isometric exercises, never letting the air build up or the blood rush to my head. In other forms of exercise, I usually breathe out with the exertion and in with the return. Breathing correctly is crucial for the health of both heart and lungs, and should always be calm, regular and unhurried. This may seem a little difficult at first, but it pays off and becomes second nature after awhile. By the same token, the mind should always be clam and unstressed, no matter what the body is doing. When I am training, all the stress is on my muscles

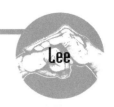

and my mind remains clam. This is how to gain the maximum from training.

Q: How has the tournament circuit developed over the years?
A: When I first started, judges weren't looking for showmanship in forms competition. Traditionally, they looked for speed and power—for how effective the form seemed—but not for how flashy or difficult the techniques were or how much showmanship the performer could generate. Of course, the forms were not originally designed for competition or entertainment, but strictly to develop certain techniques. In the first tournaments I participated in, musical forms were not even permitted. We were the first ones who included music in demonstrations, and from there it gradually filtered into competition as well—there was a music division in many tournaments only for the last few years of my competitive career. But what happened was that martial arts movies started coming out and monopolizing

"In the first tournaments I participated in, musical forms were not even permitted. We were the first ones who included music in demonstrations, and from there it gradually filtered into competition as well—there was a music division in many tournaments only for the last few years of my competitive career. Personally, I didn't add the music as a nice little touch for the audience. I usually train with music, too."

the showmanship element of the martial arts. People in the movies were starting to display more showmanship than people in live demonstrations. Today, there are still a lot of tournaments that try to exclude the more theatrical aspects of forms from competition, but at least nowadays people in a live demonstration can be compared favorably to what's being done in film. Personally, I didn't add the music as a nice little touch for the audi-

Kung-Fu Masters

"Training to music should be a total creative experience. This is not something that is easy to achieve, especially not on the strength of just listening to a song once. But if you listen to the music 20 times or so, and really begin to get to know it, you can reach a new plateau of creativity."

ence. I usually train with music, too. For one thing, it makes training more fun, just as it makes the performance more entertaining for the audience.

There is nothing wrong with having a good time in martial arts. But the musical rhythm also helped me to develop my own internal cadence for the form. As you follow the music, you'll get a feel for the rhythm of your own performance, and that adds to your creative impulses and spontaneity. Training to music should be a total creative experience. This is not something that is easy to achieve, especially not on the strength of just listening to a song once. But if you listen to the music 20 times or so, and really begin to get to know it, you can reach a new plateau of creativity. You get to where you can vary your movement rhythm any time you want. Naturally, you shouldn't rely on music, but it can be a significant part of forms training. In forms competition today, the tempo, the rhythm and the performance are becoming ever more significant and the people are getting better at it all the time.

Q: Where are your current goals?
A: I try to live my live to my fullest. Sometimes you run into people who bring negative energy into your life and you have to keep them away from you. You might say that I'm addicted to working out and I need the martial arts in my life to be happy. My goal is to develop myself more in the internal arts, to become more knowledgeable about the internal aspects of kung-fu. Probably this is a natural progression due to my age. Now I know how to build energy from inside, and I have learned to use it in a more efficient way than when I was younger. Look at nature and you'll find the right way of doing things in your own life. Try to find a balance in life. Go out with friends and have a social life too. Some people only want to be by themselves in an isolated environment and spend all their free time training in martial arts. This is not good—you have to bring balance to your life by relating to other human beings and enjoying other things in life that are not martial arts related. Then you really will succeed in kung-fu—because kung-fu is, after all, simply a matter of proper balance in life.

Q: What direction do you see martial arts going in the future?
A: I think people will go more and more into the cross-training approach I mentioned before. What they have to understand is that in order to become good in this approach, you must spend time with a good teacher to build a foundation. Don't jump from one style to another without a good foundation. After you have that strong base, give always credit to your teachers and move on to other styles that you feel may bring something good to you. Remain open and enjoy your friends and your life because that's also part of a good kung-fu practitioner. And don't forget to think happy.

Masters Techniques

Sifu Lee faces an attacker (1), who grabs his neck (2). Lee reacts by controlling the grabbing hand and hitting the attacking arm with an upward strike (3), followed by a backhand blow to the neck (4). He then places his right arm under the attacker's left arm (5), and applies an arm lock to bring the aggressor to the ground (6), for final control (7).

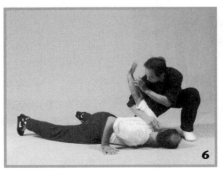
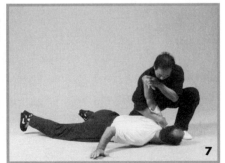

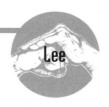

From a ready stance (1), Sifu Lee simultaneously blocks an aggressor's left punch and controls his chambered rear hand (2). He follows with a right punch (3), and a left backhand strike to the side of the opponent's neck (4). Lee then moves his right leg forward (5), and sweeps the aggressor's front leg and takes him to the ground (6).

Masters Techniques

Sifu Lee covers an attacker's punch and simultaneously strikes with his right hand (1). He follows by placing his hand around the neck (2), and hooking his opponent's head (3). He then positions his right foot (4), in order to sweep the aggressor's front leg (5), take him into the ground (6), and finish with head control (7).

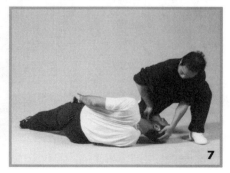

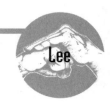

Sifu Lee faces an opponent (1), who tries to tackle him. Lee blocks the action by controlling the opponent's shoulders (2), and then takes him to the ground (3). Lee then jumps over him (4), positions himself behind the attacker (5), sits on his back (6), and applies a finishing neck crank (7).

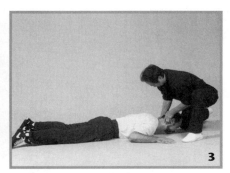

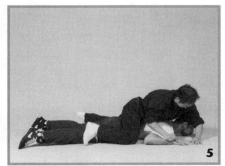

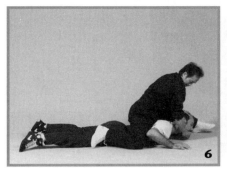

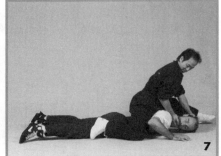

Wong Shun Leung

The Logic Behind Wing Chun

ONE OF THE TOP WING CHUN FIGHTERS AT YIP MAN'S HONG KONG SCHOOL, SIFU LEUNG TAUGHT BRUCE LEE PRIVATELY FOR ONE-AND-A HALF-YEARS AND RECALLED "HIS KUNG-FU WAS NOT VERY GOOD—HE COULDN'T FIGHT." LEUNG'S OWN INTRODUCTION TO THE WING CHUN SYSTEM WAS LESS THAN STELLAR—HE CHALLENGED YIP MAN TO A TRIAL BY COMBAT, CONVINCED HE COULD DEFEAT HIM. WHEN MAN EASILY WON, LEUNG BECAME A LIFELONG BELIEVER AND DISCIPLE OF THE SYSTEM THAT BRUCE LEE WOULD EVENTUALLY TURN INTO THE MOST POPULAR KUNG-FU STYLE EVER TAUGHT. YIP MAN, SEEING MORE IN LEE THAN OTHERS, PREDICTED TO THE INCREDULOUS LEUNG THAT, "THIS LITTLE KID WILL MAKE WING CHUN FAMOUS."

A DEDICATED AND TALENTED STUDENT, LEUNG WENT ON TO BECOME YIP MAN'S PERSONAL ASSISTANT AND WAS PUT IN CHARGE OF PASSING ON THE ART TO THE SCHOOL'S JUNIORS. LEUNG, DESPITE HIS INITIAL MISGIVINGS ABOUT THE WILD AND YOUTHFUL LEE, EVENTUALLY DEVELOPED A PERSONAL RELATIONSHIP WITH "THE LITTLE DRAGON" AS THEY BOTH MATURED. HE REFUSED, HOWEVER, TO APPEAR IN THE *GAME OF DEATH*, LEE'S LAST UNFINISHED PROJECT, BECAUSE HE FELT THAT BEING DEFEATED IN A MOVIE WOULD REFLECT POORLY ON HIS TRUE SKILL. HIS RELATIONSHIP WITH BRUCE LEE WOULD LAST UNTIL THE END OF THE ACTOR'S LIFE.

WONG SHUN LEUNG WAS A CHARISMATIC TEACHER AND A DYNAMIC LEADER, WHICH IS WHY LEE RESPECTED HIM. LEUNG'S DEEP KNOWLEDGE OF WING CHUN MADE HIM ONE OF THE MOST SOUGHT-AFTER INSTRUCTORS OF HIS ERA. ANALYTICAL, INQUISITIVE, AND PERCEPTIVE, HE WAS SAID BY YIP MAN TO BE "THE LOGIC BEHIND WING CHUN."

Q: When did you start training under Yip Man?
A: My father had friends who practiced wing chun. One of them was a man named Chan Wah Sun. He would always tell me how good his teacher, Yip Man, was. I didn't believe him, so I decided to go to Yip Man's school and challenge him. He was around 50 years old and I was 17, strong, and in good shape. To make a long story short, he beat me up easily, which really surprised me. I just couldn't believe this little old man was so good.

Kung-Fu Masters

"I don't need to talk about my past. I don't see any point in proving to people how tough you are. Being a good fighter depends on how hard you practice, and how much time you put into it. Fighting abilities are based on perseverance, confidence, and physical power—not talk."

Q: You were considered one of wing chun's best fighters, right?
A: That's what they say, but I really don't like to talk about it very much. Many people, when they get old, start talking about how great they were when they were young and sometimes they say a lot of thing that are not true. If you were really good, then people will know already—you don't have to talk about it. If I tell stories about how I used to fight, it means that I can't fight anymore. If I can still fight today, I don't need to talk about my past. I don't see any point in proving to people how tough you are. Being a good fighter depends on how hard you practice, and how much time you put into it. Fighting abilities are based on perseverance, confidence, and physical power—not talk.

Q: Did you ever consider competing in combat sports?
A: I have always liked boxing—I like anything about fighting—but my kind of fighting is not the sport version—it is real fighting where there are

"Wing chun is a skill. If you describe it as an art, there is no way to determine if it is effective or not. For example, you might like Picasso's work more than Monet's paintings, but it is purely subjective and just a matter of preference. In combat, the fighter left standing is the winner."

no rule, no restrictions, and your life is hanging in the balance. If you put on gloves then it becomes a matter of winning points, which is not total fighting. Martial arts techniques can be adapted to be used with gloves, but is not the same. However, it is true that contact training and sparring can be a very revealing experience for the student. Fighting with martial arts skills is partly a branch of learning, and partly an art. Perhaps Chinese martial arts should, taking into account the realistic social environment, formulate a set of competition regulations that would allow what I call the "trial of skills" to be brought into full play.

Q: Why did you stop boxing?
A: I was sparring with my instructor and I hit him very hard. He got real mad and came at me very hard. I fought back with wing chun and he ended up bleeding. Boxing was over for me!

Kung-Fu Masters

"Bruce was totally aware that jeet kune do is very hard to do because it depends on the student's capabilities. This can be really confusing for the students, especially if they lack a strong base and deep understanding."

Q: Do you look at wing chun as a philosophy or an art?
A: For me, wing chun is a skill. If you describe it as an art, there is no way to determine if it is effective or not. For example, you might like Picasso's work more than Monet's paintings, but it is purely subjective and just a matter of preference. In combat, the fighter left standing is the winner. It is not a matter of likes or dislikes—the skills can be proved. So I look at wing chun more as a skill than an art. Taken in that context, there nothing wrong with using your skills if you have to.

Q: You were one of Yip Man's top assistants. Did you ever teach Bruce Lee?
A: I taught Bruce Lee privately and also watched him train under Yip Man at the school. William Cheung introduced Bruce Lee to the wing chun system. Bruce trained and studied wing chun from me for over one-and-a-half years.

Q: Did you keep in touch with Bruce after he moved to the United States?
A: He used to write me telling me how he was doing and the direction his research was taking. Sometimes he would ask for clarification of a wing chun technique or principle. When he came back to Hong Hong to do movies, we would meet and talk about martial arts for hours. We had a very good relationship until the very end.

Q: Did he ever explain jeet kune do to you?
A: Yes. Bruce was totally aware that jeet kune do is very hard to do because it depends on the student's capabilities. This can be really confusing for the students, especially if they lack a strong base and deep understanding. Jeet kune do was simply a personal format Bruce used to apply his knowledge and experiences. I told him most likely there was a missing link in his research and that he was trying to cover too much distance in too short a time. On other hand, there has been only one Bruce Lee and no one could play like him—some of the old rules didn't apply.

"Wing chun method is ugly for movies but very good and very logical for real fighting. When your are young you like to fight. As you grow, you look at fighting in a different way. You have a different point of view about physical confrontations."

Q: How did you see the evolution of Bruce Lee from wing chun to jeet kune do?
A: First of all, Bruce didn't get to see the best part of wing chun during his early days of training under Yip Man. He then came back to Hong Kong, and truly learned the foundation of what would eventually become his own style. He was a very naughty boy at times but also very smart. So once in the United States, he filled in the blanks in order to make things work for him.

In the later days of his life Bruce said to me, "If I could take back jeet kune do, I'd take it back." He realized that he could make the movements work, but that was because his style was designed for his own specific talents. His students, however, had problems making the techniques work under real situations. While jeet kune do was a significant art for Bruce, it has not been that way for other people who followed his method.

Bruce was a good fighter, but not as good as movies have portrayed him—almost invincible. People used to see Bruce Lee and have kung-fu dreams. They wanted to do the same things he did and duplicate his methods. Unfortunately, it seems nobody wants to wake up.

Kung-Fu Masters

"As long as it stays logical it doesn't matter what you call it or what you're actually doing. If it is logical, if it works, use it! Make the art your slave, and never allow the art be your master."

Q: Have you made any changes to the wing chun system?
A: Basically I teach the same method I learned from Yip Man—but I would say that I teach it in a more systematic way. At the same time, though, I'm still very intuitive in my teaching.

Q: Most people associate you with the principle of *lut sao jik chung*. Why?
A: Because it is probably the most important concept in the whole wing chun system, perhaps the only exception being the *bart cham dao* techniques. As soon as the opponent offers an opening, the hand should attack instantaneously.

Q: Is it true that Bruce offered you a part in one of his movies?
A: Yes, he did. It was for *Game of Death*, but I declined because I thought that the moves of wing chun style wouldn't look good on film. I think the wing chun method is ugly for movies but very good and very logical for real fighting.

Q: Have you changed your overall view of the art since you were young?
A: Of course. When your are young you like to fight. As you grow, you look at fighting in a different way. You have a different point of view about physical confrontations. It is important to educate the students about this. Unfortunately, if a student wants to fight, there's really nothing you can do about it.

Q: Are you a traditionalist?
A: I firmly believe that wing chun is something very logical. As long as it stays logical it doesn't matter what you call it or what you're actually doing. If it is logical, if it works, use it! Make the art your slave, and never allow the art be your master.

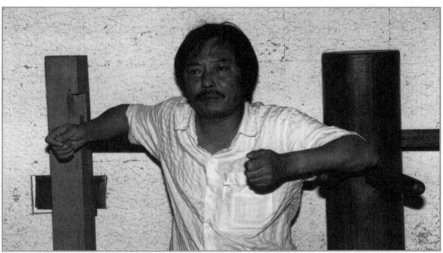

"Wing chun theory is flawless if you can execute it perfectly. But a theory is just a theory. It means nothing if you can't put it to work. You might have a better fighting theory behind you system, but if your skill level is lower than your opponent's skill, you'll be easily defeated. All the theory in the world can't save you from losing."

Q: Why do you think wing chun is so popular around the world?
A: I think Bruce Lee contributed a lot to that! But if a martial art system is not logical, simple, and useful it will disappear. It's just a matter of time. Think about the many countries or political systems that don't exit anymore. If there is something lacking in meaning and purpose it will definitely fade away. Wing chun is growing all over the world—so that should tell you something.

Q: When you teach in a different country, do you change your method?
A: I have to adapt my mentality to the country. Of course the Chinese customs are different from the American or European, but the wing chun system is taught the same. The approach can be different but the techniques are the same, and the philosophy as well. Anyone who learns martial arts must be combat-minded. If one learns martial arts' skills, but does not pay attention to fighting, then they are neglecting the essence to pursue trifles—since martial arts are not just physical exercises. To learn and to try skills are the two stages of martial arts training, and I think there's

Kung-Fu Masters

"If you have to fight in the street the kind of food you eat is not going to be that relevant so. But if you are a professional fighter or are you planning fighting in the ring, then the food will affect your energy and performance."

nothing wrong with that. One should be encouraged to test the skills as long the purpose is to study and learn from others. But it is a pity that many people have distorted the meaning of the trials of skills, and take it as a way to show their power—or even to bully people around!

Q: Do you feel that *chi sao* is an important part of wing chun?
A: Chi sao is very important in wing chun, but too much emphasis is placed on the idea of "sticking" to the hands—this causes the student to end up chasing the hands instead of punching and trapping. This mistake totally contradicts the wing chun basic principles. Wing chun theory is flawless if you can execute it perfectly. But a theory is just a theory. It means nothing if you can't put it to work. You might have a better fighting theory behind you system, but if your skill level is lower than your opponent's skill, you'll be easily defeated. All the theory in the world can't save you from losing.

Q: Are you happy with the way wing chun is being taught?
A: Well, I have seen some instructors turn simple things into big mysteries, misleading their students. They not only deceive themselves but other innocent people, too. They'd do better teaching the students how to not make mistakes in real fighting.

Q: Do you follow any particular diet?
A: If you have to fight in the street the kind of food you eat is not going to be that relevant so, I don't. But if you are a professional fighter or are

you planning fighting in the ring, then the food will affect your energy and performance.

Q: Do you have a martial arts philosophy?
A: There is an old Chinese saying that goes, "Courage first, strength second, and kung-fu third." To secure victory in a face-to-face fight with fist and kicks, one must be courageous. The courage comes from one's own self-cultivation and is one of the purposes of trials of skills. The second is strength and vigor. The kung-fu you see in real combat is only a few actions. What counts in real combat is determination, courage, and vigour. If you're superior in this aspects, then you can often knock down you opponent with two or three simple techniques. The prolonged fighting seen in martial arts movies is artificial. Bruce Lee was a master of kung-fu in his own right, but the kung-fu he actually mastered should not be confused with what you see in the movies. There are wing chun disciples whose achievements in martial arts are not even second to those of Bruce Lee. But they never made movies and got famous so no one knows them. Movie fans only know Bruce Lee because his movies are shown all over the world.

"There are wing chun disciples whose achievements in martial arts are not even second to those of Bruce Lee. But they never made movies and got famous so no one knows them. Movie fans only know Bruce Lee because his movies are shown all over the world."

Q: Do you think people respond well to your teaching methods?
A: I can only say that I try to share wing chun in an honest way. I teach in a logical manner because the art is very logical. I can't talk about what other people may do or say. I'm only responsible for my own acts.

James Lew
Breaking the Mold

JAMES LEW IS ONE OF THE FEW KUNG-FU PRACTITIONERS WHO USED THE MARTIAL ARTS AS A SPRINGBOARD TO A SUCCESSFUL CAREER IN THE ENTERTAINMENT INDUSTRY. AS A TOP-CALIBER FORMS COMPETITOR, LEW INCLUDED REVOLUTIONARY GYMNASTICS AND EXTREME FLEXIBILITY TECHNIQUES INTO HIS ROUTINES. THIS NOT ONLY SHOCKED AUDIENCES AND JUDGES, BUT IT ALSO ATTRACTED TELEVISION PRODUCERS WHO EVENTUALLY OFFERED HIM JOBS IN FILM. AS A REBEL AHEAD OF HIS TIME, LEW FOUGHT AGAINST THE IDEA OF ALWAYS REPEATING TRADITIONAL FORMS IN COMPETITION AND BEGAN TO DEVELOP HIS OWN CREATIVE ROUTINES INCORPORATING ELEMENTS NEVER SEEN BEFORE. HE HELPED TO LAY DOWN THE FOUNDATION FOR THE CREATIVE FORMS THAT THE AMERICAN TOURNAMENT SCENE ENJOYS TO THIS DAY. ON THE BASIS OF HIS PHYSIQUE ALONE, HE HAS LANDED COUNTLESS MODELING ASSIGNMENTS AND HE IS PROBABLY THE MOST PHOTOGRAPHED MARTIAL ARTIST IN THE WORLD. HIS HANDS, ARMS, LEGS AND FACE HAVE APPEARED IN *INSIDE KUNG-FU* COMMERCIAL ADVERTISEMENTS SINCE THE MAGAZINE'S INCEPTION IN 1973. TODAY, JAMES LEW IS AN ESTABLISHED HOLLYWOOD ACTOR AND STUNTMAN WHO HAS WORKED WITH SUCH TOP NAMES AS JACKIE CHAN, MEL GIBSON AND JET LI—AMONG MANY OTHERS. BUT DEEP INSIDE, HE IS STILL THAT BRASH AND CONFIDENT KUNG-FU PRACTITIONER WHO SHOCKED THE WORLD AND REVOLUTIONIZED FORMS COMPETITION FOREVER.

Q: How long have you practiced martial arts?
A: My formal introduction began when I was 14 and my first martial arts style was a combination of taekwondo and tang soo do—that was during junior high. When I got to high school a very different martial art was offered at the school karate club. It was a style developed by a Green Beret combat instructor who blended the best of the modern military fighting techniques with the traditional Chinese martial art of *choy lay fut* kung-fu. My natural curiosity to learn more also took me to another style called *bak mei pai* (white eyebrow) kung-fu. It remains one of my favorite styles today. I also studied traditional five animals Shaolin kung-fu.

Kung-Fu Masters

"My focus was on sparring. As it turns out, my interests completely reversed and I eventually found forms to be a much more satisfying challenge. I discovered that this would be the area that would create a name for me on the competition circuit."

Q: Were you a natural at kung-fu?
A: When I first started martial arts I was horrible in forms. Looking back, I think it was because that was the one aspect of training that didn't appeal to me. My focus was on sparring. As it turns out, my interests completely reversed and I eventually found forms to be a much more satisfying challenge. I discovered that this would be the area that would create a name for me on the competition circuit.

Q: What reaction did you get when you modified traditional forms for competition?
A: What really got me into trouble was that I put in moves the judges had never seen before. Back then they wanted to see a traditional style. My scores were mixed—either very high or very low. They either loved me or hated me. I included gymnastic moves and extreme flexibility techniques that surprised the audience as much as the judges. I have always believed that you should always enjoy what you do. That's why I began creating my own forms and putting together my favorites techniques. That way I could actually enjoy the form. Don't forget I didn't feel very happy doing forms! When you are having fun doing forms, that attitude helps you to look good. But once it becomes work, you trudge through it just like anything else and your moves aren't as good. However, if you actually love to punch in a certain way, then you are going to enjoy practicing that form because you get to use the punch. So I'd try to let the fun carry over into the audience. I'd always remember that there were people out there watching. The form should be more of an entertainment thing for them—something fun.

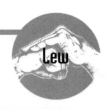

Q: What advice would you give to someone interested in creating his own competition forms?

A: Competition forms are a very visual means of communication—the way you look counts. Bodybuilding is a great complement to forms competition—just for the esthetics of it. Someone who is built a little better naturally looks stronger doing the moves. A good physique is better than having to count on the audience's ability to see your internal strength. Clothing is another important aspect. You shouldn't go out there wearing something too elaborate. When your uniform looks too flashy, it will detract from your movements.

Appearance means more than just the way you dress and the way you're built. It also includes your stage presence. Your performance begins when you approach the stage. You should always be alert and come to attention. Turn on your "game face." Look at all of the judges directly and confidently in the eyes and announce your name, style and form loud and clear. Wait for the head judge to acknowledge permission to begin your form. Then move directly to your spot where you will begin your form. And whatever you do, always pick the

"You shouldn't go out there wearing something too elaborate. You should maintain a degree of moderation in everything you do. Appearance means more than just the way you dress and the way you're built. It also includes your presence and the way you come into a room and walk up to compete. You should always be alert and come to attention."

exact place you are going to stop. A lot of people will walk back, stop and turn around. Then they will shuffle back and forth to settle into their place. This is a sure-fire way to make the judges focus on your awkwardness instead of concentrating on your technique.

Q: When and how should acrobatics be used?

A: You have to be careful with acrobatic moves. I always frown on movements which don't seem to fit in—like when a guy all of a sudden does a flip for no apparent reason. The best time to use an acrobatic technique is when the audience can picture what you are doing—like when you dodge somebody's weapon. It's also important that when you land an acrobatic move that you flow easily into the next technique. If you land real hard and off balance, the judges will say you were vulnerable at that

Kung-Fu Masters

"The main thing is to look upon kata as a showpiece and try to make it as realistic as possible. Show power and grace at the same time. Pinpoint imaginary targets with your eyes. This will help the audience follow your actions. Most of all, look upon your performance as something to have fun with. Then just go out there and have fun."

point. You've got to simulate being in combat because this is a martial art and you've got to make it look like your movements could hurt somebody. That's part of the realism.

Q: Kung-fu forms appear soft compared to karate. How did you overcome that?
A: It's true. Kung-fu fighters are always put down for not having power. So I decided to really emphasize that aspect in my forms. To start off, you have to put together in your mind your favorite moves and kicks. You throw them all into a little imaginary bucket. Then you start to pick them out. For instance, you go back maybe to one of your very basic forms and lift the movement pattern of the footwork. You know, an "L" or "H" shape or whatever. Now you add your favorite moves at key spots and link these movements with filler techniques of some kind. Try to use techniques which will emphasize the key moves. It's like you break the form into little chapters. You should off something different each time.

The overall form should stress power but at the same time it must show elegance and grace, like a dance. Grace comes from your body balance and how you flow into the different moves. That's where a little bit of ballet training is very helpful. Ballet teaches you how to make your hands flow with your body and how to establish your body language.

The main thing is to look upon kata as a showpiece and try to make it as realistic as possible. Show power and grace at the same time. Pinpoint imaginary targets with your eyes. This will help the audience follow your actions. Most of all, look upon your performance as something to have fun with. Then just go out there and have fun.

Q: Were the circular movements of kung-fu easy for you?
A: When I began kung-fu my martial arts training was already fairly advanced and the natural flowing movements of the Chinese styles felt like an art that was awakening from within me. The fluid circular-based movements of soft-style kung-fu flowed easily from my body. Being born and raised in the United States I consider myself a Westerner. My first impression of traditional Chinese training was that it was very tedious and not suited for commercial exploitation in America. But once I discovered the value in traditional training, it became apparent to me that it had its place. Traditional training not only builds a solid foundation in the fundamentals of the martial arts but it also develops the mental spirit that a true martial artist must have.

Q: When you taught martial arts, what did you emphasize?
A: When I used to teach, it was very boring and not very inspiring to me. I think the reason for that is because I have always been more of a performer and player rather than a spectator or coach. The other reason that I initially felt that teaching was not my cup of tea was that I was teaching only for the money. It is my belief that the only real way to teach martial arts is with the attitude of giving something valuable to a student. I have never viewed the art as my personal kung-fu, but rather as my personal life spirit. From that viewpoint, martial arts has truly immersed and blended with my everyday life and philosophy. More than just techniques, that life spirit was what I eventually shared with my students.

"It is my belief that the only real way to teach martial arts is with the attitude of giving something valuable to a student. I have never viewed the art as my personal kung-fu, but rather as my personal life spirit. From that viewpoint, martial arts has truly immersed and blended with my everyday life and philosophy."

Q: Do you think there are still pure styles of kung-fu?
A: If you really consider the way the masters traditionally taught their students, always retaining some secret techniques for themselves, then the

Kung-Fu Masters

"I feel different martial arts styles are not only important, but also necessary. It is only logical that a certain martial arts style is better for someone physically and mentally best suited for that style. Southern styles are better for shorter and more powerful physiques. Northern styles are better suited to tall and rangy body shapes."

evolution from generation-to-generation has always changed. So within that context of change, I feel there are still some pure styles left—or as pure as they be. Keep in mind that from the beginning of martial arts, each master brought their own personal flavor to the art they handed down to their students—even if they didn't intend to do it. I feel different martial arts styles are not only important, but also necessary. It is only logical that a certain martial arts style is better for someone physically and mentally best suited for that style. Southern styles are better for shorter and more powerful physiques. Northern styles are better suited to tall and rangy body shapes. We all need to have respect and appreciation for all the different styles of the martial arts.

Q: What is your opinion of combat sports like the UFC and K-1?
A: They definitely have their own place in the world of martial arts. I feel that combat sports have tremendous entertainment value and have raised the level of martial arts all over the world. There is a place for martial arts as a sport as long as the philosophy and traditional martial arts is not overshadowed. Free fighting or free sparring gives a strong foundation to develop the instincts and skills necessary for the streets. Although it is difficult to create the same intensity as a real street fight, free sparring is the next best thing and tests your skill under controlled environment. This is good as long as you know how to draw the proper conclusions from these experiences.

Q: Do you think that kung-fu in the West has caught up with the Chinese technical level?
A: Think of what used to be the stigma attached to eating Chinese food in the West and with having a genuine Chinese meal in Hong Kong. It was quite different many years ago but now that the masters of Chinese cooking have immigrated to the West and have the best ingredients avail-

able this gap has been closed. The same has happened with the quality of Chinese kung-fu—we now have some of the best Eastern masters teaching students in the West.

Q: Do you agree with kung-fu being treated as a sport?
A: I am more familiar with the style of Chinese *wushu* being referred to as a sport. It has been developed and promoted with competition in mind. I believe that most kung-fu practitioners still practice their style as an art, although they can compete in the sport aspects of the art.

Q: Do you think it helps open-hand forms when you train with weapons?
A: I cannot say enough about the merits of learning martial arts weapons. My love of the martial arts weapons is not only because of the important link it provides to the traditional combat arts, but also the benefits it brings to a practitioner's empty-hand skills. The theory of becoming one with your weapon and making it an extension of your body is very powerful. It also develops a keen sense of concentration because you must focus your movements or you may hurt yourself. When using a martial arts weapon the mind, body and weapon must become one.

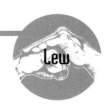

"I cannot say enough about the merits of learning martial arts weapons. My love of the martial arts weapons is not only because of the important link it provides to the traditional combat arts, but also the benefits it brings to a practitioner's empty-hand skills. It also develops a keen sense of concentration because you must focus your movements or you may hurt yourself."

Q: What can kung-fu personally give people?
A: My personal experience, through many years of training in the martial arts, has given me some very enlightening revelations. Martial arts should become part of your being for the rest of your life. It is like a true friend. You can always depend on it or even go away for a while, but it will be there when you need it and the friendship will become stronger the more you put into it. The other important advice that I can give is to have fun

Kung-Fu Masters

"The martial arts are so vast and varied that it is truly a lifetime study. I believe that everything that we can learn to better ourselves as a human beings outside of the martial arts will enhance and improve us as complete martial artists."

with the martial arts. When someone begins taking martial arts there is usually a particular reason they want to learn. But as a true martial artist progresses, they will find that the balance of all the elements—self-defense, sport and tradition—will help the other. The martial arts are so vast and varied that it is truly a lifetime study. I believe that everything that we can learn to better ourselves as a human beings outside of the martial arts will enhance and improve us as complete martial artists. It is all in your viewpoint. We are always students in both the martial arts and in life.

Q: What do you consider to be the major changes in the art since you began training?
A: With the popularity of full-contact fighting shows and the inclusion of taekwondo in the Olympics it seems the emphasis has been placed on the pure fighting aspects of the martial arts and less on the traditional training and philosophy. I truly enjoy watching the combative side of martial arts. On the flip side, I will always do my part to promote the philosophy and the health benefits of martial arts. There is a place in the world for the complete circle of martial arts to exist in harmony.

Q: With whom would you have liked to train, but have never had the privilege?
A: Definitely with Bruce Lee. He was ahead of his time and brought fresh air into the martial arts. In fact, many of the modern approaches to training are the direct result of his influence in the late '60s and early '70s. He was a turning point in martial arts history and I would loved to have the opportunity to train under him.

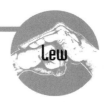

Q: What keeps you motivated after all these years?
A: Learning new techniques, learning new styles, relearning old techniques, developing new techniques, and discovering new benefits and meanings in all aspects of the martial arts. It is the same desire to grow as a human being that keeps me motivated in life.

Q: What is your opinion about mixing kung-fu with other styles?
A: My martial arts background is a very mixed range of kung-fu styles and other martial arts styles. I feel that the richness of my knowledge in many styles has made me what I am today. If you think of learning different styles as a form of cross-training, then you can truly realize the advantages of learning different styles. And speaking of cross-training, I cannot stress how vital it is to improving your martial arts. My training in track and field, football, gymnastics, swimming, weight training, boxing, ballet and many other sports has played a tremendous role in giving me the edge in martial arts.

"Watching Bruce Lee in the movies was and still is my biggest inspiration. It is not only because of the physical prowess he displayed, but the incredible martial spirit he possessed. The practice of kung-fu or any martial arts at the ultimate level of achievement is being able to live in harmony with not only yourself but with others."

Q: What has been the biggest inspiration for your training?
A: Watching Bruce Lee in the movies was and still is my biggest inspiration. It is not only because of the physical prowess he displayed, but the incredible martial spirit he possessed. The practice of kung-fu or any martial arts at the ultimate level of achievement is being able to live in harmony with not only yourself but with others. In the words of Bruce Lee, "It is fighting without fighting."

Q: What are the most important attributes of a student?
A: An open mind that can absorb the knowledge a teacher gives you, coupled with an inquisitive mind that asks questions to truly understand

Kung-Fu Masters

"I believe the martial arts are here to stay. The first understanding that one must have when comparing martial arts in the cinema to real life self-defense is that movies is about creating the illusion that we are hurting our opponent. The biggest difference a martial artist must adapt to in cinema martial arts is that the moves must be telegraphed for the audience."

what they are learning. A practitioner who embraces the enjoyment of training and the growth as a human being through the martial arts is the most successful. Unfortunately, many students stop training after a short period of time. When a student begins their martial arts training with the idea that they are either going to earn a black belt or learn martial arts to be able to beat someone up, then they are starting their training on the wrong road. That road leads to a dead end because once their goal is reached there is nothing to look forward to because they are only seeking the end result. A student with the wrong viewpoint will find the martial arts journey not satisfying and quit. The best advice I can give students is to train hard and practice other sports as much as possible. I completely believe that my diverse training in sports and different martial arts styles is the reason behind my success in martial arts.

Q: You work regularly in Hollywood and have appeared with such stars as Jackie Chan, Jet Li, Mel Gibson and others. How different is movie kung-fu from real kung-fu?

A: The popularity of Chinese kung-fu in the Western world is at an all-time high. The high profile Chinese kung-fu movie superstars like Jackie Chan and Jet Li and movies like *The Matrix* and *Crouching Tiger, Hidden Dragon* have helped make Chinese kung-fu a worldwide phenomenon. I believe the martial arts are here to stay. The first understanding that one must have when comparing martial arts in the cinema to real life self-defense is

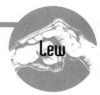

that movies is about creating the illusion that we are hurting our opponent. The biggest difference a martial artist must adapt to in cinema martial arts is that the moves must be telegraphed for the audience. It is very difficult to see a martial arts technique on the screen if it is not overemphasized. It is pretty much the opposite of what martial arts training has instilled into your fighting skills.

Q: What are your thoughts on the future of kung-fu?
A: Martial arts have become accepted throughout the world. The popularity of the martial arts in movies and as a sport has given it mainstream appeal. Because of the global economy and the huge part the Asian countries play in that economy, the Asian cultural experience is shared throughout the world. I can only feel positive about Bruce Lee's of using the martial arts to help unite the world in peace. I am very aware of the power that martial artist actors have due to entertainment industry exposure. It is my quest to utilize that exposure to be the best ambassador for martial arts I can and bring the world together as much as possible. Live by the philosophy of the martial arts—learn to fight so you don't have to fight.

"Martial arts have become accepted throughout the world. The popularity of the martial arts in movies and as a sport has given it mainstream appeal. It is my quest to utilize that exposure to be the best ambassador for martial arts I can and bring the world together as much as possible."

Henry Look
The Virtue of Honor

Kuo Lien Ying. Han Hsing-Yuen. Professor Yu Peng Shi and his wife, Madam Yu. Chen Xiaowang. Chang Tung Sheng: All great masters, all great teachers with whom Henry Look has sought guidance and found answers to his internal martial arts questions.

For nearly a half-century, Sifu Henry Look, born Look Moon-Hong in 1927 in Sacramento, California, has been delighting crowds with his internal mastery of tai chi chuan, hsing-I and I-Chuan Standing Meditation. Although he studied martial arts as a child in Guangdong, China, his years following World War II were spent as one of the world's most-successful architects. His specialty was Japanese restaurants, where he has 26 Benihana's to his credit.

But soon the pressure of creating another masterpiece, combined with constant overseas travel, began to take their toll. Doctors told him in the early 1960s that unless he found something to calm his nerves, he might not live much longer. That's when he discovered master Kuo Lien Ying, who was teaching Guang Ping Yang tai chi chuan.

It was a martial arts marriage made in heaven and consummated on a daily basis in San Francisco Chinatown's famed Portsmouth Square Park. The deeper Sifu Look dove into the seemingly benign movements of tai chi, the more layers he found. And the more layers he found, the more excited he grew about the discovery process.

His life as a student has been to find the meaning hidden within internal martial arts. His life as a teacher has been to help students find the pure pleasure in practicing something so simple, yet so complex.

Sifu Look has become one of America's most-respected and honored masters because he is known as a man of honor, a man of tradition, and a man of unswerving dedication to his students and the Chinese martial arts.

When asked to describe the qualities inherent in a good martial artist, Sifu Look explained, "They should have the five virtues of life: respect, loyalty, integrity, humility and honor." Sifu Henry Look has built a reputation by practicing those qualities every day of his life.

Kung-Fu Masters

"All the students wanted to learn his techniques, but he refused to teach them. The sifu wanted to teach the dim mak techniques to my uncle, but he refused to learn it because he did not want to be responsible for killing someone with his own hands."

Q: How long have you been practicing martial arts?
A: I was 8 when I began learning southern style kung-fu and the two-man staff from my mother's brothers, Third Uncle and Ninth Uncle. Third Uncle was reputed to be one of the best and most-skillful kung-fu fighters in the region, but he had a quick, violent temper. Ninth Uncle, who had a mild temper, learned kung-fu to protect himself against his elder brother. Ninth Uncle's sifu was highly respected for his special skill in dim mak techniques. All the students wanted to learn his techniques, but he refused to teach them. The sifu wanted to teach the dim mak techniques to my uncle, but he refused to learn it because he did not want to be responsible for killing someone with his own hands.

Q: What is your martial arts background?
A: I began with southern style kung-fu while growing up in Guangdong, China, in the 1930s, shortly before World War II. When I was a teenager in the early 1940s, after our family returned from China and lived in San Francisco, I learned boxing from the firemen at the firehouse across the street from where we lived. In the summer of 1945, before the end of World War II, I was drafted and served in the U.S. Marines. Some of my Marine Corps training includes tactical hand-to-hand combat and bayonet fighting. After the war ended, my tour of duty was in northern China, where I learned judo privately from a sergeant who was a former AAU judo champion. Then I had more formal training in competitive boxing skills. After

"In the late 1960s, my first exposure to internal martial arts came in Hong Kong where I saw many people practicing tai chi and many martial arts. At that time, Bruce Lee and I frequently crossed each other's paths. Although we were never formally introduced, we lived in the same apartment complex and shared a common central courtyard. We nodded to each other as we passed to and from our apartments."

winning six bouts (five KOs and one decision) I told the boxing coach I wanted to quit because my nose was too flat already.

In the late 1960s, my first exposure to internal martial arts came in Hong Kong where I saw many people practicing tai chi and many martial arts. At that time, Bruce Lee and I frequently crossed each other's paths. Although we were never formally introduced, we lived in the same apartment complex and shared a common central courtyard. We nodded to each other as we passed to and from our apartments.

Q: Who were your first teachers?
A: I will only include my teachers after I formally started training in tai chi chuan: Kuo Lien Ying, Han Hsing-Yuen, professor Yu Peng Shi and his wife, Madam Yu. I also wish to honor and pay my utmost respects to Chen Xiaowang, for teaching me the Chen taiji short form, and Chang Tung Sheng, for his private intensive training in shuai chiao techniques.

Kung-Fu Masters

"One month after I left Master Kuo because of personal reasons, I was very fortunate to meet Master Han Hsing Yuen, a senior disciple of Wang Xiang Zhai, the founder of Da Chang Chuan."

Q: Would you tell us some interesting stories of your early days in kung-fu training?

A: One day Third Uncle was teaching kung-fu in his house's front courtyard. A local sheriff appeared with three deputies, forced their way in, and wanted to arrest Third Uncle for smoking illegal opium. The first two deputies who tried to arrest him were punched to the ground. The sheriff and his remaining deputy chased Third Uncle, who was running through the side yard to the rear of the house. When the sheriff and deputy surrounded him, the sheriff quickly got smashed in the solar plexus and the deputy was kicked into a nearby 24-inch round by 18-inch tall "honey pot." His clothes were completely drenched and he was covered from head to toe with smelly urine and waste. He ran screaming through the side courtyard and down the street, jumped into the nearest fish pond and washed himself clean.

One month after I left Master Kuo because of personal reasons, I was very fortunate to meet Master Han Hsing Yuen, a senior disciple of Wang Xiang Zhai, the founder of Da Chang Chuan (I-Chuan). The first training session with Master Han consisted of I-Chuan or "8 standing meditation postures." Twelve reputable sifu from the San Francisco Bay area were in attendance for this first class. Standing in a slightly crouched position with our arms raised, we simulated embracing a giant ball for five minutes in each position, which meant a total of 40 minutes without breaks. After 10-to-15 minutes, everybody began to sweat profusely; some even shook uncontrollably up and down. I was fortunate to have trained in the standing meditation posture "universal post" each day for seven years with Master Kuo. And so I just stood there for 40 minutes without any discomfort.

Q: Were you a natural at martial arts? Did the movements come easily to you?
A: I'm not sure I could have been called a "natural." Martial art movements come easily for me because of the many other sports I had participated in during my young life. I was fortunate and blessed with good coordination.

Q: How has your personal martial arts developed over the years?
A: "The more I know, the less I know." Knowledge gained through martial arts development helped me to appreciate and gain a deeper understanding so I could pay more respect toward others and to myself. This has helped me gather more strength—physically and mentally—in my daily life.

Q: With all the technical changes during the last 30 years, do you think there are still "pure" systems, such as tai chi chuan, choy lee fut, wing chun kung-fu, etc.?
A: I believe all martial art styles have their good points, advantages and disadvantages. How do we recognize what is pure? Master Kuo taught me two simple, important martial arts philosophies, which I live by and use in my practice, training and teaching. In analyzing your movements, ask yourself: "What is efficiency?" and "What is the shortest distance between two points?" If you can answer those questions in your movements and applications, then the art is simple and pure in its effectiveness.

"Knowledge gained through martial arts development helped me to appreciate and gain a deeper understanding so I could pay more respect toward others and to myself. This has helped me gather more strength—physically and mentally—in my daily life."

Q: Do you think different "schools" are important?
A: To carry on the true lineage of any art, it is important the true basic foundation and philosophy are consistent. Though the methods may differ, it is important the basic philosophy remains intact.

Kung-Fu Masters

"We have a host of good, qualified teachers in this country and it doesn't matter whether they migrated from the East or trained in both the East and West. They were trained here as well as in the East and are better than many teachers from the East or West. Plus, they can communicate instructions better because they have a better command of the English language."

Q: What is your opinion of other sport competitions such as kickboxing and the Ultimate Fighting Championship?
A: I think it is great and interesting to see different sports with different techniques. All sports have certain limitations of competition in longevity. I could play many sports when I was in my late teens and early 20s. Now I would not think of attempting to play those sports. Certain sports or martial arts you can do almost forever. Take, for example, my friend and idol Gene LeBell. He was my favorite in the annual AAU Judo Championship more than 50 years ago. We met again recently in an *Inside Kung-Fu* photo shoot and I found he is still spectacular! All sports are good if forms and techniques are trained properly with a good teacher or coach.

Q: Do you think that kung-fu in the West has caught-up with the East as far as skill level?
A: It is difficult to say. In this country, our discipline, daily life, educational system and training regimen are vastly different. Given the same condition and environment as was found in China, we in the U.S. can produce unlimited kung-fu skills that will equal or surpass our martial arts forefathers. We have a host of good, qualified teachers in this country and it doesn't matter whether they migrated from the East or trained in both the East and West. For example, my good friends S.L. Martin, Glenn Wilson and Mike Patterson are all great teachers. They were trained here as well as in the East and are better than many teachers from the East or West. Plus, they can communicate instructions better because they have a better command of the English language. Another major difference between the East and West is their training schedules. Young, talented people in this country either have to attend school or work full time, while in China many young talents are orphans being trained in

temples or receiving financial assistance from the government. Many young people in America today are beginning to show signs of interest in martial arts because China is hosting the Olympics in 2008. If we can produce so many great athletes in this country, why can't we also produce great martial artists?

Q: Martial arts today are often referred to as a sport. Would you agree with this definition?
A: Today, some teachers consider martial arts a sport. In the old days, taking martial arts to learn self-defense was a way of life. If you talk about self-defense, it is not a sport. As for wushu? If you mention wushu as a sport, many teachers and practitioners feel offended. In my opinion, it is not perfection in performance, it is the true expression of the art.

Q: Do you feel that you still have further to go in your studies?
A: Yes! Definitely. I traveled this difficult road for over 15 years before I got a feel for internal strength and began to better understand the art. Even after studying for 30 years, I still feel I have a long way to go in my development.

"Today, some teachers consider martial arts a sport. In the old days, taking martial arts to learn self-defense was a way of life. If you mention wushu as a sport, many teachers and practitioners feel offended. In my opinion, it is not perfection in performance, it is the true expression of the art."

Q: Do you think working with weapons will help the physical side of kung-fu?
A: Yes, because weapons are an extension of the hands. The training helps focus the mind and body coordination with directions of power projections.

Q: Do you think the practitioner's personal training should be different than his teaching schedule as an instructor?
A: All teachers should be truthful and share their genuine art with students. Unfortunately, there are many disloyal and dishonest students who forget who planted the seeds for them. For that reason, many teachers are skeptical in training untested students the so-called secrets.

Kung-Fu Masters

"Dedication with honesty to oneself. Training in martial arts is a long road to success. There is no shortcut in leaning the proper skill in any style. Today, too many students are not willing to sacrifice enough time or be patient enough to train properly."

Many years ago, my teacher, Master Han from Hong Kong, sent me written permission, which allowed me to teach hsing-i chuan in this country. He also included a message: "You now have the ability to teach, but you must be very discreet in choosing your students, because hsing-i chuan is considered one of highest and effective kung-fu systems. If trained properly, the energy you project can blow up Tai Shan Mountain." (Tai Shan Mountain is one of the biggest mountains in China.)

Q: What is your best advice to martial artists everywhere?
A: Dedication with honesty to oneself. Training in martial arts is a long road to success. There is no shortcut in leaning the proper skill in any style.

Q: What do you consider to be the major changes in the arts since you began your training?
A: Today, too many students are not willing to sacrifice enough time or be patient enough to train properly. Another major change is the law. Teachers are limited in their methods of training, because the risk of being sued is so great.

Q: If you could train with one person, dead or alive, who would it be?
A: My Sifu Han's elder brother, Han Hsing-Chao, who himself is over 90 now and lives in Pearl River, a small city near Macao next to Hong Kong. I also would have liked to study more shuai chao with Chang Dung Sheng. Upon my discharge from the U.S. Marines after World War II, I returned to China and lived with my grandmother and uncle for a year. I wish I would have started learning kung-fu from my uncle at that time.

Q: What would you say to someone who is interested in learning martial arts?

A: If you are really serious about learning authentic martial arts, spend time researching the styles that interest you. Visit different schools, making sure to observe the styles and the quality of instructors and their teaching methods. Do not get carried away by fancy moves and cheap talk. Start only when you feel comfortable with certain styles. And most of all, be patient and dedicated. If you do not have desire to become a quality martial artist, take up dancing.

Q: What keeps you motivated after all these years?

A: One of my motivations is health related. Back in the late 1960s, I suffered from health problems tied to my business responsibilities. Tai chi was my first motivation to better health. Along the way I learned other martial arts which continued to help my daily existence. The older I got the more I learned, and the more I understood the true value of these arts. Now with the knowledge I have gained through martial arts, I wish to share my good fortune with others.

"Along the way I learned other martial arts which continued to help my daily existence. The older I got the more I learned, and the more I understood the true value of these arts. Now with the knowledge I have gained through martial arts, I wish to share my good fortune with others."

Q: Do you think free-fighting is necessary to achieve good street-fighting skills?

A: Definitely! If you want to achieve good fighting skills in the streets, it is a must to practice free-fighting without rules. There is no shame in getting a bloody nose or black eye in practice. If you have never experienced or seen stars nor heard birds chirping in your head, you will never know what it is like to be hit or thrown on your head. This experience will always help you to be cautious. Naturally, when we are young with more brawn than brains, we always think the fist is the answer to all conflicts.

Kung-Fu Masters

"My training philosophy is to have continued health and a better understanding of others. All the years of practice in martial arts has led me to appreciate all the good things I have gained through the years of disciplined training of the mind and body."

Q: What is your opinion about mixing styles? Does the practice of one nullify the effectiveness of the other?
A: I have no objection to people wanting to mix styles. I think it is good to have some understanding of different styles. However, it is very difficult for any beginner to have a fair understanding and judgment of the basic principle of each art. Whether it is business or martial arts, one who understands his special skills and knows how to utilize that knowledge will eventually be ahead of the game. I do not believe any normal human intelligent mind can become super-efficient in every endeavor it undertakes.

Q: What is the philosophical basis for your training?
A: My training philosophy is to have continued health and a better understanding of others. My late mother always reminded us, "If you have your health, you have everything." I always tell my students, "If you practice your martial art correctly, it will be correct for your health." And vice versa.

Q: Do you have a particular martial arts experience that inspired your training?
A: When I engaged in hsing-i pushing hands with Professor Yu, he always lifted me a couple of feet off the ground without grabbing my hands—no matter how I tried to keep rooted to the ground. It is hard to believe, but it is true. One day I accidentally ran into Kuo as he was walking through a doorway. Although he was over 83 at the time, he just bounced me up and sent me sailing through the air. I must have landed 12 feet away. That was my first experience in fa-jing.

Q: After all your years of training and experience, can you explain the meaning behind the practice of kung-fu?
A: All the years of practice in martial arts has led me to appreciate all the good things I have gained through the years of disciplined training of the mind and body.

Q: How do you think a practitioner can increase their understanding of the spiritual aspect of the arts?
A: Make a life commitment to integrate and unite the mind and body for a healthy life.

Q: What are the most-important qualities of a successful martial artist?
A: A successful martial artist will possess the five virtues of life: respect, loyalty, integrity, humility and honor. I would say to use your skill and knowledge to help others.

Q: What would you tell students about supplementary training?
A: Whatever you do, you have to have good balance with yin and yang. Practice lots of standing meditation such as i-chuan, which will complement any martial arts training and beyond.

"Make a life commitment to integrate and unite the mind and body for a healthy life. We need qualified, responsible instructors to produce students with proper character. With qualified instructors, martial arts will acquire a high level of respect and good standing in the world."

Q: Why do many students leave the martial arts after two or three years of training?
A: There could be many reasons—a lack of motivation, inadequate teachers, et cetera. After teaching for so many years, I realize all students need help staying motivated—fresh ideas with innovations and involvement. This is especially true for today's students, who are more intelligent and educated but lack patience, motivation and commitment.

Q: Have there been times when you felt fear in your training?
A: No! Not in training. Fear of what? Normally, my mind is concentrated on my practice; there is no time for fear.

Q: What are your thoughts on the future of the martial arts?
A: We need qualified, responsible instructors to produce students with proper character. With qualified instructors, martial arts will acquire a high level of respect and good standing in the world.

Yang Jwing Ming

The Correct Way of Life

Dr. Yang Jwing Ming was born in Hsinonou, Taiwan, in 1946, shortly after the end of World War II. He began his kung-fu training at the age of 15 under the Shaolin White Crane master Cheng Gin-Gsao. He entered Tamkang College in Taipei Hsien to study Physics at 18 years of age and began his study of Shaolin Long Fist under Master Li Mao Ching, eventually becoming an assistant instructor. Two years later, suffering stomach problems caused by childhood malnutrition, Master Cheng advised him to study tai chi chuan from Master Kao Tao, who worked as a high school teacher.

Dr. Yang came to United States to study at Purdue University in Indiana. In 1975 he founded the Purdue Chinese Kung-Fu Club and taught Shaolin long fist and tai chi. When his white crane master passed away in 1976, Dr. Yang felt he had not even learned half of what Master Cheng had to teach. Because of this, he decided to not let the same thing happen to his knowledge—so he began to write books to preserve the knowledge for future generations. Now an internationally-know martial arts author and the president of one of the largest kung-fu organizations in the United States, Dr. Yang currently resides in Boston, Massachusetts, with his family.

Q: When did you decide to teach in the United States?
A: It was in the mid-70s, while attending Purdue University. I wanted to know how Chinese martial arts had developed in America. So I visited many school and I realized that there were many "masters' who did not know anymore than I. Therefore, I decided to organize the Purdue Kung-Fu Club.

Q: You felt a need to begin teaching so young?
A: Not really. Mainly, it helped me to get extra money to send to my mother. My motivation at that time was to earn money for her.

Kung-Fu Masters

"When you are that age you like to fight all the time. You want to be a hero. It was after studying for over a year that my mentality started to change. My teacher's philosophy changed my mind slowly. I began to be deeply influenced by him."

Q: How did you start training in the martial arts?
A: I began when I was 15. I went to learn from a white crane teacher. He lived in the mountains so I had to run all the way up the hills to get to his school. You know, Taiwan is not very big, but it was still very tiring.

Q: Were you attracted to the internal arts for spiritual reasons?
A: No. I just wanted to fight—to show off. That's why I chose white crane kung-fu. When you are that age you like to fight all the time. You want to be a hero. It was after studying for over a year that my mentality started to change. My teacher's philosophy changed my mind slowly. I began to be deeply influenced by him. Of course, this feeling were very different from what I originally expected and believed in.

Q: When did you start learning the internal arts?
A: It was because of my white crane teacher that I began studying tai chi chuan. I had stomach ulcers due to poor nutrition when I was a child. He said that the only way to cure this was to learn tai chi.

Q: Under whom did you study?
A: A man from Peking who was only 29 years old. I knew he was teaching the Yang style that he learned from his father, but I did not really know or care about tai chi's philosophy or history. I went into tai chi only to cure my stomach ulcers—not for its own sake. After only six months the ulcer disappeared and never came back.

"I learned long fist and also tai chi from the same teacher. I was very happy training in long fist, because it is a Northern style and looks very athletic and poetic. It is a beautiful style with a lot of complex kicks."

Q: Did you study any other styles?
A: Yes, I went to Taipei to college. There I learned long fist and also tai chi from the same teacher. I was very happy training in long fist, because it is a Northern style and looks very athletic and poetic. It is a beautiful style with a lot of complex kicks.

Q: How long did you study with him?
A: For over eight years. Every winter I used to go back home and continue my white crane training with my master. I studied white crane under him for over thirteen years. I was with my tai chi teacher for only two-and-a-half years, though. He used to teach soccer in the high school next to mine. One day his soccer team came to our school for a game. I left for few moments and when I came back I saw him fighting against six of my high school students. I thought that a true master wouldn't lose his temper so easily—so I stopped going to his classes.

Kung-Fu Masters

"Tai chi is for helping you to calm your mind and circulate the internal energy, not to torture you. So the major purpose for tai chi study is to train your mind to the correct way of life. The goal is not the training itself."

Q: So you have bad memories of him?
A: Not at all! When I came to United States, almost twelve years later, I realized that my tai chi foundation was very good compared to other people—and it was because of him. He gave me a deep understanding of the art and taught me the secrets of relaxation and meditation.

Q: What do you emphasize in your tai chi classes?
A: I don't teach tai chi for the first month. I just teach how to concentrate, calm the mind, and loosen the body. If the student can't do these things, he's wasting his time trying to learn tai chi.

Q: These are the most important points in tai chi?
A: Basically. Concentration, relaxation, and a good breathing technique. Only with these can the *chi* circulate around your body. After a month of this, the students will have experienced a little bit of the basics and can decide whether to stay or leave. If they stay, the next step is teaching them the form. This takes around four months to learn and over a month to correct. Then, if the student want to practice tai chi for health he can go home and train by themselves, but if they want to learn self-defense then I start teaching them push hands.

Q: Why are there so many different tai chi forms?
A: It is not that there are that many, but that many people have modified the original form. For instance, if you practice tai chi for health you don't need to learn the whole form comprised of 200 movements. Tai Chi is for helping you to calm your mind and circulate the internal energy, not to torture you. So the major purpose for tai chi study is to train your mind to the correct way of life. The goal is not the training itself. A person could learn ten different forms and still ignore the key points of the art if they are not careful.

Q: Do you think Bruce Lee's movies helped kung-fu?
A: Bruce Lee's movies increased the martial arts market but they also encouraged teenagers to fight with *nunchakus*. Because Bruce Lee was actually using a mixture of kung-fu and karate that he called *jeet kune do*, many martial artists and kung-fu practitioners were misled by his films and started training and fighting like a karate man. Because of this, the Chinese kung-fu society lost its traditional roots. Even today, a lot of people are confused about what traditional Chinese martial arts really are. All the movies emphasized killing—and that gave the impression that kung-fu is inherently violent.

"Bruce Lee was actually using a mixture of kung-fu and karate that he called jeet kune do. *Because of this, the Chinese kung-fu society lost its traditional roots. Even today, a lot of people are confused about what traditional Chinese martial arts really are."*

Q: Can you tell us about the spiritual aspects?
A: I always say that tai chi is a spiritual art. It is impossible to describe the greatness of a Picasso painting, you have to reach certain level of artistic awareness to really understand his genius. The same is true with tai chi—the higher one gets, the deeper the satisfaction.

Q: Why is tai chi so popular in China?
A: Many people think it is because of the martial aspects, but it is not. The reason is that in tai chi, the internal power is stronger that in the other arts. In tai chi, every movement has to be exactly right and has to be in accordance with the internal energy. For every movement there is "intention." Because the intention is strong, the chi is strong. This is very different from other styles, because they don't emphasize intention as much.

Q: Why is intention so valuable?
A: In qi gong training, the first thing you do is regulate your body. You learn to become relaxed so you can regulate your breathing and regulate

Kung-Fu Masters

"There is a great mystery around Chinese martial arts, I don't know why, but that's the biggest obstacle to true learning. We must strip away the mystery and teach the people everything behind the art."

your mind. Only when you have mastered these three elements is your mind calm and strong enough to lead the chi. After that, you regulate the spirit. Don't forget that tai chi is part of Chinese qi gong.

Q: How does this help people?
A: The thing is, you must first educate people about the art—how to relax and breathe correctly. Just by knowing and doing this, high blood pressure drops and other problems go away. In six months a person can start to tell the difference.

Q: Do you still work as an engineer?
A: No. I quit my engineering job sometime ago because I didn't like to be pushed around. I decided to focus on researching and writing. I wrote the books as a way of sharing information and knowledge. For instance, I compiled everything I knew about *chi na* and wrote a book. Later on, I realized I had put together everything in a more systematic order than how it was taught to me. I was happy because it helped the students—and I also got money for it!

Q: It seems that you don't hide anything you know. In Chinese martial art this is not very common.
A: There is a great mystery around Chinese martial arts, I don't know why, but that's the biggest obstacle to true learning. We must strip away the mystery and teach the people everything behind the art. If you teach something, then it's not a secret anymore. A secret is something that

everybody hides—if you talk about it and teach it, it is no longer a secret. My first teacher told me that you have to learn from different sources and then compare them. This method is not accepted by many traditional teachers.

Q: Why is it so difficult to organize kung-fu competitions?
A: There are two major reasons. First, the original purpose of kung-fu was to attack vital points. Of course, in a competition both fighters must be protected, so the original purpose of training and sparring is already lost. If you have been training hard and those techniques are part of your natural, instinctive reactions, it is very hard to control them. Second, there are more than 100 different styles of kung-fu, and each one specializes in something different. So it is very difficult to decide what kind of techniques you have to ban because that would limit the fighting ability of some competitors.

Q: Do you think there is such thing as the "best" style?
A: No, and I'll tell you why. We have many styles in kung-fu. For many years they have been fighting with each other. Sometimes this one wins, the next time that one is the winner. Style doesn't matter, the important thing is how good the fighter is. There is no best style, only good students and bad students. I like to say that even the lousy styles have good students, and good styles have lousy students.

Q: What's the relationship between tai chi and the Tao?
A: That's very difficult to explain but I'll try to do my best. Tai chi derives from the Tao. When you come to the end of tai chi, you play tai chi. You're nothing without tai chi. The final goal in tai chi, in the classical sense, is the discovery of one's center point. This is the way to the enlightenment—the center point—so one's life is not affected by emotions. The spiritual side of tai chi derives from Taoism. So we can say that the final goal of tai chi is to become neutral—unaffected by spiritual, emotional, or physical attacks.

Gerald Okamura

Heart of the Dragon

HE IS A MASTER OF WEAPONS AND AN EXPERT AT THE FEARED ART OF KUNG-FU SAN SOO. WITH MANY YEARS OF UPPER-ECHELON MARTIAL ARTS TRAINING UNDER HIS BELT, GERALD OKAMURA IS STILL GOING FULL STEAM AHEAD. WHEN TALKING TO HIM, IT IS OBVIOUS THAT HIS FAVORITE TOPICS OF CONVERSATION ARE THE STATE OF MARTIAL ARTS AND THE ACTIVITIES OF HIS CLOSE-KNIT FAMILY. BUT DESPITE HIS MANY MOVIES AND TELEVISION APPEARANCES, OKAMURA IS EMINENTLY APPROACHABLE—A MAN WHO WOULD JUST AS SOON SHARE A JOKE OR FUNNY STORY AS TEACH A LETHAL TECHNIQUE. HIS ENTIRE PERSONALITY IS TYPIFIED BY THE FACT THAT HIS FAVORITE PERSON TO MAKE FUN OF IS HIMSELF.

BOTH A MARTIAL ARTS EXPERT AND ONE OF THE MOST RECOGNIZED STUNTMAN IN HOLLYWOOD, OKAMURA IS A SUPERB TECHNICIAN, A CONSUMMATE TEACHER AND A DYNAMIC SHOWMAN. HIS FANS KEEP CLOSE TABS ON HIS CAREER AND HIS DRAGONFEST CHARITY FUNDRAISER IS ATTENDED BY MANY OF THE TOP MARTIAL ARTISTS, ACTORS, AND STUNTMAN IN THE WORLD. ONE REASON FOR THIS SUCCESS IS OKAMURA'S MODESTY—HE DOES NOT SEEK THE LIMELIGHT FOR AND REFUSES TO GET INVOLVED IN ANY POLITICAL CONTROVERSIES. HE STRIVES FOR A LIFE OF TRANQUILITY AND CONTENTMENT, AND IS REFRESHED BY THE GREAT SATISFACTION HE DERIVES FROM PURSUING THE MARTIAL ARTS WITH TOTAL COMMITMENT AND DISCIPLINE.

Q: How did you get started in martial arts?
A: I started judo when I was 12. Kawasaki sensei taught me lessons at the local church. Many of my friends got into it so I decided to take the classes too. I remember that aikido was also being taught at the church but you had to be invited to that particular class. We would sneak in and watch because in the 1950s martial arts training was very secretive.

From judo I moved to kendo at the local YMCA and taekwondo during my three-year tour of duty with the U.S. Army. I was stationed outside of Seoul as part of a military advisory group and a lot of U.S. servicemen learned Korean martial arts during their stays in Korea, including Chuck Norris, whom I worked with later on in the movie "The Octagon."

Kung-Fu Masters

"Kung-fu san soo doesn't limit the practitioner to just one form of combat. It is a method that opens your mind and helps you to see the opportunities that lie ahead."

Q: How did you start kung-fu san soo?
A: I got a job with McDonnell-Douglas Aircraft and in 1962 I picked up a flyer from the late Jimmy H. Woo's kung-fu san soo School in El Monte, California. Having come from traditional Japanese and Korean martial arts where everything is very structured, the versatility and freedom of this style really appealed to me. In 1965 I received a black belt from Jimmy Woo and later on I established my own school and began to teach in East Los Angeles.

Q: What style does san soo most resemble?
A: Many of the movements are very similar to aikido, while other are purely san soo but there really isn't one particular style to san soo. There are no rules to limit applications or techniques. I think this style was a natural stepping stone for me since I was able to incorporate it into my previous training. My judo background also helped to make me a well-rounded martial artist. For most martial artists, hitting the ground is not something familiar. A judo, jiu-jitsu, or aikido man, or a wrestler, knows how to react and move under those conditions. If someone tries to throw me, at least I am somewhat familiar with the technique and I can try to counter or adapt properly to the attack. Kung-fu san soo doesn't limit the practitioner to just one form of combat. It is a method that opens your mind and helps you to see the opportunities that lie ahead. Unfortunately, a lot of people at that time were very close-minded about their training and that limited the way they thought.

Q: What was Jimmy Woo's teaching philosophy?

A: He used to tell us that everyone uses the same alphabet to learn how to construct a word, then they use these words to construct sentences. After mastering those, the individual uses them to form their own ideas about the world and themselves. From this point, the possibilities for growth are unlimited. Once you acquire this knowledge, you combine the different aspects of the art to form your own identity. In the beginning you imitate the moves of a higher level performer, but after a while, you develop your own moves that work with the way you're built or the way you move. The key is you come up with your own identity. Someone can spell your name, but only you can sign your name.

"I have been making weapons for all these years and I dare to say that I came up with several interesting variations of a number of traditional types of weaponry. I used to call them my toys; but once they are out of the bag, they are not toys anymore!"

Q: You are known as a master weapon-maker. How did you start?

A: One day I went to buy a pair of *sai* but I couldn't find any that fit right or felt comfortable in my hands. So I made my own. I have been making weapons for all these years and I dare to say that I came up with several interesting variations of a number of traditional types of weaponry. I used to call them my toys; but once they are out of the bag, they are not toys anymore! Different martial artist that I knew seemed to enjoy all the things I made so I kept doing it. I'm more into ninja-type weapons that can be concealed. Utilizing everyday things gives you the element of surprise which gives you an edge. The philosophy behind san soo is that you fight with whatever you have and as far as weapons is concerned, I was

Kung-Fu Masters

"I had long hair at that time but they made me wear a scull cap and I had to have it on all day. It was hot as hell but it got me started. That was my introduction to the limelight. Not all that glamorous."

taught not to disregard or discard anything you have at hand. Use what you have until you have no use for it.

Q: How did you get started in the movies?
A: One day Jimmy Woo was called by David Chow, who at that time was the technical advisor for the *Kung-Fu* television series during its first year. David said he wanted someone to play a Shaolin monk in the series. Jimmy didn't know the industry so he requested that someone come to pick him up in a limousine at his house, then he asked for a lot of money, too. So when David couldn't come up with the money Jimmy declined the offer and next day came into class and told me to go in his place. Not knowing the business and being naïve at the time, I just went over to Warner Brothers and I introduced myself to David Chow, who could have just as easily sent me home because I wasn't Jimmy H. Woo. But I guess he thought I could fit the role so I got a job. I worked on it for one day and played a Shaolin monk in one of the flashback scenes, and that's how I got started in the business. I had long hair at that time but they made me wear a scull cap and I had to have it on all day. It was hot as hell but it got me started. I came in at 6:30am, got into make-up, stayed in make-up all day, and then didn't get in until overtime for just a few minutes. That was my introduction to the limelight. Not all that glamorous.

Q: How long did you work on *Kung-Fu*?
A: Just that one episode—it was pretty much at the end of the first year. The second year, the executive producer was going to introduce another level of Shaolin monks called disciples. So he interviewed for those positions but they never got around to working the disciples into the script.

The next year another san soo instructor got hired for a movie called *The Killer Elite* with James Caan. It was a good movie but it could have been better. It was too early, number one, they held Sam Peckinpah to a PG rating instead of going all the way to an R rating. At that time, just

showing *nunchaku* gave you an R rating. It was crazy. My audition for the part actually came about when my friend asked me if he could borrow some of my weapons for the try-out. So I said, "They're my weapons, and if they go on an audition I'm going along with them." So I took two suitcases and a couple of duffel bags and we had an audition at Samuel Goldwyn Studios with Sam Peckinpah and some stunt coordinators. I came in with this whole array of different weapons and I did a whole show for them. I even had a cane that was a blow gun.

In one of the scenes I read for in *Killer Elite* they had a assassination attempt at the airport. So I came up with the idea of concealing a stainless steel rod in an arm cast. I had friends who worked on an ambulance, so one Sunday we made an arm cast, and concealed the rod in it. But it was too ninja-like for the times and they didn't use it. But a few

"They interviewed a lot of top martial artists from a lot of different styles for Killer Elite. *Sterling Siliphant wrote it and he had experience in the martial arts, but people just didn't get the concept. But in a way it was good. It was 1978 and things weren't as tough as they are now for martial artists to break in."*

years later when some of the ninja movies came out, things like that became hot. So *Killer Elite* was just too much ahead of its time. I don't think the stunt coordinators had very much experience in that kind of fighting.

They interviewed a lot of top martial artists from a lot of different styles for *Killer Elite*. But if you couldn't sell a punch or a kick they sent you

Kung-Fu Masters

"After Killer Elite *I met a lot of big people including Burt Young. He gave me a bump on the head and I still remember that bump."*

packing. If you were too quick and they couldn't see the punch they sent you home. Sterling Siliphant wrote it and he had experience in the martial arts, but people just didn't get the concept. But in a way it was good. It was 1978 and things weren't as tough as they are now for martial artists to break in.

Q: So it was easier to get into the movies then?
A: Oh, yeah. There just wasn't that many high-level martial artists in L.A. who were going after acting parts. Now its tough. After *Killer Elite* I met a lot of big people including Burt Young. He gave me a bump on the head and I still remember that bump. But then the following year I got a part in a B movie called *Chesty Anderson* for a day. A lot of girls and lot of big boobs—and I guess the biggest boob was me. All I had to do was be an instructor at a training facility. But I was working, you know? Then I think I did a lot of small things like *Matt Houston, TJ Hooker,* and *Knight Rider*. Because of my look, I always played a heavy.

Q: How was your training going during this time?
A: Well, just around this time I got promoted up to 5th degree with Jimmy. And after the 5th degree I got out of the organization and never got tested again so that's where I stand right now. As I mentioned before, I started my own school when I was still with Jimmy, but we've been there for 30 years, since about 1970. When the first article came out about me in *Inside Kung-Fu* in about 1975 or so, I think there was a little jealousy from Jimmy. I was never a threat to him or disloyal to him in any

way, but that seemed to open a gap between us. But I have nothing but good feelings for Jimmy.

Q: During this whole time you still kept the McDonnell Douglas job?
A: I would take vacation to do all the movie parts; but in the beginning a lot of the parts got cut out. So the joke was always that my part was probably on during the commercial. So I guess the family life was a little tough, but the wife did a good job of keeping us together. But I would work for a whole week and then only be on for two or three seconds. So when you would have to watch an hour show just to see yourself for a few seconds a lot of people would laugh—but, hey, I was proud of it, you know? And it still excites me.

Now that I'm a little more known a lot of my stuff appears on the cable channels so I get seen a little more. I've done things like *Blade*, *The Shadow*, and *Lethal Weapon 4*. I did that last one for about 3 weeks and then I'm hardly ever seen in it. My family had to watch the tape 10 times, back and forth in slow motion, just to find me. And out of everyone I was the only one out of focus. But I didn't care because at least I was in the movie! Same with *Blade*—I didn't have a speaking part and I didn't get to fight but I got to sit around a table as part of The Council, so I got a lot of screen time. I actually got a lot more in the theatrical release than on the rental.

"I would work for a whole week and then only be on for two or three seconds. So when you would have to watch an hour show just to see yourself for a few seconds a lot of people would laugh—but, hey, I was proud of it, you know? And it still excites me."

Kung-Fu Masters

"The movies appearances are good for all the kids I see at the tournaments I go to. When they see me they ask for autographs and it gives me something I can do for them to give them a positive impression of martial arts."

I've also got this on-going character in a series of B-movies, as a CIA agent named Fu. I started out being the bad guy then turned into a good guy, so I don't die. In one of the movies, *Day of the Warrior*, I play an Elvis impersonator in Las Vegas. I think I make a pretty good Elvis. The way it started was that a man called me up and said, "I hear you do a bad Elvis impersonation." I said, "You got that right. You been talking to some of the people on my other sets." So it comes down that he's looking for an Elvis and he says, "Now you've got to be bad—bad bad—not good bad." And I say, "You've got your man." They rented out the lounge at the Maxim and I had to do the Elvis moves to lip sync. I looked really awful up there, and guys from work just laughed like crazy.

But the movies appearances are good for all the kids I see at the tournaments I go to. When they see me they ask for autographs and it gives me something I can do for them to give them a positive impression of martial arts.

Q: Is this where the idea for Dragonfest came from?
A: In a way. I saw how much the kids liked to see me due to the movies and TV, and I thought why not give them a chance to see even more actors and martial artists. My son-in-law Gabe Frimmel and I started it. The problem is that martial arts celebrities are never around in one place for the public to meet. So Gabe and I got some tables and we rented a little hall and we got some other guys to come down and sign autographs. We don't pay them anything because it's for several different charities like pediatric aids. So they can sell their pictures, video tapes, or whatever or just sign pictures for free. The people can talk to the stars just like I'm talking to you. And we have vendors who rent tables and sell martial arts gear also. It's just an informal get together to give something back to the

public and help out kids by doing it. I really think it's a neat idea.

Q: It sounds like you get along with everybody.
A: I have a good rapport because many celebrities are trained in some kind of martial art. Erin Gray, for example, called and said she wanted to be part of this thing. And I found out from speaking to her that she also teaches tai chi. The first year we started small, but got good response. Then the next year was bigger and we moved into a bigger place, and then we went into the Glendale Civic Center. The rivalries that exist between styles can all be put aside for a day. So it makes me feel really good that the martial arts community, as well as the public, can get so much out of it.

Q: What was it like training with Jimmy H. Woo?
A: More important than anything else was the ability to execute the techniques. Forms were kind of secondary for him. He felt that is was a sort of isometric exercise. The biggest difficulty was his language. His used to call the "temple," the "dimple." And I couldn't figure out why the hell we were hitting the guy in the dimple for. What if the guy doesn't have a dimple, then what do you do? Many times I would go with him to do demos and I always felt honored to be his dummy. I learned a lot from doing that.

Q: How often did you train?
A: I used to go there 4 days a week, and I'd be there from right after work to about 9 pm, for about 3 or 4 hours. Jimmy's mindset was that as long as you had a toned body that you didn't have to be muscular. You see, the whole philosophy behind the application of san soo is to get the work done the easiest and quickest way. So as far as endurance went it was up

"I saw how much the kids liked to see me due to the movies and TV, and I thought why not give them a chance to see even more actors and martial artists. The people can talk to the stars just like I'm talking to you. And we have vendors who rent tables and sell martial arts gear also. I really think it's a neat idea."

Kung-Fu Masters

"The whole philosophy behind the application of san soo is to get the work done the easiest and quickest way. So as far as endurance went it was up to the individual."

to the individual. He felt that as long as you could pinpoint your target that you don't have to worry about how hard you hit it. Most of the things that other people emphasize we didn't worry about so much. We stretched, for example, but we didn't take it to the extreme. Everything went around the individual's physique. So the beginning you might imitate him, but in the end you did things a little differently. The whole philosophy behind san soo was that everybody starts out with the ABCs. You put those block letters together and you got a word. Then from the block letters you start scribbling. And your signature will be different from mine.

You might write an A that is different-looking than my A, but it is still an A, just altered for how I write. So in san soo you learn the basics and combine them how you want.

Q: Was there any emphasis on philosophy?
A: The only philosophy he ever really stressed was that you should build up self-confidence. But at the same time he also said you needed to add a little humility or you would become arrogant and fall over the other side of the fence. But you had to build up self-confidence—he always stressed that. The other thing that he stressed was that the art is there for anybody. You don't have to look good to get the job done, just get the job done the easiest way you know how. You have to be mature enough to use the art in the sense that it's not for show. If you get into a confrontation and kill a person, he said that you still had to face the laws of society. So were you the winner or the loser? It's funny that he said that because his way of life was just the opposite. He didn't care. So I guess he got mature enough to pass onto us a more mature outlook on life, and at the same time never give up self-confidence.

"You don't have to look good to get the job done, just get the job done the easiest way you know how. You have to be mature enough to use the art in the sense that it's not for show."

Q: Jimmy Woo taught out of the books that were passed down to him from the Shaolin Temple. Do you feel that this makes san soo a pure art?
A: I thought it was originally. But I have since talked to other Chinese people just to interpret the words "san soo." And they say it is more like "garbage disposal." It grabs everything and anything and then you decide what to use. So to me its very generous and I think it takes a mature mind to grasp what you want from it. And that's the beauty of the whole thing. If I don't want one thing then I just move onto something else. You just use whatever works.

Kung-Fu Masters

"When I look at an opponent, I look from the top of their head to the bottom of their feet to see what I can do to him. You have your critical attack points and you have a way of getting to those points. It is almost like a game to figure out how reach them."

Q: So he was teaching san soo long before Bruce Lee ever started JKD?
A: Yes. But not taking away from Bruce, and never having met the man himself, but having worked with both his son and his daughter, and not knowing the real reason why he did what he did, my opinion is that Bruce's martial art was simply for Bruce. Bruce would take anything and use it if it would make him a better fighter. Which to me is what san soo is. We don't call the art "judo," we don't call it "jiu-jitsu," we don't call it anything. For us, the application is the principle. Individual techniques have never been associated with words other people are familiar with. San soo shoots out in all different areas in all different directions. I think the most important quality is that you can utilize the art with any other martial art you know.

Q: So san soo is always evolving?
A: In a way, that's true. When I look at an opponent, I look from the top of their head to the bottom of their feet to see what I can do to him. You have your critical attack points and you have a way of getting to those points. It is almost like a game to figure out how reach them. When you talk about evolving the art you probably need to do that to face other trained martial artists, but as far as the guy on the street, you're not worried about him.

Q: What would you say to people who say that kung-fu san soo is dirty fighting?
A: My philosophy is that I will not turn the other cheek. I will throw the first punch if the situation requires it. In the past it used to be that if you were a martial artist you didn't throw the first punch. Well, the first punch that other guy throws might be enough to put you down. So my philosophy is that if my life or my family's life is threatened I will take the attacker out first. Call it whatever you want, but it's going to keep me safe. So whatever adjective you want to use with san soo—clean, dirty, smooth, rough, whatever—it is an art that will keep you safe.

"My philosophy is that I will not turn the other cheek. I will throw the first punch if the situation requires it. In the past it used to be that if you were a martial artist you didn't throw the first punch. Well, the first punch that other guy throws might be enough to put you down."

Masters Techniques

Master Okamura faces an opponent who attacks with a knife thrust to the midsection (1). Okamura sidesteps and deflects the attack (2), disarms the aggressor, hits him with the handle of the weapon (3), and finishes with a painful wrist-lock (4).

From an on-guard position (1), Master Okamura blocks an attacker's punch with his right hand (2), and follows with a left chop to the neck (3). Stepping inside the attack angle (4), Okamura delivers a finishing elbow attack to the aggressor's midsection (5).

Master Okamura faces an opponent (1). When the aggressor steps in with a punch, Okamura sidesteps and kicks to the outside of the lead leg (2). This brings the attacker down, allowing Okamura to control his head with the left hand (3). He follows with a hammer fist to the neck (5), which finishes the attacker (6).

Masters Techniques

From a ready stance (1), Master Okamura blocks an attacker's roundhouse kick (2). Okamura counters with back fist to the head (3), and follows with a hammer fist to the leg (4). This downs the attacker (5), and allows Okamura to finish him with a claw to the stomach (6).

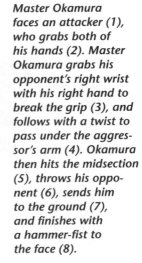

Master Okamura faces an attacker (1), who grabs both of his hands (2). Master Okamura grabs his opponent's right wrist with his right hand to break the grip (3), and follows with a twist to pass under the aggressor's arm (4). Okamura then hits the midsection (5), throws his opponent (6), sends him to the ground (7), and finishes with a hammer-fist to the face (8).

Vernon Rieta

The Shaolin Journey

AFTER YEARS OF UP AND DOWNS IN THE WAY OF SHAOLIN, RIETA KEEPS WALKING THE SAME PATH, IMMERSING HIMSELF IN THE PRACTICE OF HIS BELOVED ART. ACCORDING TO RIETA, BEING ALL CHINESE, PART CHINESE, OR ANY NATIONALITY SHOULD NOT MATTER. IF YOU CAN UNDERSTAND THAT EVERYONE IS CREATED EQUAL, WHAT DIFFERENCE DOES OUTSIDE APPEARANCE MAKE IF THE SPIRIT, MIND, AND BODY ARE TRULY IN LOVE WITH THE ART OF KUNG-FU? "IN ANALYZING SHAOLIN KUNG-FU, I FELT WE SHOULD ORGANIZE A GROUP OF KUNG-FU PRACTITIONERS WHO CAN CONTRIBUTE AND SEE THE BIG PICTURE. MY MAIN CONCERN IS NOT TO BECOME A MILLIONAIRE FROM TEACHING KUNG-FU. IF THAT WERE MY BIGGEST CONCERN I WOULD HAVE TRULY FAILED. WE MIGHT NEVER BECOME FINANCIALLY RICH AT THIS ART, BUT THE CHANCE TO EXPLORE A TREASURE OF KNOWLEDGE HAS ALWAYS BEEN WHAT DRIVES MOST TEACHERS."

WITH ONE FOOT PLANTED IN THE PAST AND THE OTHER ROOTED IN THE PRESENT, RIETA IS CONSIDERED BY MANY TO BE ONE OF THE BEST HUNG GAR KUNG-FU INSTRUCTORS IN THE WORLD. BUT VERNON RIETA'S GOAL HAS NEVER BEEN TO GLORIFY HIMSELF, BUT RATHER TO PRESERVE ALL THE KNOWLEDGE PASSED ONTO HIM BY HIS TEACHERS IN ORDER TO PERPETUATE THE ART OF THE SHAOLIN TEMPLE.

"COMING FROM A PURE ART BACKGROUND," SAYS RIETA, "I CAN APPRECIATE THE UNIQUENESS OF BEING DIFFERENT. THE FUTURE SHOULD BE AN EXTRAORDINARY ADVENTURE THAT CAN SIGNAL RARE AND FANTASTIC VISIONS OF THE ACCUMULATED KUNG-FU KNOWLEDGE SITTING AT OUR DOORSTEP. THOSE LEADERS AMONG US SHOULD BE ABLE TO LOCATE AND LEARN FROM SUCH CONTRIBUTING INDIVIDUALS, TEACHERS AND MASTERS. THE ONGOING EFFORT TO PROBE OUR PERSONAL INTELLECT, PHYSICAL ABILITIES, AND SPIRITUAL POWERS SHOULD NOT CEASE IN OUR LIFETIME BECAUSE OF INTERNAL OR EXTERNAL LIMITS. THE WORD "KUNG-FU" LITERALLY MEANS "HARD WORK," AND WORKING AT WHAT YOU LIKE BEST CAN BRING A TRUE HAPPINESS THAT SHOULD BE SHARED WITH THE REST OF THE WORLD.

Q: How long have you been practicing martial arts?
A: I would say around 41 years, since 1961. I was 11 years old when I formally started and I was strongly influenced by my older brothers. At 6 years old, I saw one of them tear a nickel in half with his bare fingers. Seeing one

Kung-Fu Masters

"My first teachers were my older brothers. All of took some sort of martial arts style—from Okinawan karate to kenpo karate to pure street fighting. I could not help but see them use some techniques from these arts. My formal introduction to kung-fu was with the Jing Mo Kung-Fu Association (Chinese Physical Culture Club)."

other brother do kenpo karate forms, and then hearing fight stories from my other brother's beach boy days in Hawaii was also very formative for me. Growing up in Hawaii, a multi-cultural society with Chinese, Filipino. Japanese, Korean, Thai, Okinawan, Samoan, American and Hawaiian all living together, made it possible for me to experience all the different cultures and all their versions of martial arts. My neighborhood of friends and family has shaped, exposed and influenced me a great deal.

Q: How many styles have you trained in?
A: I have studied many Chinese kung-fu styles, but mainly the Southern-style five families comprised of mok gar, fut gar, hung gar, choy gar and

lau gar. I've also learned choy li fut (long-hand style), paqua (eight diagram palm), tai chi chuan (yang style and ng style), monkey, white crane and praying mantis. Most of the kung-fu schools would mix different kung-fu styles and made them available to all the students. The other styles I was expose to were Japanese Zen archery and judo, Filipino kali-escrima, muay Thai and Brazilian capoiera. All of these styles take years to master, but trying to acknowledge their history and main techniques has been an enjoyable part of the research. Much has been gained by a open-minded attitude that gave me no prejudice. The one style that I truly enjoy is hung gar, because of its accumulated history. I could never run out of material to extract from it. It is the one style that has always taken me to phenomenal introspection and has been a home base for my years of study. Between my teachers, friends, students and research, I have gained a wealth of information that has contributed to my own comprehension.

"The one style that I truly enjoy is hung gar, because of its accumulated history. I could never run out of material to extract from it. It is the one style that has always taken me to phenomenal introspection and has been a home base for my years of study."

My first teachers were my older brothers. All of took some sort of martial arts style—from Okinawan karate to kenpo karate to pure street fighting. I could not help but see them use some techniques from these arts. My formal introduction to kung-fu was with the Jing Mo Kung-Fu Association (Chinese Physical Culture Club). The teacher was Master Lau. He was teaching five families style—mok gar, fut gar, choy gar, lau gar and hung gar. I was a member of many other kung-fu schools in Hawaii, like the Kung Ming Tang Association, and many others. In my younger days of kung-fu training I was such a fanatic I would go to as many kung-fu schools as I could squeeze into a week. Three separate schools within the week—Monday and Wednesday, Tuesday and Thursday, and Friday and Saturday. I concealed my connection to the different schools until the

Kung-Fu Masters

"Most people always look at knowledge as coming from someone who is older. I felt so guilty for being so young that I made the students call me si-hing, instead of the proper protocol of sifu."

Chinese New Year came along and the various associations would require the students to shake the lion head for the Chinese New Year celebration. I would not show-up for Chinese New Year events! But when I was younger I had my share of shaking the lion head during Chinese New Year. I absolutely enjoyed the fireworks, the excitement of being with my friends, and doing kung-fu demonstrations at community celebrations.

After Master Lau, my first teacher, died, I found Bucksam Kong's school in 1965. I really liked him. The style he was doing was hung gar kuen, which was very familiar to me because it is a southern style very similar to my previous method. It blended perfectly into the other styles I was practicing. I stayed with him for many years and eventual helped him to open his mainland branches of siu lum pai in California. Being 21 years old with my own school was heavy task. The people would come up to the office and ask who the head instructor was—I would always get a stare. Most people always look at knowledge as coming from someone who is older. I felt so guilty for being so young that I made the students call me *si-hing*, instead of the proper protocol of *sifu*. I managed to train 180 students by myself. I taught every day for 6 years straight, with schedules from 8:30 AM to 11:00 PM, sometimes six days a week! These extensive and continual days helped me to closely examine how and what I was teaching. Whatever it was that I would be demonstrating for the upcoming months had to be planned in advance so I could research everything I had in my curriculum. It truly made me think for myself and made me stronger as a teacher and as a researcher. My own curiosity made me question what I was teaching and made me more of a perfectionist. This helped me to

answer any questions that the students might throw at me regarding kung-fu.

Even when I had my schools, I was still going to see, learn and study many other styles like jiu-jitsu, escrima, Japanese archery, muay Thai boxing, Hawaiian lua and capoeira. I began to understand human physiology and see the common cord that combines all the abilities we have in our bodies. Like any student finishing university and earning a degree, the journey had just began. Now it was time to fully understand knowledge and think for myself. When exploring physics, I often read about Albert Einstein and physics books to find the answers to my questions. Some times we don't realize that we are what we are because of the people who came before us, and because of our own experiences and development. My fine arts background helped me to think three-dimensionally and see what others don't when looking for techniques that are hidden in the forms. To view what kung-fu is all about in the present, we should understand why it was created and the manner we received it from past masters.

"Martial arts imitates life in many ways. You are there to learn about your mind and how the human body works. Learning how to defend yourself is a given in martial arts, but the real experience comes from the other aspects such as harmony, persistence, confidence, humility, self-respect, courage, and the pursuit of perfection."

Q: Were you a natural at martial arts?
A: Yes, to a certain extent. Some movements came very easy to me and some others I needed to practice over again until I could satisfy myself with my level. I think the best part of me has always been my memory. I could learn a whole kung-fu form in one class session. This was truly help-

Kung-Fu Masters

"I think we need to develop more educational skills because this will give us a more academic status to match the status kung-fu has in the East. Making a living teaching kung-fu has given me the opportunity to devote an extensive amount of time toward education. By doing kung-fu everyday, you will increase your skills more rapidly than if it is practiced occasionally."

ful for me, because I could retain many forms from different schools and teachers. I was like a collection book, storing information I could extract data from and then cross-reference movements to different arts. Of course, analyzing teaching methods and researching philosophies came later. The video camera was not invented when I first started, so having a gifted memory helped my study of kung-fu vastly. That unique skill gave me the ability to learn and study many forms. Being able to execute different kung-fu styles at will made it possible for me to sharpen related moves when practicing a form or a technique.

Q: Who would you have liked to train with?
A: The monks at the Shaolin Temple. It would be nice to meet and train with the kung-fu masters who dedicated their lives to the study of this great art. It would be wonderful to meet the founder of the Shaolin Temple, the great Tamo.

Q: What would you say to someone who is interested in learning martial arts?
A: Martial arts imitates life in many ways. You are there to learn about your mind and how the human body works. Learning how to defend yourself is a given in martial arts, but the real experience comes from the other aspects such as harmony, persistence, confidence, humility, self-respect, courage, and the pursuit of perfection. Walking with your body, mind and spirit eventually becomes a way of life. You will find yourself

dealing honestly with all your own shortcomings. Staying the course, no matter what steps into the road in front of you, is the first movement of your journey. Competition might make it exciting but between the trophies and medals comes self-satisfaction. When you see yourself growing old and stop accepting challenges, it comes another part of your journey to succeed as a human being. Martial arts has always given me all the rewards I need to be fulfilled. You will not be disappointed in martial arts if you give them a chance.

For me, kung-fu is an endless fountain of knowledge and wisdom. Trying to understand what makes us live longer and healthier is just one stop on that trek. You never stop learning about yourself and the things that make your body perform at remarkable levels of skill. The exploration of the mind gives me much excitement. To wonder and conjure up places and things that can be possible with the power of the mind is just incredible. The fruit of the garden is our body and the glow of our effort is the soul.

"For me, kung-fu is an endless fountain of knowledge and wisdom. Trying to understand what makes us live longer and healthier is just one stop on that trek. You never stop learning about yourself and the things that make your body perform at remarkable levels of skill. The exploration of the mind gives me much excitement."

Q: Do you think kung-fu in the West has caught up with the Orient?
A: I think we need to develop more educational skills because this will give us a more academic status to match the status kung-fu has in the East. Making a living teaching kung-fu has given me the opportunity to devote an extensive amount of time toward education. By doing kung-fu everyday, you will increase your skills more rapidly than if it is practiced occasionally. The assorted ways that kung-fu is taught in the East and West are very different. If you're learning kung-fu in Hong Kong it is very limited when it comes to workout space, but each student gets better attention from the teacher.

In the United States you have huge facilities, more group activities, and more private lessons for people who can afford them. The open interaction with other students makes for an open forum that increases kung-fu knowledge—the East doesn't have that. Whenever you fund teachers

Kung-Fu Masters

"Each instructor will teach what he thinks will make his student a better practitioner. It is like standing on top of a mountain with ten people. Each one would give a different opinion on what the best view was. No one would be wrong but they would all help each other to see different things."

(sifus) you support their own study as well as provide the training facilities necessary to broaden, advance, and refine the art. The many schools and full-time teachers help the students also. Fighting rings, kung-fu apparatus and punching bags all become a common environment that bring out the best of the art. Seeing the martial arts in books, events, competitions, and movies has made the West vital to martial arts growth. This has helped to increase the kung-fu foundation in the West. To be totally honest, I would have to say kung-fu development depends on each individual, teacher, and school regardless if you are from the West or East.

Q: Do you think there are still pure systems in kung-fu?
A: I think some accumulated knowledge might have gotten watered down. But if there is one place we can draw information from, it is from the old kung-fu masters. I think we all strive to study a pure system, but we should always include the present and the future. But I am convinced that the ancient forms in kung-fu are universal and can be used by all.

Q: Do you think different schools of kung-fu can co-exist?
A: I think every teacher can shed a different view on the same style. Each instructor will teach what he thinks will make his student a better practitioner. It is like standing on top of a mountain with ten people. Each one would give a different opinion on what the best view was. No one would be wrong but they would all help each other to see different things. I feel cer-

tain that the contribution of different schools is a great asset to everyone.

The main difference is that each style has its own method of training, and each school teaches ways that are unique to their own style. Everyone's priority is different. If you focus on health you might change your style to fit your age. All forms of knowledge are good and the journey is always more important than the destination. Human physiology is the same no matter what style you practice. I look at the applications common to all human traits, condition, mannerism, emotions and attitude. This help to disband the blinders you wear when switching styles or schools.

Q: What is your opinion of sport competitions like kickboxing and the UFC?
A: Sport is really about challenges in a friendly environment.

"Reality starts in the mind and can affect your body if your practice is done without any limitations. The many fighting forms of kung-fu have documented these ideas and principles. That inventory of knowledge and history should be dissected and analyzed better."

There are many differences between a sport and real fighting. No one dies or get seriously injured in a sport except accidentally. The possibility to compete in an event gives you just another road of development. Rating your skill against someone else has always been what drives perfection. What you have to remember is that this is not the only method that can drive perfection. There are many traditional ways as well.

Q: What is the philosophical basis for your martial arts training?
A: The study of Chinese culture has helped me to look at the philosophical principles related to kung-fu. The vast history of China is what makes

Kung-fu Masters

"How I practiced during my teens is different from what I did in my 20s, 30s, 40s, and 50s. What I find interesting in kung-fu is that all the knowledge that has been passed down is contained in the forms. This boundless amount of treasure had made me anxious to open the forms and dive into the minds of the old masters."

kung-fu unique. China's culture, symbolism, mythology, philosophies and religions have created a wonderland to explore and ponder. You have a Buddhist thought, Taoist thought, Confucius thought and many mixtures of them. When I first concentrated on the meaning of kung-fu, I realized that the experience would lead me to investigate Chinese culture. The one thought that echoes most loudly in my mind is that true self-cultivation brings enlightenment. As Lao Tze said, "correct persistence brings good fortune," and "an enlightened person will carry things out to completion." The words of Chinese philosophers and scholars has always been an inspiration to my training.

Q: Is it necessary to engage in sparring to achieve fighting skills?
A: I certainly feel any fighting experience can contribute to your fighting skills. There are two schools of thought—one can move when the apple hits your head, or one can look up and move before the apple hits your head. Both manage to accomplish the job of moving but the one that can surpass any physical limit is the mind. The mind has the power to create scenarios that you might never experience in real life. When it comes to the mind we seldom voyage beyond what is given to us from our teachers. Let's look at form training, for example. I think most people do not feel it is vital to giving you fighting experience. But forms training can be used to train for a real fight by using the imagination to match a real fight scenarios. Students often do not make this mind/body connection. The use of a person in front of you is very important for timing, accuracy and a real life experience, but I do not think the training should stop there if you are looking for real self-defense moves.

The Chinese use a lot of visualization when describing martial movements. They took on the mannerisms of certain animals to help make that mind/body connection. When imagining a crane fighting, you have to become light, stand on one leg, and be ready to strike with the beak. The tiger will leap on an attacker and claw the victim, and a leopard will strike from above or behind.

A kung-fu fighter can practice his fighting every time he uses to conjure up an opponent. Western boxers do it all the time when they shadowbox. Reality starts in the mind and can affect your body if your practice is done without any limitations. The many fighting forms of kung-fu have documented these ideas and principles. That inventory of knowledge and history should be dissected and analyzed better, and is the one place most practitioners have overlooked.

Q: Did you have an experience that inspired you to train?
A: I remember in 1966 when I was practicing kung-fu at a Buddhist Temple in Hawaii—the Nuuanu Temple. I to class early and saw a monk in the kitchen preparing dinner for the other monks. So I thought this would be a great opportunity to ask a real monk about kung-fu. I approached him and asked if he ever did kung-fu. He replied, "Everyday." The he left to serve the dinner. I finally saw the head monk who spoke English quite well and asked him about the monk in the kitchen. "His kung-fu must be really great." I said. The head monk smiled and replied that he was the best cook at the temple. That one reply taught me that any great skill should be considered "kung-fu." I now regard everything I do and can master as "kung-fu."

Kung-Fu Masters

Q: What does the practice of kung-fu mean to you ?
A: Kung-fu is a deep part of my life. But sometimes you feel that you will never master it because your body and mind change as you grow older. How I practiced during my teens is different from what I did in my 20s, 30s, 40s, and 50s. What I find interesting in kung-fu is that all the knowledge that has been passed down is contained in the forms. This boundless amount of treasure had made me anxious to open the forms and dive into the minds of the old masters. The ability to practice independently without holding someone responsible for my exercise is a great help. I also like the idea of living a longer and fuller life by practicing a healthy form of exercise. Kung-fu has been a significant way to help me to achieve these multiple goals and control my own destiny.

Q: Do you think it helps to train with weapons?
A: Yes, quite definitely. I think it completes an evolution to engage in weapons. It will develop different timing and give you functionality. The ability to know the vulnerable parts of the human body is also part of weapons training. Striking with a sword is much different than using a staff. The chain whip will give you a understanding of circular movement and the double swords will make you aware of your footwork. The 18 weapons of kung-fu are a unique assortment of tools that can change your physical abilities and create mental discipline. First comes the mind, then the body, and later the weapons as an extension of the own body. At the very end, of course, comes the environment.

Q: Should an instructor's personal training be different than their teaching schedule?
A: All training should be individual. The ability to achieve greater skill lies in your personal needs. A class session will involve several people, but you are there for your own personal growth and achievement. The sifu's ability to instruct and execute moves needs to be enhanced by class participation. So each student needs to participate fully in order to progress individually. My teaching schedule has always focused on a multiple-year curriculum. My personal training time, on the other hand, is for my own personal needs. But when you have a curriculum of sixty sets, and the technical level varies from student to student, you will find yourself switching sets to make the teaching spontaneous and challenging for everyone.

Q: Do you have any general advice for martial artists?
A: The most important thing to know is that you have given knowledge as well as received it. After spending years training, your abilities to think on your own and make contributions are an important key to the success of the next generation of teachers and practitioners. Albert Einstein said, "Imagination is more important than knowledge." I have to agree with that. It's nice to explore the frontier of the mind. We all need to grow and advance. I'm not saying to give up traditional martial arts, but just to look closely at what you have in your possession. Sticking to the same route is safe, but venturing outside that route could give you new experiences that you could share with other martial artist. Take the time to explore the forms of the past, for it is the door to knowledge. To perform kung-fu is nice but, to be kung-fu is divine.

Q: What are the most important qualities of a successful martial artist?
A: Have a good character with strong moral base, persistence, courage, understanding, humility, patience, and self-control. Persistence is the path to any success, but it mental or physical. Courage allows you to take a step beyond the ways of your average day—to be unafraid to try new ways. Be humble about yourself and not be too eager to prove something right or wrong. Control of your anger—don't criticize less-than-perfect performance or behavior from others. Patience will allow you to work though any problem, and humility will keep you from looking down on others just because they are not exactly like yourself. These traits are special, but like anything in life, you have to work at them and practice in order to succeed. These are just some of the steps in becoming a successful martial artist that I think carry through to other parts of life.

"Albert Einstein said, 'Imagination is more important than knowledge.' I have to agree with that. It's nice to explore the frontier of the mind. We all need to grow and advance. Take the time to explore the forms of the past, for it is the door to knowledge. To perform kung-fu is nice but, to be kung-fu is divine."

Kung-Fu Masters

"The idea of stretching and weight training take on entirely new meaning when done with kung-fu as its base. The resulting method must be focused on making your martial arts skill complete. I do not see supplementary training as a problem if you do it the right way."

Q: What's your opinion of supplementary training?
A: I have always known that cardiovascular exercise is important. I integrated cardiovascular exercises into my workout long ago with kung-fu principles, and it worked perfectly. The idea of stretching and weight training take on entirely new meaning when done with kung-fu as its base. The resulting method must be focused on making your martial arts skill complete. I believe when you go shopping you must pick the right ingredients in order to create your desired meal. I do not see supplementary training as a problem if you do it the right way.

Q: Have you felt fear in your training?
A: I haven't felt fear with any training that I've done. The only time I had a glimpse of fear was when I was a novice. I had to fight someone bigger and I was afraid of his strength and size. I have friends who stopped practicing kung-fu because of the fear of hurting their body through chi kung practice. Internal exercises should always be done with an experienced sifu. One thing I always remember is that when the door swings open it can also do harm as well as good. If you went to a doctor for sickness or injuries and he gave you the wrong prescription, then it might do more harm instead of good. The only one who knows if it feels good or bad is yourself. This inner power to distinguish the difference requires a perceptive mind.

Q: What keeps you motivated after all these years?
A: My strongest motivation has been to be the best and to find knowledge. To be perfectly honest, I never found anything that comes close to making me feel as contented as kung-fu. It makes me feel good after the workout is done and it exercises my mind to when I try to understand what makes these techniques work. The chi kung part of kung-fu emphasizes various health benefits and the information contained in the many forms of hung gar and kung-fu in general would take a lifetime to extract. The acoustic form in hung gar has taken many years to understand—not to mention the five emotions part of the form. When you had a place like the Shaolin Temple, where people could share and exchange knowledge and learn together, you can see how knowledge would grow. The picture of a old Chinese sage reaching for that last book of knowledge seems to exemplify my own personal attainment and drive to reach perfection. I may never attain it but I will never stop learning or trying.

Q: What is the future of martial arts?
A: Like any art form, it will be up to the new martial artists to break the mold into another dimension. If you look at the many ways martial arts has contributed to mankind, you will see that it is a great part of our past. The power to physically defend ourselves and our families, cities and countries against all enemies put this art form in a different place. It has helped us to succeed in understanding our own bodies, to create positive minds, and push us towards exercise for health and longevity. To be one with our body, mind and spirit is truly what drive us to be alive. The efficiency to live a fuller and longer life makes any knowledge handed-down even more important. The possibility to create and expand our perception using martial arts is one great way for the future generations to grow kung-fu. Because of modern technology, we can better communicate between students, teachers, cities, countries and the world community. All this has all helped to improve the old and given us power to extract past knowledge through research. What a grand future awaits all martial arts' players who unite together for common knowledge.

Masters Techniques

Sifu Rieta faces multiple opponents (1). When the first aggressor punches, Rieta blocks the attack (2), and redirects him (3), into the aggressor on his left side (4), where he is thrown off-balance (5), and goes to the ground (6). Rieta turns immediately to block the final attacker's front kick (7), and then throws him to the ground (8).

From a ready stance (1), Sifu Rieta defends two simultaneous attacks by hitting one of his opponents in the face and then deflecting the other attacker's front kick (2), with a hooking motion (3), followed by a hand claw to the face (4). He then executes a crossing kick to the attacker's supporting leg (5), which brings him to the ground (6), where Rieta finishes him with a kick (7-8).

Masters Techniques

Sifu Rieta is attacked by two men (1). The one from behind tries to bear hug him (2). Before he complete the action, though, Rieta elbows him in the chest and covers the other aggressor's actions with his left hand (3), which blocks an incoming punch (4). Rieta follows with a front kick (5), and a left hand strike to the head (6). This opens the angle for a hook to the attacker's left arm (7), which allows the execution of a shoulder lock (8), and body twist (9), which throws the attacker to the ground (10).

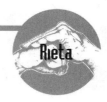

Sifu Rieta faces an opponent armed with a spear (1). When the aggressor thrusts the spear, Rieta blocks with his forearm (2), and counters the action with a circular motion (3), which brings the weapon to the right side. Simultaneously, Rieta hits the opponent with a left-hand palm strike (4), then steps in with his left leg (5), which turns into a sweep (6), that brings his opponent to the ground (7).

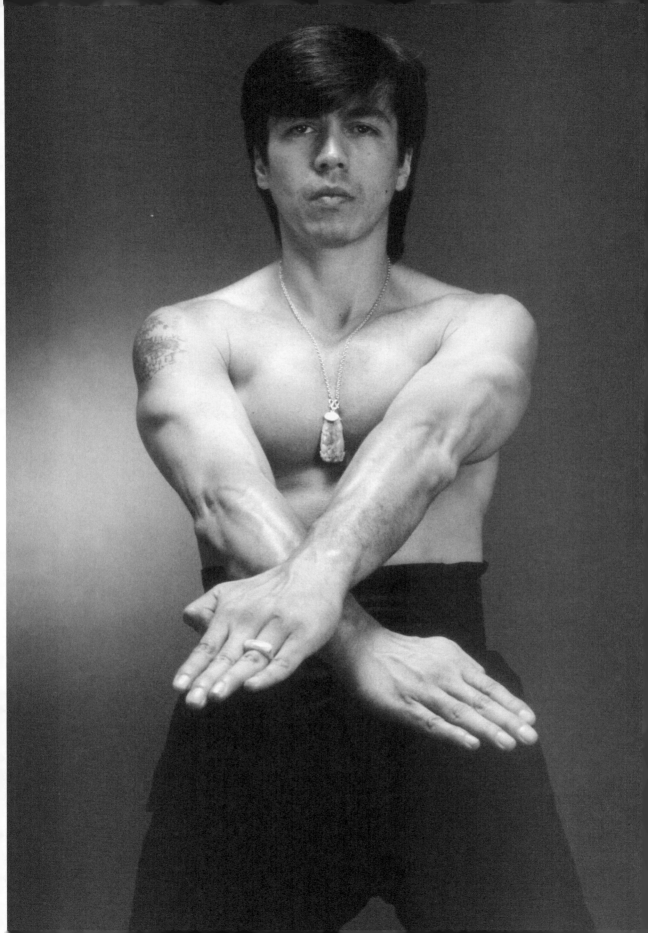

Randy Williams

A Wing Chun Crusader

RANDY WILLIAMS IS ONE OF THE MOST PROLIFIC WING CHUN INSTRUCTORS IN THE WORLD. PRECISION AND ACCURACY—IN EVERY TECHNIQUE HE PRACTICES AND IN EVERY BOOK AND VIDEO HE PRODUCES—ARE HIS SIGNATURE TRADEMARKS. HE IS ONE OF A DISTINGUISHED GROUP OF KUNG-FU MASTERS WHO HAVE BEEN ABLE TO ADAPT AND INTEGRATE MODERN COMBAT ELEMENTS INTO THEIR FIGHTING SYSTEMS WHILE PRESERVING THE TRADITIONAL INTENT AND FLAVOR OF THEIR ANCIENT ARTS. OVER THE PAST THREE DECADES, THOUSANDS OF STUDENTS HAVE LEARNED AND RECEIVED INSTRUCTION UNDER HIM. HIS INDELIBLE MARK ON THE WORLD OF KUNG-FU WILL ALWAYS BE REMEMBERED AND NEVER BE ERASED. WITH A HAPPY-GO-LUCKY ATTITUDE AND KEEN SENSE OF HUMOR, RANDY WILLIAMS HAS TRAVELED THE WORLD VISITING SCHOOLS IN EUROPE, AMERICA, AND ASIA MORE FREQUENTLY THAN MANY OTHER INSTRUCTORS TEACH CLASSES AT THEIR OWN SCHOOLS! RANDY WILLIAMS IS THE PERFECT EXAMPLE OF A TRADITIONAL KUNG-FU MAN FOR WHOM THE STRUGGLES OF THE PAST HAVE BECOME THE SUCCESSES OF THE PRESENT.

Q: How long have you been practicing the martial arts?
A: I have been training in martial arts for more than three decades. God, that makes me feel old! Although I enjoy all the martial arts, I have only trained in two systems—wing chun kung-fu and jeet kune do with Sifu Ted Wong.

Q: Who was your first teacher?
A: Sifu George Yau Chu from Hong Kong. I met him when he walked by and stayed to watch while I was hitting and kicking a bag in my garage. He was my neighbor in L.A. Chinatown. Coincidentally, so was Sifu Ted Wong. Since I knew he was a member of Bruce Lee's College Street group, I used to beg him to teach me when I was a kid and I'd see him in the neighborhood, but he always refused until many years later. Years later, a friend who trained with him arranged for me to meet him at a private dinner when I was in my early thirties. I said, "Wong Sifu, it's an

Kung-Fu Masters

"My sifu was absolutely brutal when he trained me. It seemed like he actually spent time dreaming up new ways to make me quit."

honor to meet you!" He replied, "What are you talking about? I've known you since you were a kid and you used to pester me to teach you."

Q: What was your early training like?
A: My sifu was absolutely brutal when he trained me. It seemed like he actually spent time dreaming up new ways to make me quit. Like making me stay in *yee jee keem yeung ma* with my pelvis up and my knees one-fist's distance apart for extended periods. To ensure I didn't waiver, he made me hold my wallet between my knees. And believe me, in those days my wallet wasn't all that thick. When I dropped it, he'd kick me hard in the shins with the sharp inside edge of his shoe and make me start over. I had to endure this kind of torture regularly, but in the end I'm kind of glad he made me do it. To this day, I have a very solid stance and strong footwork, although I went home from many a lesson with bruised, bleeding shins in order to get them that way.

But my favorite war story involving my teacher had to do with jogging. Of course, all of us Bruce Lee fans have been told many times that Bruce considered jogging the "king of all exercises." So of course, I wondered why my own sifu wasn't doing any jogging. Since I jogged regularly, I must have asked him dozens of times why he didn't, and the last straw was when I asked him just before practice at his house. He finally said something like, "OK, Boy—he always called me "Boy," never by my name—since you think jogging so great, you gone take a nice big jog!" He then sent me out to his back yard to pick up two large bricks. He told me to take off my shirt and shoes, and then to hold one brick gripped in the fingers of each hand. He marched me out into his front yard and

pointed out some road cones way in the distance and told me to run all the way there and back, and not to stop because he'd be watching. I said, "You've got to be kidding, right?" But he replied that he was dead serious and to "get the hell going." So off I took, barefoot, without a shirt, carrying bricks, running down the street in a drizzle with all the passers-by pointing and laughing at me. By the time I rounded the cones, I was actually whimpering and considered stopping, but a quick glance back at the house revealed the old sifu watching me intently, perhaps with the hint of a smile. So I kept on going.

When I got somewhat near the house, I saw him run inside and shut the door. I made it to the front porch and knocked, but there was no answer for a while. So I

"My Sifu wasn't going to learn English anytime soon, so he made me learn at least some basic Chinese before he'd even consider taking me on as a student. Again, I'm very glad he made me do that as my ability to speak Chinese has helped me in my business life as well."

stood there, shirtless and barefoot, shivering, hands scraped up and permanently paralyzed into claws. But he finally came to the door, opened it and chucked a pitcher full of ice cold water on me. Then he ordered me to get into the garage and practice *siu leem tau* on the cold cement floor, which I did for what seemed like hours. Needless to say, point taken, Sifu.

Q: Were you a natural at martial arts?
A: No, I had to work very hard to develop certain skills, and still do. Plus, I had a language barrier to overcome. My Sifu wasn't going to learn English anytime soon, so he made me learn at least some basic Chinese before he'd even consider taking me on as a student. Again, I'm very glad he made me do that as my ability to speak Chinese has helped me in my

Kung-Fu Masters

"As in all other forms of science and technology, I believe that wing chun must move forward. The inventors of the system never had to consider combat against the many modern and non-Chinese arts that a fighter may encounter today, such as Thai boxing, shootfighting, Brazilian jiu-jitsu and sambo just to name but a few."

business life as well. I overcame my initial awkwardness through sheer stubbornness and repetition training—thousands upon thousands of punches, blocks, kicks and footwork. I still do a *siu leem tau* or *chum kiu*, a 45-minute footwork pattern, and a thousand kicks and punches at least once a week to this day. Plus a lot more other drills and exercises since I am now back to full-time teaching and training.

Q: How has your personal martial arts changed over the years?
A: I have freely used my own common sense and experience to help me derive certain applications and principles of the system that are not as obvious as others, and to use these to help me deal with modern combat situations not encountered and therefore not considered by the founders of the system. As in all other forms of science and technology, I believe that wing chun must move forward. The inventors of the system never had to consider combat against the many modern and non-Chinese arts that a fighter may encounter today, such as Thai boxing, shootfighting, Brazilian jiu-jitsu and sambo just to name but a few. In the past, certain acknowledged ancestors made additions and improvements to the system, and it is my belief that the system will have to be continually modified and upgraded in order to keep pace with today's ever-changing combat technology.

"Although your father may have taught you to speak, I still know it's you on the phone when you call and not your father. I believe martial arts is the same. Your expression of the style will be somehow different than your teacher or fellow students regardless of how closely you follow the traditional patterns."

When you see an effective technique, you can't be afraid to work backwards and to break it down and see why it works—then try to use movements from your own style to create a similar application. I believe you owe it to yourself to be the most effective fighting machine you can. Blindly ignoring the beauty of an effective technique simply because you were never shown it as a "classical" example of the principles of your style is cheating yourself and your style. An old proverb of wing chun says that its techniques are "limitless in their application." That means if you can think of it and it works, it's an application. So what if you didn't think of it first? You didn't think of any of the rest of it first either. And no one owns a style of martial arts they didn't create. Thus, no one can tell you that you can't use the movements of your style in any given way.

Kung-Fu Masters

"When I was beginning, it was very difficult to find anything about wing chun in print. There were few books in English and videos weren't born yet. The real martial artists are out there training and getting the job done, not just constantly chatting about it on the Net. And if the real guys have a beef with you, you'll know about it, not read about it."

Q: With all the technical changes during the last 30 years, do you think there are still pure systems?
A: Whether we want to believe it or not, almost all systems are modified through the years, even if inadvertently. It can be compared to learning your mother language from parents—you can't help but add your own personal flavor to the language when you speak it. Your voice, the neighborhood you grew up in, the current slang, and other factors creep into your speech patterns. Although your father may have taught you to speak, I still know it's you on the phone when you call and not your father. I believe martial arts is the same. Your expression of the style will be somehow different than your teacher or fellow students regardless of how closely you follow the traditional patterns. If you put bags over ten of my top students' heads, I could still almost immediately tell you which one was Wayne, which was Bert, and which was Jerry simply by watching them move, although I taught them all the same. So in my opinion, nearly every major system is somehow flavored by its various instructors through time, but the essence will remain pure in many cases.

Q: Do you feel that the Internet has helped or hurt the martial arts?
A: Both—it has obviously made martial arts' information much more accessible to the public. When I was beginning, it was very difficult to find anything about wing chun in print. There were few books in English and

videos weren't born yet. But on the downside, I think the Internet chat rooms have also given a large number of armchair experts a wide-reaching medium for disrespectful and often libelous criticism and character assassination without having to back up their words. They remain hidden behind their computer screens and user names. Some of my more scrappy students contact many of those people asking for *goang sau* matches to give them a chance to prove their superior skills, but not surprisingly not a single one of them has ever risen to the challenge. They typically hide behind excuses like, "I'm not famous, so I don't have to be tough," or "A fight like that would be illegal." More common is the, "I'll call the police if you come anywhere near me." Or my favorite—used a lot by pseudo wing chun computer guys— "I'll call your ISP and have your service discontinued if you threaten me." As one of my students so aptly puts it, "Don't let your mouth write checks your butt can't cash!"

The real martial artists are out there training and getting the job done, not just constantly chatting about it on the 'net. And if the real guys have a beef with you, you'll know about it, not read about it.

"I constantly review all of my old notes from years gone by and I never fail to pick up on some concept, technique, or drill that I hadn't thought of for decades. The older and more senile I get, the more sense the statement, "I've forgotten more about wing chun than you'll ever learn," makes to me."

Q: Do you think different schools or styles of the same method are important?
A: Yes—after all, why would everyone want to do everything the same? There must be differing slants on each art, and students will tend to gravitate towards the approach that suits them the best. For example, certain instructors place more emphasis on actual combat applications, while others stress the more spiritual or artistic aspects of a system. A potential student can then decide which extreme or middle ground is more appli-

Kung-Fu Masters

"Nowadays, the general public is much more sophisticated in regards to martial arts and is very aware of what works and what doesn't. And the UFC has also forced the martial arts world to take a closer look at what is actually effective in combat."

cable to their own situation and desires.

Q: What is your opinion of sport competitions like kickboxing, and fighting events such as the Ultimate Fighting Championship?
A: I think they have brought a much-needed element of reality to the martial arts. In the '70s, you could strike a karate pose and frighten off a number of potential opponents who thought that just because you were trained in a martial art you were a deadly fighter. Nowadays, the general public is much more sophisticated in regards to martial arts and is very aware of what works and what doesn't. And the UFC has also forced the martial arts world to take a closer look at what is actually effective in combat. For example, the overall importance of ground fighting skills has been almost universally acknowledged and is now a part of the training regimen of nearly all true combat-minded martial artists.

Q: Do you think that kung-fu in the West has caught up with the East?
A: It depends on your context. If you mean pure fighting skill, then I would have to say that it is fairly safe to say that Westerners continue to dominate nearly every form of combative competition—be it fencing, boxing, wrestling or NHB fighting. Of course, there have always been, and will always be, many individual exceptions to this. But if you are talking about pure skill in terms of deep-rooted knowledge of concepts and principles, it would be difficult to give a blanket answer. The true skill levels of the originators of the many various styles of martial arts remains

largely unknown. For that matter, the same is true of many modern-day masters as well.

Q: Martial arts are often referred to as a sport. Do you agree with this definition?
A: Not in general, but certainly as the term pertains to various forms of competition, from forms to point fighting to NHB. In fact, the word "art" as part of the term would seem to discern it from sport. I think it would be better to say that sport is only a small facet of the full spectrum of meaning covered by the term "martial arts."

Q: Do you feel that you still have further to go in your studies?
A: Always—although I'm not sure I will get there. At this point, after so many years of training, I have to struggle to maintain the skill level I have already attained. I constantly review all of my old notes from years gone by and I never fail to pick up on some concept, technique, or drill that I hadn't thought of for decades. The older and more senile I get, the more sense the statement, "I've forgotten more about wing chun than you'll ever learn," makes to me.

"I would advise a student to pick his style and teacher with the utmost care and attention. You must weigh certain factors and decide which are the most important to you. At some point, every bird must leave the nest, but it would be nice to pick a teacher who won't push you out and then try to eat you."

Q: Do you think it helps kung-fu practitioners to train with weapons?
A: Yes, the weight and additional snap of the weapon can help develop empty-hand power. But having said that, I do feel that there are much more efficient methods available today if physical training is the objective—even as it relates to the specific motions of kung-fu.

Kung-Fu Masters

"I personally train in the martial arts at least in part not to be beaten up. So it doesn't make a lot of sense to me to purposely expose myself constantly to damaging punches and kicks to the head and body."

Q: Do you think the practitioner's personal training should be different than their teaching schedule as an instructor?
A: It has to be. Teaching beginning and intermediate level students will keep his basics sharp, but an instructor must also focus on his own personal maintenance and development of advanced techniques, as well as focusing on his own personal weaknesses—which aren't necessarily the most important areas for his students to work on. For example, if the teacher needs work on his stop-kick skills, it would be better for him to focus on that aspect in his own personal regimen, rather than use to large a portion of valuable class time that would be better spent on those things needed by a group that's not ready for such things.

Q: Do you have any general advice you would care to pass on?
A: Besides the obvious "train hard," "use your knowledge for the right reasons," "respect your elders and superiors in the art," and the old favorite "wax on, wax off," I may have some tips to offer. In your training, try to keep mind, body and spirit in balance. It is easy to train the body with forms, drills, sparring, weight training, et cetera. The mind is a little harder to train, though. But reading, watching videos, learning about the culture and language of the country your art comes from are all ways of improving mental strength.

But to train the spirit is even a much more intricate process. Each person is different, and must strive to find the things that make them stronger spiritually. Some people find it in religion, others in charity work. But whatever it is that you need to do to make yourself feel "clean" and

"deserving" will also serve to strengthen your spirit. Some people work extra hard on only the physical aspects, like bodybuilding. Others can literally be rocket scientists, but are extremely out of shape. A religious figure may be both spiritually and mentally strong, but lacking in physical fitness. But a true martial artist should strive to be strong in all three arenas to be complete. In this way, when confronted by an opponent, you will have the strength to deliver effective techniques, the knowledge to make them succeed, and the self-worth to say, "Dammit, I deserve my place on earth as much as you do. I'm not gonna let you harm me."

I would also advise a martial arts instructor to remain a good student for his entire life. If you are a meticulous note-taker and have a great memory, coupled with actually going home and diligently training what you have learned, seen and heard, it is possible to improve your skills even without constant supervision from an instructor. You can even surpass the skills of those that live in the same city with him, but that don't have the same learning potential and drive that you have. For example, I have students in Italy, Germany, Singapore, and many other places whose skill levels are higher than those local students who train with me much more regularly but who aren't as driven.

Lastly, I would advise a student to pick his style and teacher with the utmost care and attention. You must weigh certain factors and decide which are the most important to you. Does this art appeal to me? Will I practice it daily? Is the school in a convenient location? Do I have the time to dedicate? Do I have potential in the art? Am I looking for self-defense, sport, spirituality or all of the above? Is the teacher someone I want to follow? You must also be careful of student/teacher relationships. In my experience, jealousy can unfortunately play a part in driving a rift between student and teacher. At some point, every bird must leave the nest, but it would be nice to pick a teacher who won't push you out and then try to eat you.

Q: What do you consider to be the major changes in your art since you began your training?
A: Widespread availability, not only of more schools and more styles, but also more information available through books, videos, and the Internet. I also feel that competition between many different schools and instructors, as well as NHB-type competition, has raised the bar in terms of quality.

Kung-fu Masters

Q: Who would you like to have trained with?
A: Yip Man, Wong Shun Leung, Moy Yat, and of course, Bruce Lee—like everyone else out there. There is also one guy that I did train with—and put my heart and soul into paying tribute to. But since he now disavows having taught me, I guess I'd have to include him on my list, too. You may be able to figure out who it is, but I can't tell you because it'll just wind him up (laughs).

Q: What would you say to someone who is interested in starting to learn martial arts?
A: If I said it promoted decency, fitness, high moral standards and character, that would imply that I was an example of those virtues. So instead, I would just tell them that it's a lot of fun and will expose you to the most interesting people and places you will ever know.

Q: What keeps you motivated after all these years?
A: Great students who are also my best friends and practically my extended family. The fact that they want to learn what I have worked so many years to develop makes me want to always be able to satisfy their drive to achieve. So I have to stay at the top of my game in order to live up to their hopes and expectations.

Q: Do you think it is necessary to engage in free-fighting to achieve good fighting skills for the street?
A: Yes, at some point in your life. At least to experience what it is to hit and to be hit, and to appreciate the importance of fitness and conditioning, as well as crucial elements of distance and timing in actual combat. But I have to qualify that statement by saying that I personally train in the martial arts at least in part not to be beaten up. So it doesn't make a lot of sense to me to purposely expose myself constantly to damaging punches and kicks to the head and body. If my training had included being hit solidly in the head at least once a day, in the course of 30 years of training I would have suffered a whopping 10,950 punches in the head—considerably more damaging blows than I might have suffered not knowing a thing about martial arts and losing even a hundred street-fights in which my opponent had hit me 20 times per fight. The first and foremost purpose of kung-fu is self defense. That doesn't just mean protecting yourself against bullies who want to beat you up, it also involves defending yourself by using your head in your training to avoid injury when you can. This inherent self-preservation is why there are so many revered masters of the martial arts who are

still actively training and teaching well into their 70s and 80s—but very few boxers can make a similar claim. Muhammad Ali, arguably the best boxer of all time is now unfortunately suffering the ill effects of just such brutal training and competition.

Q: What is your opinion about mixing martial arts styles?
A: Cross-training has already proven to improve a fighter's effectiveness in a competitive environment. But in terms of keeping an art systematic and preserving its original essence, there have to be dinosaurs like myself who keep the arts separate and to some degree pure and original. Take your pick.

"Why would everyone want to do everything the same? There must be differing slants on each art, and students will tend to gravitate towards the approach that suits them the best. For example, certain instructors place more emphasis on actual combat applications, while others stress the more spiritual or artistic aspects of a system. A potential student can then decide which extreme or middle ground is more applicable to their own situation and desires."

Q: Do you have a particularly memorable experience that inspired you to train?
A: I have a number, but an experience I had at the San Francisco school of white crane system Sifu Quentin Fong probably had the most impact on me and sticks with me the most. Fong Sifu was on the cover of the very first *Inside Kung-Fu* magazine I ever read, and to me, he embodied everything that kung-fu was supposed to be. So I convinced my mom to let me take a bus trip all alone from LA to San Francisco to visit his school.

After the long bus trip up, I found his school just off the cable car route. When I knocked, a couple of the students who came to the door were really mean to me and wouldn't let me in. But since my bus wasn't leaving until later that night, I decided to sit outside and wait. When Fong Sifu showed up later, he asked me where I was from and why I was sitting outside instead of inside watching the class. When I explained, he took me inside and asked, "Which one of these guys was it? Was it him? What

Kung-Fu Masters

"My first instructor inspired all kinds of fear in me. His teaching methods could be brutal at times, with the result of a missed block being a black eye, a lump on the head and/or a fat lip. And there's always fear before a real fight. It never goes away completely, and maybe that's good."

about this one?" He then scolded the guys and made them stand in very low stances until their legs shook. Then he had them clamp quarters between the handles of those springy hand-gripper things and made them throw hundreds of punches, arms fully extended with the grippers held tightly closed so as not to drop the quarters. When they were sufficiently humbled, he had the entire group demonstrate forms for me—empty hand, weapons, and even one with a sawhorse-like work bench.

Afterwards, he took me into his office and picked out a nice T-shirt with a picture of a crane on it and the Chinese characters for white crane kung-fu written in red across the chest, which he gave to me. Then he insisted on driving me back to the bus station and waiting for me to get on before he left, because it was on a bad part of Market Street. He waved goodbye as he drove off. I still have that shirt and the memories of that day, many years ago. Had he not taken the time and effort to treat me with such kindness, I might have lost my passion for kung-fu long ago.

Q: After all your years of training, what does the practice of kung-fu mean to you?
A: It's a way of unifying mind, body and spirit. A way of building strength, confidence and lifelong relationships. A path to attaining the courage to stand up and fight when it's absolutely necessary, and the courage not to when it isn't, without fear of being called a coward. A constant gauge by which to measure your personal progress and growth. A quest for knowledge. Tapping into the mystique of Asia and its culture. Pride in your stu-

dents' development and achievements, and pride in passing the art down to another. It's a doorway to countless adventures and journeys around the world. An opportunity to see the world, to meet new people, and to beat them up (laughs). No, seriously, it's all of the above wrapped up into one, plus more that can't be easily put into words.

Q: What are the most important qualities of a successful martial artist?
A: That depends on what you consider successful. If you mean skillful, I think it's important to set a goal and remain focused. I have always known from a very young age what I wanted to do and be in the martial arts, and I stayed focused on that. So I would advise you to put yourself into a situation conducive to the success you're after. If you want to be an actor, move to Hollywood. In martial arts, it is also very important that you find the right teacher. Then, above all, self-discipline is the most important quality. A martial artist cannot afford to be lazy. To be a good student, and eventually a good teacher, takes many, many hours of hard work and many gallons of sweat.

I have always felt that having a good sense of humor can help you rise to the top of any field, not just kung-fu. In my opinion, you need to have the ability to *not* take yourself too seriously. I learned something about humility from Sifu Quentin Fong, and I try to follow his example by taking the time to answer every letter, phone call or e-mail I receive, and to treat everyone who contacts me with questions about wing chun with respect and friendliness.

If success for you means commercial success, then I would advise you to put out a good product, be it instruction, books, videos or magazine articles. I can tell you from experience that you will have to look at that article and those photos for the rest of your life, so you better do the best you possibly can, or you'll regret it for many years to come. And although I'm not sure it helps all that much commercially, at least in the short term, you have to be able to guide a student in what he needs—not necessarily what he wants. You must demand from them almost as much as you demand of yourself; this will lead to quality, not quantity.

Q: How do you feel about supplemental physical training?
A: I am a strong believer in weight training. But you have to be careful how you use weights. It is very possible to train with weights and to actually *increase* your speed. It may slow you down if you aren't training right for the sport you're in, but I find that most of the guys who say it'll slow you down aren't that fast or strong to begin with (laughs). My rationale is

Kung-Fu Masters

this—if two guys are the same size and skill level, the stronger and fitter one will win nine times out of ten, so it just makes sense to be the strongest and fittest you can be, on top of whatever skill level you are able to achieve. I also believe in jogging—but if you see Sifu George Yau, please don't tell him!

Q: Why do a lot of students fall away after two or three years of training?
A: Kung-fu is not as easy to learn as many people might think, and not everyone has the intestinal fortitude to put in the hours of sweat required to achieve a high level of skill. They often come in thinking it'll be like "The Matrix" and quit when they realize they aren't going to be Jet Li anytime soon.

Q: Have there been times when you felt fear in your training?
A: Of course. My first instructor inspired all kinds of fear in me. His teaching methods could be brutal at times, with the result of a missed block being a black eye, a lump on the head and/or a fat lip. And I already told you about his propensity for shin kicking. And there's always fear before a real fight. Of course, you can use that fear and channel it into faster, more powerful techniques. But it never goes away completely, and maybe that's good.

Q: How important is lineage in a martial artist's credentials?
A: My own view of what is important in wing chun can at times be very different from many other traditional kung-fu instructors. Although I certainly appreciate and respect the history of wing chun and the importance of its lineage as handed down from generation to generation, I am personally more concerned with the more tangible aspects such as skill, knowledge and performance. In other words, I respect my elders and seniors in the system, but I do not necessarily believe that *when* someone began their study or *with whom* they studied is the primary criteria for their ranking or status in a system.

Instead, I look at the person's skill level, ability to explain their system in detail and—most importantly—their ability to perform. In other words, I take a more practical approach—almost an American sports attitude. For example, if one looks at the game of football, most fans probably do not care who taught Jerry Rice to catch a football, that he may not know the entire history of football, or that he may not have a genealogy of all of the players which passed it down to him from the founders of the game.

What is important to the fans is that he is the best wide receiver of all time. He may have learned from his father, or more likely from just getting out there and playing the game. But above all, he got out there and did the job, head and shoulders above the rest. That is what makes him an all-time great.

It is my belief that wing chun in the modern world has become much the same, and rightfully so. With the abundance of instructional materials available today, virtually anyone with an earnest desire to learn wing chun can do so with relative ease. Personally, I am more interested in watching a player who can do his job with excellence rather than watching a player whose coach, father or grandfather was a star player, but who may himself not be exceptional. Similarly, I respect those that can actually "get out there and do it" much more than those who just talk about it. I feel that martial arts is one of the few fields where many of us are graded by whom we have trained with, instead of what we have achieved, published or produced.

"I have always felt that having a good sense of humor can help you rise to the top of any field, not just kung-fu. In my opinion, you need to have the ability to not take yourself too seriously. And although I'm not sure it helps all that much commercially, at least in the short term, you have to be able to guide a student in what he needs—not necessarily what he wants."

Q: What are your thoughts on the future of the martial arts?
A: I believe that martial arts will always move forward with the times, as they must. As in all other forms of science and technology, I believe that wing chun and martial arts in general must move ahead, adapting and improving to keep pace with the rest of the world. After all, would you want to go to a doctor from 300 years ago, from the present, or from 300 years into the future?

Masters Techniques

Sifu Williams faces an opponent (1), and blocks his attack with a left **bong sau** *(2), followed by a right-hand trap and left* **fark** *sao to his neck (3). Williams then scoops his left arm (4), and puts the attacker into a neck crank (5).*

From an on-guard position (1), Sifu Williams block the attacker's punch with his left hand (2). He then follows with a side kick to the midsection (3), a left-hand trap and right punch to the face (4), and a trap and left punch (5).

Ark Y. Wong
Grandmaster of Shaolin

ARK WONG CAME TO THE UNITED STATES IN 1921 AND OPENED A KUNG-FU SCHOOL IN SAN FRANCISCO. AFTER BUILDING A REPUTATION IN THE BAY AREA, HE WAS ASKED BY A GROUP FROM LOS ANGELES TO COME TO SOUTHERN CALIFORNIA TO TEACH THE ART. HE MOVED TO LOS ANGELES IN 1929 AND TAUGHT EXCLUSIVELY FOR THE WONG FAMILY FOR THE FIRST TWO YEARS. BUT DUE TO THE SIZABLE DEMAND FOR HIS INSTRUCTION, HE EXPANDED HIS CLASSES TO INCLUDE ANY SINCERE STUDENT WHO HAD THE DESIRE TO LEARN. HE BECAME ONE OF THE MOST SENIOR KUNG-FU INSTRUCTORS IN THE WESTERN WORLD AND WAS LEGITIMATELY CONSIDERED A GRANDMASTER BY THOSE WHO KNEW HIM. HE TAUGHT VARIOUS CLASSICAL KUNG-FU STYLES, BUT WAS MOST OFTEN ASSOCIATED WITH THE FIVE ANIMALS SYSTEM. HE BEGAN CHARGING $20 PER MONTH FOR LESSONS WHEN HE OPENED UP IN 1921 AND THE LAST DAY HE TAUGHT AT HIS *KWOON*, HE WAS STILL CHARGING $20. "SAME PRICE FOR MORE THAN 60 YEARS," HE SAID. "I NEVER CHANGE."

Q: Grandmaster, what can you say about your beginnings in kung-fu?
A: I started to train at a very early age, 7 years old. I learned kung-fu and Chinese herbal medicine from Lam Ark Fun. I also learned mau gar kung-fu from Ho Ark Yeng. Both teachers were hired by my grandfather to teach traditional kung-fu exclusively to the members of my family. The country was wide open and the surroundings quite dangerous. Later on, I went to school in Canton where I met the chief monk of the Canton area. His name was Pung and I studied under him for a year and a half. He taught me the very important elements of internal kung-fu. When the civil unrest broke out in Canton I went back to my village and opened a kung-fu school for my family and children of the area. Then in 1921 I came to the United Sates of America.

Q: Is kung-fu an art that can be practiced by everybody or does it require certain types of physical characteristics?
A: I need to explain few things here. Kung-fu is a great form of exercise for the human body. It's similar to water; you put water in a bottle and if you don't change it from time to time, it gets dirty. Well, the body is the

Kung-Fu Masters

"The rank is something that you have to give to the student based on their attitude and dedication, not simply because they have been in the school for six months. Time doesn't mean anything to me if you don't use it wisely and put all the effort you possibly can into your training."

same. Through exercise the blood flows and feeds the body. You need to know what kind of exercise is good according to your age. It should be different for a 25-year-old student that is for someone over 50. For instance, *tai chi chuan* is great for someone old, but I don't think it is good for a young practitioner. A young body needs a different kind of physical activity and I honestly believe that if you put a 20-year-old kid to train in tai chi, it will spoil him! That person needs a different style. For someone like me, old men and weak people, then it is good.

Q: How do you approach ranking and grading in your school?
A: My ranking policies are very conservative. I only have testing sessions every six months and many times I decide to postpone them. The rank is something that you have to give to the student based on their attitude and dedication, not simply because they have been in the school for six months. Time doesn't mean anything to me if you don't use it wisely and put all the effort you possibly can into your training. For me, character, self-control, honesty, sincerity and other ethical qualities are far more important than how high you can kick or how strong you can punch the heavy bag. My ranking system covers five grades and these grades correspond to five different colors: gray, green, red, blue, and black.

Instructor ranking is a whole different thing and only my black sash students are granted the right to teach the art. Regardless of your previous training, if you enter in my school you have to wear the gray sash at least

for the first six months. I think is simply fair; you may have a lot of ability but out of respect for a new school you should know what your position is and you must pay respect to everyone who has trained here before you.

Q: How can forms can help the practitioner?
A: My primary training method is still the practice of the traditional forms. I teach six basic forms plus the five animals forms. Many people disagree with the practice of forms, but I believe they are missing the point. All these are simply immature comments from people who never went deep into the art and are simply thinking about fighting. The traditional *kuen* (forms) not only keep all the traditional techniques for future generations, but also stimulate the heart of the practitioner sufficiently high for improve cardiovascular fitness. Forms have a place in the training of a kung-fu practitioner but you need to know what they are meant for.

The old masters did have some idea of what they were doing, regardless of what some describe as a classical mess. The forms contain very useful fighting information and techniques for those perceptive enough to pull the techniques out and apply them according to the situation. Only someone with a very superficial knowledge will make such kind of derogative statements against the traditional forms. Where do they think they are getting the techniques they use for combat? From the outer space? You have to break the form up for fighting, although the beginner will never be able to figure those things out by himself. It takes years of training to develop the right understanding to learn from the forms.

"The old masters did have some idea of what they were doing, regardless of what some describe as a classical mess. The forms contain very useful fighting information and techniques for those perceptive enough to pull the techniques out and apply them according to the situation. Only someone with a very superficial knowledge will make such kind of derogative statements against the traditional forms."

Kung-Fu Masters

"I teach traditional kung-fu so my methods can be described as 'traditional.' I would like to advise the new generations to reexamine some of the 'old' ways of training and to focus on the ideas behind them."

I know these days people get tired very easily and instructors need to develop 'newer' and 'fancier' training methods to keep the students coming back to classes. The training methods have evolved radically in the last decades but definitely my training methods are very different. I teach traditional kung-fu so my methods can be described as 'traditional.' I would like to advise the new generations to reexamine some of the 'old' ways of training and to focus on the ideas behind them.

Q: What is the main goal of kung-fu training?
A: First of all, I must say that I don't like to talk about kung-fu, or martial arts in general, as a sport because they are not. The main purpose of kung-fu training is self-defense, and improving health is secondary. For me, the sport tournament is not good. That's not fighting and may mislead the student to believe that they can rely on techniques that won't work under real situations. Sometimes they don't even hit and get points anyway. Many of them are simply fancy fighters, jumping around and bouncing in and out without a serious approach to fighting. All you have to do is wait until they get tired and then hit them hard and solid. They will go down, I guarantee you. All those fancy movements are useless in a real fight.

Q: So you just like the basics?
A: Well, I don't like to teach the fancy stuff, that's for sure. For instance, you won't see too much stretching in my classes because all that stretching will weaken a person's joints in the long run and will produce a per-

"Stretching will eventually loosen your tendons, ligaments, and other important tissues that should be strong when you get older. You have to understand what is good for your body and what is not. All stretching routines are meant to allow the student to kick high. Well, why does he need to kick high? It's better to kick low and punch high!"

manent degree of elastic strength. Look at some practitioners who have been over-stretching for years—they have to get surgery to fix or replace their hips. Why? Because they overdid something that is not good for your body. Stretching will eventually loosen your tendons, ligaments, and other important tissues that should be strong when you get older. You have to understand what is good for your body and what is not. All stretching routines are meant to allow the student to kick high. Well, why does he need to kick high? It's better to kick low and punch high! My goal is self-defense and believe me, there is sense in using kicks to the head in a real situation. Kick low, break his "family" with kicks; kick the groin. Kicking to the head is as senseless as punching to the feet!

Q: Would you tell us about the traditional training methods used in your school?
A: Sure. For instance, I don't believe in mats so the floor of my school is a normal surface. We train with shoes because you don't walk barefoot in

Kung-Fu Masters

"I believe that practical weapons can be found anywhere if the person has been trained to see them. Anything can be used as a practical weapon—a broom, a chair, et cetera. They may not be considered classical, but if the situation arises and you have been properly trained in traditional weapons, then you'll be able to use them."

your daily life. On the floor you can see different geometric patterns that we use for learning the proper footwork. It's a guide to learn stance and footwork combinations. We use baskets holding gravel-like substances of various degrees of coarseness to condition the hands and fingers for thrusting and poking attacks. I remember that my teachers used to have a pole pounded into the ground so we could practice the foot-sweeping techniques. The whole idea was to break the pole off at the ground level in order to demonstrate some degree of proficiency. I don't use this anymore, though.

Q: Do you teach traditional weaponry in your school?
A: Yes I do. I believe that practical weapons can be found anywhere if the person has been trained to see them. Anything can be used as a practical weapon—a broom, a chair, et cetera. They may not be considered classical, but if the situation arises and you have been properly trained in traditional weapons, then you'll be able to use them. The principles learned though the traditional weapons can be applied to other similar tools. In my classes I don't like to teach weapons unless the student has been training consistently for a minimum of six months. If the student doesn't have the proper foundation, then it will be useless to teach him the weapons. He needs to know how to use the body so he can transfer the power into the weapon with the right body mechanics.

Q: You are very active and in an exceptional shape for a man of your age. What's your secret?
A: No secret! I don't drink, smoke, or gamble. Nothing far out. I enjoy life but I also take care of myself. When I leave my school every night, I go home but I don't sit there for two hours watching TV. No fool around. Have rest. Today, young people fool around too much—too much wasted time and energy. They love to touch girls. For instance, you practice kung-fu today; you feel good and strong. You feel the energy going throughout your body. Then tonight you touch girl and tomorrow you walk around feeling sore. You feel chunky, you feel empty, you lose life energy. You have to learn how to balance everything in your life. If you know how to do it, then you'll live for a long time and feel strong even if you are old. I like to say that if I have a secret, it's rice and exercise. If I feel a sickness is coming on, I use my Chinese herbs to prevent it getting worse. I am a certified acupuncturist and have an extensive knowledge of herbal medicine.

"You have to learn how to balance everything in your life. If you know how to do it, then you'll live for a long time and feel strong even if you are old."

Q: Is it true that you had some problems with the use of needles in the past?
A: Yes. In 1924, I opened an herbal specialist office in Oakland on Market Street and many people were coming to me for treatment. I used acupuncture and Chinese medicine to treat them. Someone put the word out that I was using needles and a detective came to my house and explained that the use of needles was prohibited without the proper license. I had to stop using them but continued as an herbal specialist. This information about herbs and acupuncture is something that in China they don't teach indiscriminately. You have to gain your teacher's trust. I trained under my teacher for ten straight years before he decided

Kung-Fu Masters

"I was the kind of student that never made trouble, never fought anyone, and he knew that I wouldn't use this knowledge to harm anyone, except if there were no other alternatives."

to start teaching me these traditional aspects of our culture. I was the kind of student that never made trouble, never fought anyone, and he knew that I wouldn't use this knowledge to harm anyone, except if there were no other alternatives.

Q: But you finally got your acupuncturist license, right?
A: Yes. In 1976 I applied for it and I sent all the documentation and I qualified as an experienced practitioner of acupuncture to the license board. They reviewed my application and granted me the license in 1977.

Q: I have heard you don't like golf. Why?
A: I really advise young people to play sports, but I don't think golf is a healthy sport. When you swing, with the twisting and pulling action of the movement you put pressure on the muscles close to the heart. In other sports like basketball, tennis, et cetera, different motions are used and blood circulation is stimulated. But in golf there is basically only one movement—swinging the club. That is not a good exercise and eventually can be very harmful.

Q: What advice would you like to give to kung-fu practitioners?
A: A true martial artist not only should have physical abilities but also ethical attributes such as humility and respect for others. I don't talk about

other styles of martial arts because I believe all of them are good if properly taught by a competent instructor. In the end, the effectiveness of your art depends on how good you are, and not on the characteristics of the style. In short, always respect your teachers and always treat your art with respect. If you do, it will serve you well. The art is not something you can take with you, it is something that I would like to leave to dedicated students.

"I don't talk about other styles of martial arts because I believe all of them are good if properly taught by a competent instructor. In the end, the effectiveness of your art depends on how good you are, and not on the characteristics of the style."

Doc Fai Wong

Deliberate, Steady, and Solid

BORN IN KWANGTUNG, CHINA, IN 1948, WONG DOC FAI IS ONE OF THE HIGHEST-RANKING KUNG-FU INSTRUCTORS IN THE WORLD. SIFU WONG ARRIVED IN THE UNITED STATES VIA MACAO AT AGE 11. ALWAYS INTERESTED IN LEARNING MARTIAL ARTS, HE GOT HIS CHANCE IN SAN FRANCISCO, WHERE AT AGE 14, WONG WAS ACCEPTED AS A DISCIPLE BY CHOY LI FUT KUNG-FU GRANDMASTER LAU BUN. THE SAME YEAR HE BECAME A DISCIPLE OF CHAN MASTER HSUAN HUA, THE ABBOT OF THE CITY OF TEN THOUSAND BUDDHAS. HE STUDIED UNDER GRANDMASTER LAU BUN UNTIL HIS DEATH IN 1967. IN 1969, ENCOURAGED TO OPEN HIS OWN SCHOOL BY LAU BUN SUCCESSOR LANG LEW, WONG BECAME ONE OF THE FIRST TRADITIONAL INSTRUCTORS TO VENTURE OUTSIDE SAN FRANCISCO'S CHINATOWN WITH A MARTIAL ARTS STUDIO. A CALIFORNIA STATE CERTIFIED ACUPUNCTURIST, SIFU WONG IS ALSO A RESPECTED INSTRUCTOR IN THE YANG STYLE OF TAI CHI CHUAN, HAVING LEARNED DIRECTLY FROM WOO VAN-CHEUK—HIMSELF A STUDENT OF YANG CHENG FU, THE GRANDSON AND BEST-KNOWN MASTER OF THE YANG FAMILY STYLE.

Q: What made you decide to get into tai chi?
A: I first studied Wu style tai chi. My teacher was a private student of Wu Gong Yi, the oldest son of the founder of Wu tai chi—Wu Jian Qien. Two years later in 1962 I switched to Yang style, learning from a teacher in San Francisco's Chinatown, named Lau Yee Sing. Since I was so young, I also wanted a more active style of kung-fu, so I started taking choy li fut from Lau Bun in Chinatown.

Q: How did you practice and learn choy li fut and tai chi at the same time?
A: I started tai chi first. When joined the Hung Sing Choy Li Fut Studio in Chinatown in 1962, learning from Lau Bun, I continued practicing tai chi. In 1964 I trained in push-hands and hsing-i chuan from Kwok Ling Jee, while still learning from Lau Bun. In 1967 Lau Bun died, so I helped his successor and my senior classmate, Sifu Jew Lang, teach and run the

Kung-Fu Masters

"Today, everyone first learns the tai chi form before moving to push hand or meditation practice. That's not the way the Yang family intended it to be taught. In ancient times, Yang family tai chi didn't start with the form. Students practiced special standing meditation postures and breathing exercises before learning anything else."

Hung Sing Studio. In 1968 I started my own classes, teaching both choy li fut and tai chi.

Q: How did you become a student of both Hu Yuen Chou and Wong Gong?
A: In 1970 I realized I was very young and should try to advance myself to a higher level in martial arts. Therefore, I decided to travel to Hong Kong and look for high-ranking teachers to study with. Fortunately I found Hu Yuen Chou, a direct disciple of the choy li fut founder's grandson for over 20 years and also a private student and disciple of Yang Cheng Fu, grandson of the founder of Yang tai chi. I applied for discipleship with him. After accepting me, Professor Hu sent me to learn even more about choy li fut and the Kong Chow branch from Wong Kong.

Q: How is tai chi practiced today compared to the old times?
A: Today, everyone first learns the tai chi form before moving to push hand or meditation practice. That's not the way the Yang family intended it to be taught. In ancient times, Yang family tai chi didn't start with the form. Students practiced special standing meditation postures and breathing exercises before learning anything else. Each training session began with an hour of standing meditation to build up chi.

Only when their chi was sufficiently developed did they start learning the tai chi martial art stances. As they progressed, they eventually combined their training sessions to include meditation, breathing and martial art stances. This lasted for two-to-three years before commencing tai chi form position work. Every three months they changed to a different mar-

tial arts stance until all 13 positions had been practiced. Some exchanged their tai chi knowledge with hsing-i and pa kua teachers, adding to the original list of 13. Each posture developed *jung* (energy) in different parts of the body, while externally strengthening their arms and legs.

After several years, they were taught the form. However, this was not the connected moving form we know today. First they had to stand and hold each technique in the form for 20 breaths. Then they changed to another form posture, repeating the same 20-breath position for each posture throughout the set.

By practising the form this way, students learned only one movement at a time. Naturally, it took a long time to finish the entire form. Students didn't learn to connect form movements until after they had finished memorizing all the postures and their applications. Subsequently, it took several years just to learn the complete form. It might have taken longer, except the Yang long form contains a number of repeat movements.

"Naturally, it took a long time to finish the entire form. Students didn't learn to connect form movements until after they had finished memorizing all the postures and their applications. Subsequently, it took several years just to learn the complete form."

Q: Were meditation, stances, and postures the only aspects in the curriculum?
A: Not at all. Students of Yang family teachers, such as Yang Chen Fu, also spent time practicing *tui shou* or push hands. Their push-hand practice included single-hand, double-hand, and something called *ba zhen tui shou* (eight front push hands) that positioned practitioners in stances similar to today's Chen-style push hands. Ba Zhen eventually became today's Yang style *da lu*, sometimes called *si zhen si yi* (four front and four corners).

After training for four-to-five years, Yang stylists put their tai chi form into continuous movement. Today, most people practice their form at a

Kung-Fu Masters

"Most people simply didn't want to devote eight years to what they considered boring training. To keep students interested, Yang opened his teaching with the moving form. Only when students became close practitioners or disciples did they learn the internal side of tai chi training."

very low speed. That wasn't the case in tai chi's early days. Back then, there were two ways to practice the tai chi form. The easiest and most popular was called *zhuo jia*, or "walking the form." The method, practiced by serious students, was known as *xing gong*, or "developing the form." *Zhuo jia* is done faster than *xing gong*. It's more like a warm-up form, compared to the chi-developing *xing gong* method that puts concentration, focus, and intention into a slow, precise forms practice. *Xing gong* is practiced much slower than *zhuo jia*. Although it takes longer and requires more work, *xing gong* practice brings greater internal development to tai chi students than the faster and easier *zhuo jia* method. At this stage, Yang style tai chi students also practiced actual freestyle sparring with students who attacked with conventional kicks and punches.

Q: How long did it take students to complete the whole training?
A: Approximately eight years. They learned moving forms and weapons, such as the straight sword, saber, and spear techniques, as the last part of their training. Then they practiced on their own. In later years, Yang Cheng Fu found that tai chi would never be popular with the general public when taught the old-fashioned way. Most people simply didn't want to devote eight years to what they considered boring training. To keep students interested, Yang opened his teaching with the moving form. Only when students became close practitioners or disciples did they learn the internal side of tai chi training.

Of course, just because Yang Cheng Fu taught the public tai chi in reverse didn't mean the rest of his family did. His brother Yang Shou-Hou, and a few other classmates of Yang Cheng Fu's, still began with the old way of standing meditation. There were more, however, who studied tai chi for health. This created two branches of Yang tai chi for health. One branch consisted of many of Yang Cheng Fu's students, who learned the

form only for health purposes and called it tai chi chuan. The other group learned only the meditation and breathing part of Yang tai chi, but not the tai chi form or push hands. They called their branch *tai-chi chi kung*, now know as *chi kung* (also spelled "*qi gong*").

Among those who practiced tai chi only for health reasons, some liked the variety and relaxation of practicing the form. Those were Yang Cheng Fu's everyday students. Others liked the simplicity and lack of need for extra space that meditation and stance training provided, hence the two ways to practice Yang tai chi for health. Only those students who mastered tai chi for both health and martial arts had everything.

Q: Didn't you once write an article about the "Ten Commandments" of tai chi training?
A: Yes, I did! In Yang tai chi we have several old writings called the "classics." The classics are compiled writings of famous tai chi practitioners. Included among them is a treatise by Yang Cheng Fu, grandson of the founder of Yang tai chi chuan. It's called "Ten Important Points for Tai Chi Chuan." These ten points describe how the tai chi form should be practiced. They are among the most important guidelines to correct tai chi form practice and you can dare to say that without them your art is not real tai chi. I translated Yang Cheng Fu's ten points directly from Chinese.

1) *Uplift energy to the top with empty feeling*: Raise your head naturally, without making your neck and body stiff. When your head is carried erect and relaxed, your spirit *(shen)*, intention *(yi)* and internal energy *(chi)* are directed through your eyes. 2) *Hold chest in and arch the back*: Relax your chest muscles, allowing your breathing level to drop closer to your lower

"Among those who practiced tai chi only for health reasons, some liked the variety and relaxation of practicing the form. Those were Yang Cheng Fu's everyday students. Others liked the simplicity and lack of need for extra space that meditation and stance training provided, hence the two ways to practice Yang tai chi for health. Only those students who mastered tai chi for both health and martial arts had everything."

Kung-Fu Masters

"In tai chi chuan the center of gravity should be in a straight line over the supporting leg. If it is spread evenly between both legs, you are double-weighted, which is incorrect. Also, if your shoulders and elbows are raised, your body will be stiff, making it easy to be pulled or pushed off balance."

abdomen; this gives you more relaxed, natural lung capacity. When you relax your chest muscles, you naturally round your back slightly, helping keep your upper and lower back straight. 3) *Relax waist and loosen crotch between two legs*: Relax the waist, giving yourself more fexibility in this region. Loosen the crotch area by opening your hips. Waist and hip action directs the power produced in the legs. 4) *Distinguish between empty and full*: If the body's center of gravity, which carries most of the body's weight, rests over the right leg, that leg is full. Since the left leg has less weight and no center of gravity over it, it is empty. In tai chi chuan the center of gravity should be in a straight line over the supporting leg. If it is spread evenly between both legs, you are double-weighted, which is incorrect. The double-weighted person is easily pulled off balance and can't move quickly and easily in any direction. 5) *Sink the shoulders and drop the elbows*: Relax your shoulders. Your elbows should point down. If the shoulders are tense or the elbows stick out, your breathing and chi levels rise, making your breathing shallow and entire body tense. Also, if your shoulders and elbows are raised, your body will be stiff, making it easy to be pulled or pushed off balance. 6) *Use intention, not strength*: Use your mind *(yi)* to accomplish your action, not tense body force. This keeps your body relaxed and supple, yielding and redirecting, rather than exerting force against force. 7) *Top and bottom follow each other*: The root of your movements start with the foot position. Energy or power is then produced by the legs. The waist and hips direct the power, which is released through the arms and hands. Each part of this sequence must be connected amd done in correct order. 8) *Internal and*

external are in mutual harmony: Internal energy *(chi)* and external power (muscle strength) are both necessary. However, you should not have an excess of one over the over. Both should balance each other. 9) *Connect together without breaking*: Each movement in the form should be a continuous expression of the tempo and speed from the previous movement. Even though the body momentarily stops between postures to change to a new posture, your intention continues unbroken. There should be no hard, fast movements followed by soft, slow actions—or vice versa. 10) *Attain motion in silence*: Although you are moving, your mind should be calm and quiet. This allows you to breathe easily, think clearly and move with agility.

Those are Yang Cheng Fu's ten principles of correct tai chi practice. No matter which form you use, if you follow these principles you will benefit from the many health and martial advantages tai chi has to offer.

"Now more people understand Chinese culture and martial arts. Although there are plenty of unqualified teachers around, Westerners try their best to learn real kung-fu and promote their systems. If Chinese martial arts have a failing in the Western world, it's because we need more qualified instructors, teaching full-time as professionals."

Q: How do you see the art today?
A: Today's kung-fu is not like 10 or 20 years ago. Now more people understand Chinese culture and martial arts. Although there are plenty of unqualified teachers around, Westerners try their best to learn real kung-fu and promote their systems. If Chinese martial arts have a failing in the Western world, it's because we need more qualified instructors, teaching full-time as professionals. Pure kung-fu schools are few and far between. When you open the Yellow Pages, you don't find too many kung-fu schools. There are plenty of schools that advertise kung-fu, along with karate, ninjutsu, and anything else you want to learn. Those are what we call *chop-suey* martial arts, taught by people who have mixed everything together, trying to sell whatever they think the public wants. They aren't pure kung-fu systems.

Kung-Fu Masters

"Many of the instructors learned a little here and a little there, but not enough for a full understanding of what they are trying to teach. They may teach fancy movements without knowing the applications, leaving their students seriously compromised in real fighting situations."

Unfortunately, for the last 20 years everybody has been trying to be the next Bruce Lee. They study several martial arts styles thinking that they can start their own system. In ten years these instructors claim to learn a dozen system, which means they spend less than a year per style. This approach will make them nothing more than long-term beginners and they will never be as good as Bruce Lee.

Q: It seems to me that you don't agree with the idea of mixing styles.
A: There is a problem with these mixed-up styles of martial arts. Many of the instructors learned a little here and a little there, but not enough for a full understanding of what they are trying to teach. They may teach fancy movements without knowing the applications, leaving their students seriously compromised in real fighting situations. They may also cause their students external and internal injuries through incorrect training practices, such as improper breathing methods or dangerous techniques. There are also a lot of Chinese teaching kung-fu from Hong Kong or Taiwan who once learned a little kung-fu. Then they leave China and work in other countries, maybe as a restaurant cook, and start teaching kung-fu or tai chi as a sideline business after working hours. Later, because these instructors were only part-time students, then part-time teachers, their schools close, leaving many students without a teacher. Unable to find a good instructor, those students try learning from a book or videotape, and the quality of their kung-fu drops even lower. This is very bad for the art and the main people to blame are those who teach without having the right knowledge.

Q: What advice would you give to these people?
A: If you want to be a good martial artist, stay in one system and learn it well. Thoroughly understand it through hard work and constant practice. By additional training you can broaden your knowledge by reading good books and quality martial arts magazines. I'm not talking only about the up-to-date mgazines, but the ones that promote the real kung-fu. Participate in and observe martial arts exhibitions and tournaments. This will help you to gain knowledge of other styles to compare their good and bad points with your own chosen style. You should also study the culture and history of the Orient for more in-depth martial understanding.

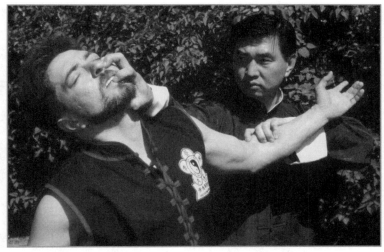

"If you want to be a good martial artist, stay in one system and learn it well. Thoroughly understand it through hard work and constant practice. By additional training you can broaden your knowledge by reading good books and quality martial arts magazines. I'm not talking only about the up-to-date mgazines, but the ones that promote the real kung-fu."

Q: What is your advice on a physical and technical level?
A: Always work on the forms. Besides this, try to find a partner to practice two-person training such as sparring and combinations. If you only know forms without knowing how to fight, then you are not a real martial artist. But if you just know how to fight and cannot do forms, you won't have the foundation of balance and coordination and will lack the basic techniques of your style. Then all you have is sloppy streetfighting. Include some conditioning exercises but don't train wrong and get hurt. There is a *wrong* way of doing everything from horse stance to iron palm training. If you do internal training, then make sure your activity is supervised by a qualified instructor. By practicing *chi kung* incorrectly you can suffer bad physical side effects.

Kung-Fu Masters

"If you just know how to fight and cannot do forms, you won't have the foundation of balance and coordination and will lack the basic techniques of your style. Then all you have is sloppy streetfighting. There is a wrong way of doing everything from horse stance to iron palm training."

Q: What's your opinion of how the art has evolved in the United States?
A: Americans have a great appetite for kung-fu. A large number of non-Chinese instructors make frequent trips to Hong Kong, Taiwan and mainland China to learn directly from Chinese martial arts experts. They do it because they know we have a need for qualified teachers here. They can recognize the differences between true traditional Chinese martial arts and *chop-suey* systems. I don't believe today's kung-fu has reached matu-

rity. The few good teachers are located mostly on the West and East Coasts of the United States, leaving the nation's Midwest kung-fu students starved. Many of this nation's chop-suey schools spring up in the areas where there are few good teachers.

Q: Is there any kind of formal exchange with top instructors from China?
A: Not really, but there are more and more Chinese teachers traveling to the United States for temporary visits, teaching and spreading their martial arts. Many of them are *wushu* coaches from mainland China who teach only *wushu* gymnastic exercises. Occasionally, traditional kung-fu experts from China visit the United States for short periods of time, teaching pure tai chi or kung-fu. The only problem with visiting instructors or with people who make one trip abroad for a few weeks or a month is that there's not enough time to learn. It's long enough to learn a *wushu* form, but not enough to understand higher training levels like fighting applications or internal strengths. Only those people who stay in Asia for a long period or make frequent serious study trips should be called qualified kung-fu teachers.

"The only problem with visiting instructors or with people who make one trip abroad for a few weeks or a month is that there's not enough time to learn. It's long enough to learn a wushu form, but not enough to understand higher training levels like fighting applications or internal strengths."

Q: How do you think the art will evolve in the years to come worldwide?
A: In another ten years, things will have changed. More Westerners will have learned good Chinese martial arts from aunthentic instructors. Their knowledge will be at a higher level. At this moment, the quality of kung-fu in the Western world depends on Western-based instructors, both Chinese and non-Chinese. We have to develop future experts from our own students. Our responsibility is to give them our best knowledge and

Kung-Fu Masters

"We have to develop future experts from our own students. Our responsibility is to give them our best knowledge and help them become teachers. If our best students don't become teachers, we won't have enough people to promote our traditional systems. The future starts now."

help them become teachers. If our best students don't become teachers, we won't have enough people to promote our traditional systems. The future starts now. I want to pass on my kung-fu and tai chi systems, not only to Chinese people but to anyone who wants to study and promote the martial arts the way they were intended to be practiced.

Q: What about the art in the United States?
A: It's the same. Americans are human beings like everybody else. Some people may say they aren't built right physically, or they don't understand Chinese philosophies, but the Chinese even say that about other Chinese. Northeners say that Southern Chinese aren't built right for Northern kung-fu. But I see a lot of Southern Chinese doing Northern kung-fu as well as Northern people, so why should Americans or any Westerner not be as good as Chinese? I have also seen Caucasian and black *wushu* stylists who do their forms just as well as *wushu* people from Mainland China.

Actually, Americans have the potential to be better than Chinese at kung-fu and tai chi. They have more leisure time, more expense money and better nutrition. Americans consider martial arts a treasure, so they put more effort into learning and understanding kung-fu than do many people in the Orient. Americans have more time for diligent practice. They have more money and freedom to travel to whatever teacher they choose. For example, the average Chinese from Guangzhou can't go to Beijing to learn from a high-level master, because they don't have the time or money for travel and study. Even if they did have the resources, what would they do with it? They can't make a living teaching martial arts in China today. At least here, people can use what they learn as a profession, giving them more incentive to research and study every facet of their martial arts, rather than just give it up after a few years. There's no reason

Western martial artists can't be better than their Asian cousins.

Q: You said once that the foot steps out in tai chi before the hands move forward. However, some Wu style practitioners say that the hand and feet should move forward together. Which is correct?

A: I do have some personal observations of three famous Wu style experts, Wu Tu Nan in Beijing, Ma Yeuh Liang in Shanghai, and Wu Gong Yi's videoclips from Hong Kong. None steps out with the hands and feet together. If they did, they would fall forward abruptly. Let's take a look at a common movement—"brush knee" in Yang, Wu or any other style. One foot must stay balanced, while the other foot steps forward. When you step out, one hand circles to a position behind the ear and waits there until the forward foot is on the ground. By the time that the hand pushes all the way forward, the forward knee will have shifted its weight forward with all movement stopping at the same time. There will be no empty and full weight distribution, meaning the knee has no chance to shift forward. This is a principle I learned from my teacher, Hu Yuen Chou, a direct disciple of Yang Cheng Fu.

"At least here, people can use what they learn as a profession, giving them more incentive to research and study every facet of their martial arts, rather than just give it up after a few years. There's no reason Western martial artists can't be better than their Asian cousins."

Q: What makes tai chi so beneficial for *chi* development?

A: The answer lies in tai chi's most important principles—relaxation and calmness. These are the keys to *chi* development. Since tai chi is done slow, smooth and even, the result is relaxation. Calmness comes from concentrating on timing, sequence and correct form.

Chi kung is not tai chi. *Chi kung* means "chi development" and is as simple as meditation and breathing exercises. Meditation requires no movement. It is standing in one place while using a variety of different arm positions. *Chi kung* meditation requires the body to be totally relaxed

Kung-Fu Masters

"Meditation requires no movement. It is standing in one place while using a variety of different arm positions. Chi kung meditation requires the body to be totally relaxed without external movement. Standing meditations are initially uncomfortable for most students, forcing them to physically relax tense muscles over the one-hour meditation period."

without external movement. Standing meditations are initially uncomfortable for most students, forcing them to physically relax tense muscles over the one-hour meditation period. Students learn to relax their mind and breath evenly. Blood circulation starts flowing evenly. This corresponds with the tai chi theory of "silence produces action."

The other facet of *chi kung* is its breathing exercises. These include the tai chi form, where the body slowly moves. Proper breathing is a must for relaxation, just as relaxation is critical for good breathing practice. If your breathing isn't even, you won't be relaxed while practicing the tai chi form. Most people don't realize that under tension or stress, they exhale longer than they inhale. If they are not relaxed while practicing tai chi, their shoulders tense and their breathing rises, throwing off the timing and smoothness of their form. Tai chi breathing exercises teach students to inhale and exhale at the same rate.

Each breathing exercises and meditation posture benefits specific parts of the body, for both health and martial arts. For example, one is good for lowering blood pressure while simultaneously strengthening the upper arms and shoulders. Another brings the three primary areas of the body energy into harmony as it develops *peng jing* or "ward off" fighting energy.

Correct tai chi practice requires both forms of meditation. Standing meditation causes relaxation and develops *chi*. Movement, including breathing exercises, activates the *chi*. For instance, the *peng yue* (carry the moon) breathing exercise stirs and balances internal energy. Through its circular pattern, it actually directs energy into the correct parts of the body by creating a magnetic field from the body movements.

After balancing internal energy through the *pen yue* breathing exercises, the meditation that follows is calm and pure, naturally lowering the body's *chi* breathing point.

Comprehensive tai chi study must include some internal (*chi*) training. Without *chi* development, tai chi would be just another external martial art or exercise. *Chi* development comes from passive meditation and stance training. It must also include *chi* and physical activity, gained from forms practice and breathing exercises.

If you practice tai chi as a martial art, you must also have push-hands practice, which requires a partner. You practice form techniques on another person. In tai chi, the martial arts aspect is impossible to learn without two-person practice.

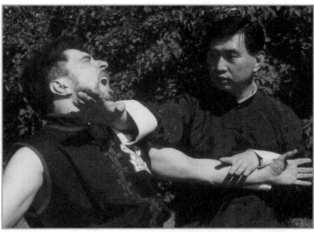

"If you practice tai chi as a martial art, you must also have push-hands practice, which requires a partner. You practice form techniques on another person. In tai chi, the martial arts aspect is impossible to learn without two-person practice."

Q: How important is relaxation in the progress of a martial artist?
A: No matter what your martial art is, if you are not relaxed while doing it, you won't reach your ultimate potential. Relaxation is more than a state of mind. When I talk about relaxation, I do not mean that you should try to make yourself as limp as cooked spaghetti. That isn't relaxation. True relaxation contains energy—like a garden hose with water flowing through it. It is a condition where your mind and muscles work together, without tenseness or stiffness, in a fluid organized manner. The benefits of being relaxed when you practice martial arts are many. Your mind is calm and alert for any required change of direction or movement. Your body is more flexible and mobile, making it easier to escape from any kind of attack. You have more power when you throw a punch or kick. Relaxation is easy to achieve, provided you exercise patience.

Kung-Fu Masters

"People tend to think that soft styles are composed of relaxed actions and hard methods use stiff movements. Nothing is farther from the truth. Take Japanese or Okinawa karate as an example. The best karate is not stiff and tense. The top karate masters project their power like dynamite—in a very explosive way."

Q: How does a relaxed physical state affect a technique such as a punch?
A: Let me say first that there are many misconceptions about what constitutes soft and hard styles. People tend to think that soft styles are composed of *relaxed* actions and hard methods use *stiff* movements. Nothing is farther from the truth. Take Japanese or Okinawa karate as an example. The best karate is not stiff and tense. The top karate masters project their power like dynamite—in a very explosive way. This is only possible by achieving a high level of relaxation before execute the technique. The reason why many karate or hard styles practitioners don't possess this power is that they don't saty with their masters long enough to learn the right way of developing this principle. And some old masters won't take time to teach the right way. It is much harder to teach beginning students, who are often stiff and tense.

Q: Northern styles are known for their high kicking and Southern methods for using the kicks in the low line. Is this perception still true in the 21st century?
A: It is not always true that Northern kung-fu styles kick high and Southern styles only kick low. For instance, in choy lee fut we kick as high as any other Northern shaolin style practitioner. The truth is that if you can kick high, you can easily kick low. However, just because you have powerful low kicks doesn't mean you can successfully kick high. In tai chi the highest kicks are to the point of an opponent's hip. Hsing-i and praying mantis also direct their kicks low. It's just common to practice to kick as high as possible in the forms for maximum flexibitlity and strength development. You don't need to be flexible to kick well, but you must be flexible to kick high.

In the Chinese southern systems we only use kicks against an opponent's lower body in a grappling situation where the hands are occupied defensively. There is a Chinese saying that translates as, "Hands give 30 percent of your power and legs give 70 percent." "However," the saying continues, "the legs give 70 percent chance of danger." This means you have a 70 percent chance of losing your balance while standing on one leg and kicking. With those odds, most Chinese martial arts systems choose to kick only as a last resort.

Q: Some Chinese styles have dozen of different *kuen* (forms). Should the practitioner's skill level be measured by the number of forms they know?
A: No. That would be a mistake. If you measure your progress based on the amount of forms you know, you are keeping yourself from ever reaching your top martial arts potential. It is not how many *kuen* you know that makes you proficient in your chosen style. In the days when choy li fut was known solely in China, accomplished masters personally only studied four or five major hand forms. Everything they needed to know was contained in those few forms.

For instance, choy li fut contains about 30 empty-hand forms and if we add the weaponry forms there are almost 100 sets in the system. But this doesn't mean that in order to master the style you need to know all the forms. Chan Heung, the founder of the system, had three teachers and that training plus his own brilliance was enough background to create a large number of organized training patterns. Knowing that I wanted to teach, my instructor, Woo Van Cheuk, sent me to several of his own-generation choy li fut brothers to learn the system from different families. Although I studied with several teachers, I spent many years practicing

"If you measure your progress based on the amount of forms you know, you are keeping yourself from ever reaching your top martial arts potential. It is not how many kuen you know that makes you proficient in your chosen style. In the days when choy li fut was known solely in China, accomplished masters personally only studied four or five major hand forms."

Kung-Fu Masters

"Some forms are for kickers and more flexible students—others for those who are more proficient with their hands. Personally, my own instense practice and knowledge of five and six forms allows me to understand all the choy lu fut's principles. Armed with that background, I can relate to other forms."

only a few special forms for my personal training. However, not all the forms are suitable for all people. Some forms are geared to small people and others for big individuals. Some forms are for kickers and more flexible students—others for those who are more proficient with their hands. Personally, my own instense practice and knowledge of five and six forms allows me to understand all the choy lu fut's principles. Armed with that background, I can relate to other forms.

In tai chi chuan it happens the same. There are people who try to learn different styles of tai chi rather to stick to one. This is fine for the physical side of tai chi—but you don't need to know more than one style to master the art.

Q: Respect is something very important in the Chinese kung-fu tradition, but sometimes Western culture steps in the way. Is there any kind of conflict between those two different cultural approaches?
A: Not really, but you need to know and understand what would be an offense to your teacher. For instance, if your teacher is a professional instructor then don't bargain with him for his fee. If you do, you'll only create a bad impression and he won't teach you all you hoped to learn. He may only correct your movements on a shallow level. The other type of instructor is well known and very knowledgeable in martial arts, but he does not have his own school. You must find a way to be outstanding in his mind. Do that by taking good care of him. Treat him special as you want him to treat you—with sincere, honest respect and money or a nice gift. But becareful because not everything evolves about money. Be the one who pours tea for him at restaurants. Serve him first, then pour tea for the others at your table. This shows respect for him and his other stu-

dents. And don't ask too many questions. Most masters don't like people who ask too many questions.

Q: What philosophical advice on kung-fu ethics would you give to modern martial arts practitioners?
A: Good martial artists listen and practice more than they talk—this is a rule of thumb. By doing this, not only will you reach your goal but also you'll keep them tangible. Don't take lessons with the intention of inventing up your own style. If you have enough experience and knowledge, your system will develop automatically. Eventually, you may develop new ways to do things, or you may find everything you desire in your original style. That's a different approach than simply making up a name for your own style.

Be loyal to your instructor from the very beginning. For example, if you are learning from one master while taking lessons from another—without anyone's permission—you are not loyal. When they find out neither teacher will trust you. The best way is like building a pyramid—start with a strong foundation and big base of knowledge and hard work. Then you will reach high and stay strong forever.

"Good martial artists listen and practice more than they talk—this is a rule of thumb. By doing this, not only will you reach your goal but also you'll keep them tangible. Don't take lessons with the intention of inventing up your own style. If you have enough experience and knowledge, your system will develop automatically."

Masters Techniques

Sifu Doc Fai Wong blocks the attacker's first punch with his right hand (1), bringing the arm downward (2). This opens a new attacking line for the opponent to throw a second punch (3), which Wong blocks with his left hand (4). Trapping both of his opponent's hands (5), Wong delivers a palm strike to the face, hooks his right leg behind his opponent's legs and takes him down (6).

Sifu Doc Fai Wong blocks an attackers left punch (1). Wong then pushes the arm downward (2), which opens a attack line (3), allowing him to execute a finger jab to the eyes (4), which disables his opponent (5).

Y.C. Wong

The Whipping Power of Hung Gar

HE IS THE CLASSIC KUNG-FU MASTER. THE KIND OF MAN THAT ANY STUDENT WOULD BE PROUD TO HAVE AS THEIR TEACHER. YEW CHING WONG HAS BEEN TEACHING MARTIAL ARTS IN THE SAN FRANCISCO BAY AREA FOR OVER THREE DECADES. IN THE MID-'70S, WHEN AN ATTEMPT WAS MADE TO UNIFY THE DIFFERENT KUNG-FU SCHOOLS INTO THE NORTHERN CALIFORNIA KUNG-FU FEDERATION, WONG WAS ELECTED PRESIDENT OF THE FEDERATION FOR SEVERAL TERMS. DELIGHTING AUDIENCES WITH HIS FAMED DOUBLE-WHIP STEEL CHAINS AND WITH HIS LIGHTNING-FAST TWO-PERSON EMPTY-HANDED OR WEAPON SETS, WONG WAS ONE OF THE PEOPLE RESPONSIBLE FOR THE FIRST LARGE KUNG-FU DEMONSTRATION IN AMERICA IN 1968. FOR MORE THAN THRITY YEARS, HE HAS MAINTAINED A PERSONAL TOUCH IN HIS KUNG-FU CLASSES. UNLIKE SOME SCHOOLS, WHICH HAVE ESSENTIALLY BECOME LARGE CHAINS WHICH USE MANY ASSISTANT INSTRUCTORS, SIFU WONG CONTINUALLY ATTEMPTS TO TEACH HIS CLASSES HIMSELF, PERSONALLY EXPLAINING THE HISTORY, PHILOSOPHY, AND TECHNIQUES OF CHINESE KUNG-FU, THE ART HE DEVOTED HIS LIFE TO.

Q: Who were your kung-fu teachers?
A: I began my training at the early age of 6 under an old man skilled in hung gar kuen, as well as in a few other Southern styles. The training was very hard and pretty soon I was able to maintain a squatting horse stance for nearly half an hour. The economic hard times and the coming of World War II soon ended all serious training, however. Finally, at the age of 18, I left China and immigrated to Hong Kong. I had long heard of the famed hung gar expert, Grandmaster Lum Jo, teaching in Hong Kong, and asked to become his student. Thus, for the next 12 years, I lived at my teacher's school, trained under his personal supervision, and became his assistant instructor. By following Lum Jo for many years, I learned and perfected the unarmed techniques and all the traditional Chinese weapons of the style. Upon nearly completing my training in hung gar, I studied the Northern Chinese style of pa kua under a close friend of my teacher. This person was Kwan Duk Hoi, the famous old master skilled in monkey style and pa kua. In 1963, I immigrated to the U.S., settling

Kung-Fu Masters

"For the last three decades, I have been active in promoting the art of kung-fu in the United States, not only teaching at my schools but also giving demostrations and seminars all around the country."

in San Francisco and starting my own school there. For the last three decades, I have been active in promoting the art of kung-fu in the United States, not only teaching at my schools but also giving demostrations and seminars all around the country.

Q: Would you give us some insight on the history of hung gar kuen?
A: According to some, Geesin Sumsi is supposedly the founder of the hung gar system of kung-fu. The truth is that maybe he is a fictional character. But since hung gar ranks with tai chi chuan as the most influential Chinese fighting art—and is the direct Chinese ancestor of Okinawan karate—the Geesin legend holds significance for most modern martial artists.

According to the story, the five surviving monks vowed to avenge the deaths of their comrades by leading China in open revolution against the Ching dynasty. They agreed to form a secret society to prepare for the rebellion, and then each dispersed to find more recruits. All members of the society were to be considered brothers under the family name of hung, which means "red," and was the name of the ruling household during the Ming dynasty.

Geesin Sumsi fled southward into Canton where he found refuge inside Canton's opera houses. Chinese opera made extensive use of the martial arts and was, therefore, an excellent ruse for a rebellious Shaolin monk. He began to teach Shaolin kung-fu to other militant patriots from the opera. The opera troupes in those days traveled down the Pearl River delta on boats. These boats were called hung ch'uan, or "red boats," in

reference to the red pants worn by the boatmen. Much of Geesin Sumsi's instruction was aboard these boats between performances. Geesin was forced to adapt his Shaolin system to less than favorable conditions. The boats were unstable and perpetually rocked back and forth. Thus Geesin taught his students to fight in very low, very strong horse stances. Also, there was not a lot of room on board, so the monk deemphasized kicking and jumping techniques because they obviously weren't very practical under those conditions.

Soon, Geesin Sumsi sent his students out on their own to organize other patriots and teach them kung-fu. And since the river boats upon which that art developed were called 'hung ch'uan,' the name of the rebel's fighting art quickly became known as "Hung Gar Kuen." Unfortunately, their numbers did not grow large to lead the revolution they dreamed about.

"Today, because the early practitioners were confined by tight spaces, the style is based on the concept of an immovable foundation. Hung gar emphasizes power and stability with strong stances and strong hand techniques."

Q: So the enviroment where the art was developed influenced the physical techniques of the style?
A: Definitely. Today, because the early practitioners were confined by tight spaces, the style is based on the concept of an immovable foundation. That is, the hung gar practitioner prefers to stand in place, using the low horse stance to remain as immovable as a boulder. Then the opponent's attacks will bounce painfully and sometimes injuriously off the blocking and guarding actions, and create openings for devastating counterattacks. At this point, the hung gar stylist can end the struggle with one powerful blow which rips muscles, breaks bones, dislocates joints, or worse kills. Hung gar emphasizes power and stability with strong stances and strong hand techniques. While some styles rely on tricks to beat the opponent, hung gar practitioners depend on speed and power as well as

Kung-Fu Masters

"I try to find that perfect balance between speed and power although we can't forget the fact that speed will allow us to hit the moving target our opponent is."

on their techniques to win; thus hung gar practitioners are traditionally known as honest fighters. Of course, the student's advancement in kung-fu as in any other mahial art depends on his intelligence coordination. and dedication.

Q: You say that hung gar bases its techniques in physical power—but is this not just one side of the coin?
A: Clearly, hung gar kung-fu was intended to be the artistic expression of power—but unfortunately at the expense of speed. It is with this inherent preference of the system that I feel that a combination of speed and power is better balanced and represents, at least to me, a better art. I try to find that perfect balance between speed and power although we can't forget the fact that speed will allow us to hit the moving target our opponent is. With no speed, there is no way we can use power because we'll never be able to catch the moving object.

Q: Does studying different styles go against the traditional princples of kung-fu?
A: I remember the early days of my kung-fu career when, as a child in Kwangiung Province, China, I was expected to study just one style from just one instructor—whether or not that style or instructor offered me what I needed in an art To learn a second art or to question the instructor's teaching was considered disrespectful and unforgivable. Fortunately, people today are not as conservative as they used to be when a man learned only one system and stuck to it. The practitioner of today wants to expand

"Traditionally, kung-fu systems are divided into two camps—the hard systems and the soft systems. This division reflects the influence of the Taoist theory of changes from classical Chinese philosophy."

into other systems, to increase his art. You see, kung-fu is like knowledge. Obviously, the more you learn, the more knowledge you have. And every system adds something to your knowledge. I don't really see anything wrong with that as long as you do it with respect and honesty.

Q: When did you start to study and analyze other systems of kung-fu?
A: It was in 1953, when I arrived to the United States, that I immediately began to look at other styles of kung-fu. Traditionally, kung-fu systems are divided into two camps—the hard systems and the soft systems. This division reflects the influence of the Taoist theory of changes from classical Chinese philosophy. Soft styles rely primarily on indirect leverage to turn the opponent's strength against himself. They are characterized by indirect tactics and speed techniques. Of course, since I come from a hard style, the first art I chose to study had to be a soft style. I chose tai chi

Kung-Fu Masters

"As the opponent attacks, you become yin, pulling him off balance. But as he attempts to retreat, you become yang and uproot him. Yin and yang are kept in constant balance."

chuan, the grandfather of all soft styles, as well as tai chi chuan's sister arts of pa kua and hsing-i.

Q: What can you tell us about these internal styles?
A: Tai chi chuan was originally developed as the Taoists' answer to Shaolin. The art grew out of the Taoist search for immortality. Taoists believed that dance-like exercise could maintain the harmonious balance between yin and yang within the body—and so increase the circulation of life-sustaining chi or inner strength. Each dance-like posture of tai chi chuan was designed to be the physical embodiment of some element of Chinese philosophy. For example, when your weight is over the rear leg, you are yin. And when your weight is over the lead leg, you are yang. As the opponent attacks, you become yin, pulling him off balance. But as he attempts to retreat, you become yang and uproot him. Yin and yang are kept in constant balance.

Pa kua and hsing-i are further elaborations on the tai chi chuan ideal. Pa kua techniques key off of "walking the circle," or circling around your opponent in preparation for a counterattack. Pa kua stresses the use of horizontal, circular movements and the open palm. Frequently, a pa kua practitioner in action will resemble a cross between a judoka and an aikidoka since many pa kua counterattacks employ graceful throws. But hsing-i is based on solid footholds. Movement is largely linear, expounding the strength of the straight line. Hsing-i stresses the use of vertical power and the clenched fist.

They are internal systems which are a special category of soft style. They rely on leverage to turn the opponent's inner strength against himself. This type of counterattack is accomplished by patiently setting the opponent up for a devastating closerange attack which catches him both mentally and physically off balance. Since the attack coincides with the opponent's moment of absolute helplessness, internal practitioners can frequently defeat an opponent without hurting him. Internal systems always embody some element of Chinese philosophy. Tai chi is the yin and yang of boxing. Pa kua is the eight triagrams boxing. And hsing-i is the five elements boxing.

Q: Do you have a training program that you could recommend?
A: Not really, although based on my own experience, I could give some type of advice for the kung-fu practitioners. Many years ago, when I was much younger, I trained extensively in the techniques of hung gar. However, after long years of hard training, I gradually realized that one should not continually overexert onself in the use of power and speed. After all, one only has a certain limited reservoir of chi energy, and overextending that would be detrimental to one's health. For many years now, I have favored what I call "balanced training." Hung gar is a hard style in relation to other kung-fu styles. Although I still practice its hard techniques, I also attempt to relax, to loosen up my body and limbs and to conserve my chi through training in such internal kung-fu styles as tai chi, pa kua, and Chinese meditation.

"For many years now, I have favored what I call "balanced training." Hung gar is a hard style in relation to other kung-fu styles. Although I still practice its hard techniques, I also attempt to relax, to loosen up my body and limbs and to conserve my chi through training in such internal kung-fu styles as tai chi, pa kua, and Chinese meditation."

Q: Do you follow any particular diet?
A: Actually, there's no special diet to help one keep in shape. Of course, there are some foods that you don't want to eat all the time; but what makes a difference is how one trains and how often you workout. You can

Kung-Fu Masters

"It is true that kung-fu, as any other martial art, can be seen as only a method for fighting efficiently. Do keep in mind, though, that kung-fu is a skill that is also part of a heritage passed down through many generations of practitioners."

have the most perfect diet in the world—but if you don't train hard you won't see any improvement. I advocate the concept of balance in everything one does, so I would say that it's important to eat moderately and balance all the different foods you take. One should not overexert and overtrain oneself. One should practice moderation in the types and amounts of food one consumes.

Q: What is your idea concerning the fighting aspect of the martial arts?
A: It is true that kung-fu, as any other martial art, can be seen as only a method for fighting efficiently. Obviously, no matter how skilled a person is, he should not make trouble or indiscriminately hurt people by using his acquired kung-fu skills. First, the purpose of kung-fu is not to hurt others but to promote one's health and to be used as self-defense only if absolutely necessary. Second, no matter how highly skilled a person is, he is bound to meet someone even more skilled than he. So it is adviseable not to brag about what you know or you don't know. Be humble and train hard.

Do keep in mind, though, that kung-fu is a skill that is also part of a heritage passed down through many generations of practitioners. Although kung-fu training is not always an advantage in this age of guns, the essence of the art should still be preserved, and the essence not only includes the ability to do good-looking moves but also the ability to use the technique effectively if the situation arises.

The usefulness of full-contact fighting depends on your purpose. If one views full-contact fighting as a sport, then it is OK—except that too many people are out for blood instead of competing in the spirit of sportsmanship and for advancing one's skill. Needless to say, some other forms of combat sports are extremely brutal and I don't think they bring anything relevant in the study and way of the true martial arts.

On the other hand, the rules of full-contact fighting—though needed for the participant's safety—are too limiting, and may not do much to advance and to bring out the use of kung-fu techniques. For instance, some styles have very effective gripping techniques, but gloves would immediately prevent the use of those techniques. The rule of no kicking below the waist is also very limiting. Some of the most effective kicks are below the belt, attacking the knee joint. Like I said before, it all depends of what you are looking for and the reason you train. If you want to make money fighting, then maybe that is the way to go, but it is not something that I personally would recommnend. My approach to the martial arts is quite different.

"Don't forget that your body changes and the techniques you practice will change too. After I was exposed to the soft styles, I began to slightly modify my own hung gar system to soften it up and round it out a bit."

Q: Have you made any innovations in your style or training techniques?
A: Actually, a major innovation was made by Grandmaster Lum Jo, many years ago. Although traditionally, hung gar practitioners practiced only a very hard style, Lum Jo began to soften the style a bit and execute his techniques with a bit more fluidity. He also added principles of Northern styles to his techniques, combining power with mobility. Lum Jo was well known for his ability to leap high and land as lightly and quietly as a cat and to execute moves with amazing power and precision.

I tried to carry on this principle and my training in Nothern pak kua emphasizes speed and mobility while hung gar stresses power and stability. The two complement each other well and provide a balance that is necessary to be able to train all your life. Don't forget that your body changes and the techniques you practice will change too. After I was exposed to the soft styles, I began to slightly modify my own hung gar

Kung-fu Masters

"There are four basic forms that I use for teaching the fundamentals of the style. The first form is called kung chi fook fu kuen *and sometimes is translated as 'cross tiger fist.' It is probably the oldest form in the system and is used as a foundation set."*

system to soften it up and round it out a bit. I made it more agile and smooth. Not that I thought there were any combat contingencies for which the classical system was inadequate, but rather that my changes did not affect the art's practical utility. Indeed, I believe that these changes would strengthen, expand and improve the art. Just because you learn how to swim, that doesn't mean you lose the ability to walk. Still, I continue to preserve the classical forms of hung gar.

Q: Which are the basic forms used in the hung gar method of kung-fu?
A: There are four basic forms that I use for teaching the fundamentals of the style. The first form is called *kung chi fook fu kuen* and sometimes is translated as "cross tiger fist." It is probably the oldest form in the system and is used as a foundation set. It is always the first form the student learns and we believe that it was developed by the great Hung Hei Gung himself. It is a very powerful form and demands a strong basic technique in the stances. It can help the student to develop a lot of power due to the technical characteristics of the form. It's a great training form to improve one's legs strength and increase the ability to use the waist in all the movements.

The second form is *fu hok seung ying kuen* and it can be considered the trademark of hung gar. This set was designed by Wong Fei Hung and in many ways we can say that it is a style in itself. He combined the most important hand techniques in the style and created a set that all the students could use to train these techniques. This set teaches not only all the hung gar hand techniques but also some movements of other kung-fu styles as well. The tiger and crane are the main animals in the form, but it also includes some others. The tiger techniques in hung gar are used for

teaching the student power, stability, courage and breathing skills, while the crane complements the tiger by giving the student calmness, concentration, agility, spirit and balance. The tiger is an external hard form and the crane provides the soft internal balance. You should strive to be like a rabbit—still but quick.

The third and next form is *sup ying kuen* and is reserved for more advanced students. It's name is translated as "ten forms" because it include five animals—tiger, crane, dragon, snake and leopard—and five elements—metal, water, wood, fire, and earth.

Q: Is *tid sien kuen* the more advanced form?
A: We may say that because it uses the techniques from the dragon but also involves the use of sounds and internal elements. It draws its name from the saying that it can be "as hard as iron or as soft as thread." Iron thread is 70 percent external and 30 percent internal. It's a form that we can describe as "balance of yin and yang." Many of the movements are intended to be isometric and isotonic exercises performed with the proper breathing techniques. When a hung gar practitioner performs this set, he makes sounds in conjunction with his breathing exercises. These sounds relate to different types of power. The high-pitched sounds correspond to external exercises and represent the yang portion of the set. Low-pitched sounds are emitted with all soft internal techniques, becoming yin.

Q: How do the sounds affect the practitioner's performance and health?
A: Well, I must begin by saying that the main goal of this form is not to develop fighting techniques, but instead to promote internal strength and good health. The purpose of the sounds is to promote a better oxygen intake to release the strain put on the practitioner by the isometric exercises. These breathing exercises are very difficult and intricate. Under no conditions should a beginner try these exercises because he would injury himself internally. The hung gar stylist has to know how to inhale and exhale properly before going deeper into the form. The form consists of ten minutes of alternately fast and slow movements. Due to these advanced breathing techniques, the stylist can keep a regular breathing pattern when finishing the form, regardless of how much power he uses in the execution of the physical movements. This set enhances the circulation and the heart action. It also helps other internal organs such as the kidneys and improves the body's metabolism. The daily practice of this

Kung-Fu Masters

form will keep the student's muscle strong and hard without the tightening and stiffening of other conventional methods like weight lifting.

The old practitioners of our style believed that those who train in this form will live long. I don't know if this is true or not, though. The bottom line is the student learns to alternate tense isometric movements with loose relaxed power and to directly control his body's responses—this is the goal of kung-fu training, regardless of the style you practice.

Q: Would you describe the five animals and the five elements used in hung gar and what they represent?
A: The tiger *(fu)* represents courage, fierceness and strength. The crane *(hok)* emits alertness, active spirit, balance and agility. The leopard *(pow)* teaches speed and power. The snake *(sare)* is tricky in nature and represents the soft and internal with special ability to change from one move to another. And the dragon *(lun)* is the spiritual king of all animals and gives the hung gar practitioner bold internal power and spirit. The five elements—water, earth, metal, fire and wood—represent more abstract principles. The right understanding of the elements gives the student the ability to form techniques that will overpower any techniques his opponent uses. Each element can counter one other element and the right use of this knowledge will provide the hung gar stylist with invaluable power.

Q: Do you consider yourself a traditionalist?
A The word "traditionalist" is vaguely defined. If you mean "traditionalist" in terms of traditional forms, I am for the most part a traditionalist because I teach a style very close to what I learned many years ago. There is virtue to traditional kung-fu as practiced by the many generations of earlier practitioners. Often there are principles built into the techniques so that if you start to change the techniques radically, you will lose the effectiiveness and essence of what you are practising. You have to be very careful if you change or alter any aspect of the art because you may be making a big mistake. But this does not mean that the order of the techniques cannot be changed. I am a traditionalist in another sense. I advocate the long-held traditional value of respecting your teachers and your style. After all, where did you learn your kung-fu? If not for your sifu, you would not know what you know now. You should keep some traditional values. In the very end they will be very good not only for your martial arts training but for your daily life as well.

Q: Is altering or modifying aspects of the art a part of the traditional approach?
A: Let me explain this in detail. If you say that traditionalism is to passing the forms down exactly from one generation to the next, then I don't feel that is correct. Traditionalism is passing the "principle" of the style. Traditional kung-fu is the usage of the style, not just the memorization of the moves. A lot of very traditional and conservative sifus prefer that the students do the forms and techniques exactly the way the founders did it. They are afraid that if they start messing around with the style it has a tendency to become diluted. And to some extent I agree with this, however, once a person becomes proficient in the art, you shouldn't be limited to just that format. The beginning and intermediate student should follow the forms

"A lot of very traditional and conservative sifus prefer that the students do the forms and techniques exactly the way the founders did it. And to some extent I agree with this, however, once a person becomes proficient in the art, you shouldn't be limited to just that format."

exactly. But the forms can evolve and change with the more advanced people. No two students will do the form exactly like each other. When you change little things, it's not a problem. But if you add acrobatics, that's not good. If it's a move that works, that still makes sense, that's fine. I think traditional forms will prevail. Somehow we have to find a way to raise the standards for kung-fu without watering down the art.

Q: Is it true that meditation is a big part of your training these days?
A: Yes. When I began doing meditation, I immediately noticed that something had been missing from my own training. For example, most of the

Kung-Fu Masters

"If the instructor is interested in just making money out of the art, then he is not going to teach other important values. But if the objective of the teacher is to pass on the art, then he will have a greater emphasis on teaching tradition."

time when you practice kung-fu, your mind is functioning at a competitive level. You train yourself to develop sufficient speed, power, and technique so that you can either defeat all of your opponents, or so that you have at shown improvement over your previous self. In other words, you're always looking for some kind of reward. But the problem with the reward approach is that you'll never find it. It's a never-ending search. But after you start meditating, you notice that you feel content and peaceful inside yourself. There's no more chasing after things outside yourself. No more comparing yourself to others, or even to yourself. You just feel good inside. You feel in harmony. And that's when you start to feel the flow of your own energy, of your potential for power. And then, you know what? Your physical techniques become stronger, faster, more powerful, but by putting out less energy. In the end there is no one superior system. All styles have their strong points and weaknesses, too. What really matters is the willingness to learn and train with the goal in mind that the greatest benefit of training is the artistic unity of the mind and body.

Q: How do you see the art of kung-fu at the present time?
A: The current trend is toward commercialism. Which usually means it gets watered down. It all depends on the instructor teaching. If the instructor is interested in just making money out of the art, then he is not

going to teach other important values. But if the objective of the teacher is to pass on the art, then he will have a greater emphasis on teaching tradition. It's an individual thing on the part of the instructor. When you teach commercially, you ususally only have about three hours per week of instruction with the same group of people. And there is not too much time for interaction with all the students. I think there could be ways to run a school successfully and still maintain traditionalism. If the teacher is passionate about the style he can make sure that traditionalism is maintained. It all depends on the teacher. My classes are small and very informal which gives me the opportunity to instill traditionalism. The instructors of old wanted to maintain the purity of their tradition. If the instructor couldn't find anyone worthy to preserve it properly, they would rather die with those secrets rather than pass on the art. Because of this, I feel that there has been a lot of wisdom that has been lost.

Q: How does respect apply to the relationship between instructor and student?
A: Respect is the fundamental attitude toward the art. As an instructor, you must instill a certain amount of humbleness in the student. It is important that the student learns how to respect the teacher and each of the other students. It's important that the students learn this to help each other. A student must learn from his sifu how to control himself and his movements. In addition, the student must always show great respect for his sifu. Practising kung-fu shouldn't be just going to the school three times a week for a lesson. You go to class to develop a relationship with the sifu and you value that relationship. Even if the student has not practiced in years, he must always respect his previous sifu. This is the beginning of traditionalism.

Q: Where are you at with your art now?
A: I have made the form movements a bit less explosive, but more fluid. I'm at an old age now. I'm not looking for anything that external. Instead, I'm looking for constant health and relaxation. I want something that will preserve my body into old age. I've noticed that a lot of hard training is bad for the heart. Also, overtraining can shorten your life. It makes you use up your vitality. But with the study of the internal systems, based on Taoism and self-healing, you learn about the radiance and the flow of energy. That's why I've included internal training with my hung gar. That is where I am at.

Li Jian Yu

The Power of the Mind

PAINTER, CALLIGRAPHER, HERBALIST, AND CHEF, LI JIAN YU EMBODIES THE HIGHEST IDEALS OF THE MARTIAL ARTS. A MASTER IN THE TRUEST SENSE, HE DEMANDS AS MUCH AS HE GIVES. NOW IN HIS LATE 70S HE STILL DISPLAYS INCREDIBLE ENERGY, BALANCE, AND POWER IN EVERY MOVEMENT. A FIRST-GENERATION, DIRECT-DISCIPLE OF *YI CHUAN* FOUNDER WANG XIAN ZHAI, HE AVOIDS THE LIMELIGHT AND DEDICATES HIMSELF TO SHARING THE KNOWLEDGE PASSED TO HIM BY HIS LEGENDARY MASTER. HE WORKS ON THE PREMISE THAT AS THE MIND STRENGTHENS, SO DOES THE BODY—HE STILL CONSIDERS HIS BODY TO BE '"WEAK" AND ATTRIBUTES MOST OF HIS PHYSICAL PROWESS TO THE POWER OF THE MIND.

EXTRAORDINARILY TALENTED, MASTER LI JIAN YU'S KUNG-FU HAS REACHED A LEVEL WHERE THE AVERAGE OR MEDIOCRE IS NO LONGER ACCEPTABLE. YEARS OF HARD TRAINING HAVE TRANSCENDED MERE COMBAT IN HIS SEARCH FOR HARMONY WITH THE UNIVERSE. TRUE POWER COMES ONLY FROM KNOWLEDGE, AND KNOWLEDGE ONLY COMES FROM WITHIN. WITH HIS POWERFUL SPIRIT DRIVING HIM TO EXPLORE THE DEEPEST SECRETS OF HIS SELF, LI JIAN YU HAS DEFINED HIMSELF IN THE IMAGE OF THE TAO.

Q: When did you start training in the Chinese martial arts?
A: I was born in 1924. I have always been very interested in the art of wushu so I started training when I was 6 years old. My first school was located in Daxing, very close to Peking. The name of my first teacher was Tang Feng Ting and the style he was teaching at that time was *hsing-i chuan*—the boxing of the five elements—one of the three major internal Taoist arts.

Q: When did you meet the founder of yi chuan, the great Wang Xian Zhai?
A: When I was 18 years old, I met a martial arts master named Hong Lian Shuen. He was around 50 years old and the first teacher Yao Zong Xun ever had. His movements were really impressive and his techniques very powerful. One day he told me that compared to Master Wang Xian Zhai he was "nothing." He always advised his top students to leave him and

Kung-Fu Masters

"I was young, with a lot of motivation and honesty, so Wang Xian Zhai was very happy to accept me as a new student. I was the only one at the school with that background. He was a very tolerant and open-minded man."

go and train under Wang Xian Zhai. In 1943 he decided that it was time for me to go train under the master. I was young, with a lot of motivation and honesty, so Wang Xian Zhai was very happy to accept me as a new student. He also appreciated the fact I came from a Muslim family. In fact, I was the only one at the school with that background. He was a very tolerant and open-minded man. At this time, Master Wang Xian Zhai was already 48 years old.

Q: What was your first impression of Wang Xian Zhai?

A: He was very quiet and elegant. At first sight it was impossible to tell that he was a martial arts practitioner—but everything changed when he adopted a stance or position. Then it was a whole different thing. He was a different person. He was amazingly fast and smooth in his actions. His techniques were direct and very economical. He needed very few techniques to finish a fight.

He used to invite me to his place. Once we were there, he liked to talk about philosophy and the different problems related to life itself. I remember that I used to stay the night at his place many times. For him martial arts was not the only thing. He wanted me to have a balanced view and perception of what life was all about, not only martial arts. He wanted me to look at the same thing from different angles—from different perspectives. Of course, when we discussed life and human relationships a lot of philosophy was expressed.

His idea was that being physically strong is not enough. He used to talk about physique and strength. He thought a person needed to accumulate strength and find the right way to use it in an explosive manner.

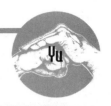

His martial arts philosophy was to be soft and calm on the outside, but powerful and fast on the inside.

Q: Master Wang Xian Zhai's reputation as a fighter was legendary. Were you present at any of his matches?
A: I remember that there was a young boxer who was bothering Master Wang all the time. Finally, Master Wang accepted the challenge and told the young man to choose the kind of combat he wanted—empty-handed or armed with weaponry. At that point, the young man got really nervous and started to insult master Wang while looking for a sword. Master Wang stayed there, looking at his opponent without moving a finger. When the young guy finally found a sword he liked he went to attack. But Master Wang just stood still as the young man approached, starring quietly at him. Before the boxer crossed Master Wang's limit he just stopped suddenly and said, "I can't fight you. I can't defeat you. I know I'm defeated already". And he left. He felt the power. He understood.

"He wanted me to have a balanced view and perception of what life was all about, not only martial arts. He wanted me to look at the same thing from different angles—from different perspectives. His martial arts philosophy was to be soft and calm on the outside, but powerful and fast on the inside."

Q: What are the fundamentals of Master Wang Xian Zhai's teachings?
A: His method is based on three basic exercises: *zhang zhuang*—the fundamental stance which prepares the physique and the intention; *shiri*—movement to test the strength; and *footwork*—which teaches the principles of mobility. Usually the first exercise is practiced during the first three years. Only after mastering the first one is the student allowed to train in the other two using different states of consciousness. To practice this style the student needs patience and strong will. After a few years the disciple will start to train in the "explosive" aspect of the system called *fa-ri* or *tui shou*—the "pushing hands." The combative aspects are learned last.

This training progression has to be followed step-by-step, otherwise the progress won't be appropriate. The little things are very important. Master Wang Xian Zhai always demanded a lot of attention be paid to

Kung-Fu Masters

"The more advanced you are, the more you make use of distance and spacing, concentration and focus, and the idea of utilizing infinity. The time-space paradox is found in yi chuan due to its apparent external immobility which cloaks a powerful and swift internal explosion."

the small details of each technique and position during training. This included the hands, the hip, the shoulder, the fingers, et cetera. It is interesting to note that Chinese boxing is based on theories and principles discovered more than 500 years ago. The more advanced you are, the more you make use of distance and spacing, concentration and focus, and the idea of utilizing infinity. The time-space paradox is found in yi chuan due to its apparent external immobility which cloaks a powerful and swift internal explosion. Both students and teachers look for the same goal—to find the perfect understanding of the three basics yi chuan principles of conception, intention, and action. These principles are the real key to learning the yi chuan method.

Q: In one of his works, Master Wang Xian Zhai criticized the direction tai chi chuan and pa kua chang were taking. Why?
A: He combined all the internal arts into one method. He took the major principles and theories and, after many fighting experiences all over China, founded yi chuan. Pa kua and tai chi were lacking spontaneity he felt. He taught that static habits become negative inertia. Due to this negative inertia, the student loses his freedom and therefore, his spontaneity. In the yi chuan system you don't want any movement on the outside but if someone tries to enter your protective limit you will respond and thereby be projected.

Q: What's the difference between the da cheng chuan system and yi chuan, and what were Wang Xian Zhai's thoughts on it?
A: There's no difference, really. At Master Wang's school there was never any misunderstanding about the perception or meaning of this. I guess the problem was more with some interpretations of the characters or

ideograms than with the real meaning. There's no difference.

Q: What do you think the future will bring to the yi chuan system?
A: Westerners are very interested in the technical aspects of the art, but not that much in the history or philosophy. They just look for the fighting aspects and combat techniques and some of them don't understand the training progression devised by Master Wang Xian Zhai himself. I understand that in the very beginning it is very difficult to realize what yi chuan is all about—I know that. The ultimate discovery of yi chuan is based on the teacher's and student's perception and intelligence. Unfortunately, this realization only comes after many years of training. Therefore, the future of the art depends on the capability of the Western students to master the principles needed to understand the yi chuan method. It is a matter of patience. By living the art instead of just practicing it in a classroom, the principles become a natural part of the practitioner and can be applied without effort.

"The ultimate discovery of yi chuan is based on the teacher's and student's perception and intelligence. Unfortunately, this realization only comes after many years of training. By living the art instead of just practicing it in a classroom, the principles become a natural part of the practitioner and can be applied without effort."

Q: What is your personal philosophy of martial arts and life in general?
A: These days it seems people are just interested in learning how to fight rather than learning how to live. It's important for the martial artist to treat the most important things in their life with the same care and concern they treat the simplest. Sometimes when the mind of an Eastern mystic is put into a Western martial arts school, this turns into a cult. The teacher is considered a God, governing his disciples' lives with pronouncements on everything. Following blindly only makes you a good follower, that's all. You need to learn to think for yourself. If martial arts is to lead you to self-perfection and self-mastery, the emphasis must be in developing your unique self—not becoming the pale shadow on your teacher. Interestingly enough, the very same desire pushing us to master the art is the desire which will prevent us from fully understanding and

Kung-Fu Masters

"You need to learn to think for yourself. If martial arts is to lead you to self-perfection and self-mastery, the emphasis must be in developing your unique self—not becoming the pale shadow on your teacher. Sometimes the teacher is ready to pass on the art and knowledge but the student is not ready to understand and learn what the teacher has to teach."

applying what the art really means and is. Sometimes the teacher is ready to pass on the art and knowledge but the student is not ready to understand and learn what the teacher has to teach. It's a matter of timing. That's the reason why sometimes the student will understand things the teacher said years later.

Q: What is your advice to all martial arts practitioners?
A: I believe martial arts is a very unique discipline and sometimes we try to make it too special. I would recommend treating your martial arts as part of your life. Make it your daily routine; breath it, feel it and enjoy it as part of the essence of your life. By doing this, you'll integrate something with your own existence and therefore it will be part of you. This is the only way that one person can keep training and enjoying it for the rest of their life. It takes many years to reach mastery in your chosen method but it takes a lifetime to really make it your own. Sometimes thinking too much is not good, we must

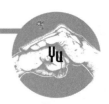

put our head aside and just train physically. The body will learn and the mind will understand through the body. Try to execute the movements correctly because this will bring a proper understanding of what you are doing. Put yourself into it and don't forget that stillness is the fastest move of all. There is no difference between the mastery of the martial arts and the way we live our own lives. If we all look at our training with a more open perspective and how this can affect the outside world, we would definitely change the way we do things in our lives.

"Sometimes thinking too much is not good, we must put our head aside and just train physically. The body will learn and the mind will understand through the body. There is no difference between the mastery of the martial arts and the way we live our own lives."

Q: What are the most important qualities of a martial arts instructor?
A: A martial arts instructor is basically the student's guide along the path. The best instructor is someone who has seen all his own weaknesses, and therefore has insight into yours. A good teacher won't insist you travel the same path he did because he will know that by doing that he will limit your knowledge. A genuine teacher will be able to convey useful lessons about life through physical movement. Unfortunately, not all teachers are good—just like mountain climbing guides who only show you the lowlands.

Teaching can be described as the art of communication and therefore spending time and money searching for the right teacher is worthwhile. Because of the great influence an instructor can have in your life you want only the best. For instance, if you're sick and need surgery you look for the best doctor, right? It is the same with martial arts. Look at the students of that particular instructor, not what he knows or how well he performs, but how good and how well his students perform.

Pay attention to his ability to speak clearly and transmit the knowledge with proper explanations and words, since this aspect will directly affect your understanding of what he is teaching you. In a nutshell, I guess the most important qualities are the ability to speak and communicate, the ability to physically perform the movements at a high level of skill, and

Kung-Fu Masters

"I guess the most important qualities are the ability to speak and communicate, the ability to physically perform the movements at a high level of skill, and the ability to speak the language of human emotions."

the ability to speak the language of human emotions. A teacher must know how to motivate and inspire the students to reach higher levels.

Q: Is there a way to distinguish real yi chuan teachers from false ones?
A: The best way to distinguish a real instructor is to see if what they teach follows the yi chuan principles. Yi chuan emphasize that power must be generated from the heels, then transmitted to the leg and up to the waist, and into the body, the shoulders, the arms, and the hands. Unfortunately, today there are many widespread misconceptions about the art of yi chuan and this is due to practitioners of the art who have not yet acquired enough years of practice and wisdom going out to teach and demonstrate.

You can't have an understanding of the art with only a year or two of practice. This is the main reason why so many do not know the history, the philosophy and the real application of the techniques they are teaching. In the old times, the prospective student spent a lot of time with the teacher. Humility was developed even before the actual physical training started.

Only after the student was proven worthy could they begin the real kung-fu training. Real kung-fu is a Chinese legacy from the past; it is a complete martial art developed and refined over centuries of time. Unfortunately, some of the real kung-fu has already been lost due to the lack of honest students.

Q: Do you feel that awareness, focus and patience are necessary to reach the higher levels of skill?
A: Perhaps the most difficult part of repeating something over and over is learning to work with boredom. When one is bored, that is the very moment a deeper learning takes place. Boredom is a deep way to study ourselves because there are many things that lie underneath each person such as disappointment, frustration, anger, clumsiness, et cetera. It's then that we can go beyond simple technical mastery. In order to achieve this we need patience and full attention to what we are doing.

"Learning requires having a quiet mind so we can focus on the work at hand. A quiet mind doesn't erase thoughts, it shuts down the internal dialogue that occupies so much mental energy. We should create that mental space so our thoughts don't represent who we are."

Attention applies to a state of mind in which we learn a movement. For the teacher it's important to emphasize the experience of doing the movement and not demand millimeter exactness and conformity to some fixed image of a physical technique. For the student, attention means being fully present in each moment, experiencing the body. This can only be achieved with a focused mind. Learning requires having a quiet mind so we can focus on the work at hand. A quiet mind doesn't erase thoughts, it shuts down the internal dialogue that occupies so much mental energy. We should create that mental space so our thoughts don't represent who we are. In the very end, what a student discovers about themselves is more important than simply performing the martial move correctly. The study of the self is the study of how we really are, and not just a narrow view of how we would like to be.

Kung-Fu Masters

Q: What is your role as a teacher?

A: I see myself as a guide. I am just a tool for my students to develop themselves. It's important to know how to teach and share knowledge according to the student's needs and abilities. Yi chuan is a style to be taught on an individual basis. You can practice as a group but the whole idea is very personal. Each student should move at their own pace. These days many people think only about fighting. Fighting is something natural for the human being and learning how to use your skills in combat is part of traditional kung-fu. But it's important to also teach how to avoid fighting.

In a way, by learning how to fight we also learn the value of not fighting. Self control is very important. Martial arts gives you a feeling of safety. No ones trains in order to attack someone or to pick on others. Training forms good reflexes and presents one with a moral code for life. Such training makes us all better human beings. I would also strongly advise not to intellectualize the art. Kung-fu can be intellectualized but the real practice is what is important. It takes more patience and hard work and less words. Finally, as Master Wang Xiang Zhai said, "He who learns from me in an original way will benefit, but he who only copies me mechanically will suffer."

"A true martial arts practitioner, like an artist of any kind—be they a musician, painter, writer or actor—is expressing and leaving part of themselves in every piece of their craft. The need for self-inspection and self-realization of who they are becomes the reason for a journey in search of that perfect technique, that great melody, that inspiring poetry, that amazing painting or that Academy Award winning performance. It is this motivation to reach that 'impossible dream,' that allows a simple individual to become an exceptional artist or master of their craft."

—Jose M. Fraguas

Notes

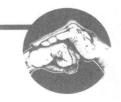

Notes